THE ICON BOOK

Visual Symbols for Computer Systems and Documentation

William Horton

John Wiley & Sons, Inc.
New York / Chichester / Brisbane / Toronto / Singapore

Publisher: Katherine Schowalter
Editor: Theresa Hudson
Managing Editor: Frank Grazioli
Book Design and Composition: William Horton Consulting

Trademarks

Aldus PageMaker® is a registered trademark of Aldus Corporation. Apple® and Macintosh® are registered trademarks of Apple Computer, Inc. Microsoft®, Microsoft® Excel for the Macintosh®, and Microsoft® Excel for Windows™ are registered trademarks of Microsoft Corporation. Many other words in this publication in which the Author and Publisher believe trademark or other proprietary rights may exist have been designated as such by use of Initial Capital Letters. However, in so designating or failing to designate such words, neither the Author nor the Publisher intends to express any judgment on the validity or legal status of any proprietary right that may be claimed in the words.

This publication is designed to provide accurate and authoritative information in regard to the subject matter covered. It is sold with the understanding that the publisher is not engaged in rendering legal, accounting, or other professional service. If legal advice or other expert assistance is required, the services of a competent professional person should be sought. FROM A DECLARATION OF PRINCIPLES JOINTLY ADOPTED BY A COMMITTEE OF THE AMERICAN BAR ASSOCIATION AND A COMMITTEE OF PUBLISHERS.

Library of Congress Cataloging-in-Publication Data:

Horton, William K. (William Kendall)
   The icon book: visual symbols for computer systems and documentation / William Horton.
         p.   cm.
   Includes bibliographical references and index.
   ISBN 0-471-59900-X (paper)   ISBN 0-471-59901-8 (book/disk)
   ISBN 0-471-02497-X (disk)
   1. Graphical user interfaces (Computer systems)   2. Electronic data processing documentation.
   I. Title.
QA76.9.U83H67 1994
004'.0148—dc20
                                                          93-38303
                                                          CIP

Printed in the United States of America
10 9 8 7 6 5 4 3 2 1

PREFACE

I wrote this book because one morning, after loading a new "easy-to-use" program on my computer, I found myself confronting a screen that looked like the control panel of an alien space ship. Dozens of colorful icons danced before my eyes—but what did they mean? They were pretty in the way an abstract painting is pretty, but their meanings were totally obscure to this 20-year veteran of some of the most user-hostile software to slither down a network. I'm no icon-basher. I've used systems with graphical user interfaces for a decade and would prefer to click on an understandable image than to enter technojargon commands—even if I could remember how to spell them. But not all icons are clear and easy to understand. Icon design should be more of a science and less of an art. Hence, this book.

Who is this book for?

This book is for anyone who designs icons for computer systems. With the proliferation of graphical user interfaces such as those for Microsoft Windows, Apple's Macintosh, and IBM's OS/2, the need for clearly designed icons has become critical. This book will guide designers in creating icons that users recognize readily, understand fully, and remember reliably.

This book is for teams and individuals actually designing icons. They design icons for a wide range of computers and graphical user interfaces, including Windows, Macintosh, OS/2, Motif, Open Look, New Wave, NextStep. These designers work in various departments and have varying titles. They include:

- Graphic designers and artists designing computer screens
- Programmers developing user interfaces for their programs
- Ergonomists and human factors specialists concerned with designing or testing products for ease-of-use
- Designers of multimedia applications and presentations
- Trainers and instructors developing computer-based training
- Designers and producers of online documents and electronic books

Others may find this book useful too. They include:

- Teachers and students of graphic design, ergonomics, human factors, software engineering, and instructional design
- Anyone designing any form of visual symbol

Everyone is welcome to read this book, but it does not try to meet the specific needs of all readers. It is not meant to be scholarly, and those in academia may find it overly pragmatic. My goal is to assist icon designers rather than to report new research or to compound new theories. What theory I have reported has been to serve more as an engineering model than to guide scientific research.

What's here?

This book collects advice, design principles, rules of thumb, thousands of examples, and just a dash of theory into a guide for icon designers. It draws on my own experience leading icon design efforts and on the work of many of my consulting clients. This book strives to report and show those good design practices that most of us discover only by costly trial and error.

It flows from general to specific, though you need not read it that way. Start with the section or chapter that best answers your questions.

Section		Chapter
What are icons and what can they do?	1	Icons in perspective
	2	How icons work
Showing ideas	3	Representing ideas graphically
	4	Showing relationships
	5	Designing an iconic language
Style and appearance of the icon	6	Drawing icons
	7	Color in icons
Fitting icons into the interface	8	Standard parts of the icon
	9	Icons for specific purposes
	10	Icons for international products
Process of designing icons	11	Managing development
	12	Testing icons
	13	Editing icons
Resources	14	Forms, formulas, and checklists
	15	Case study in icon design
	16	Icon starter set

Who is the author?

William Horton applies ergonomics and human factors to guide users of computer systems. A registered professional engineer and graduate of MIT, he specializes in engineering effective electronic media.

As founder of William Horton Consulting in Boulder, CO, he works with corporations and other business and educational organizations in designing more effective communications. He conducts public and in-house seminars on subjects ranging from online documentation to visual literacy.

William Horton is also author of *Designing and Writing Online Documentation*, *Secrets of User-Seductive Documents*, and *Illustrating Computer Documentation*.

CONTENTS

6   DRAWING ICONS   137

7   COLOR IN ICONS   163

8   STANDARD PARTS OF THE ICON   183

11   MANAGING DEVELOPMENT   269

12   TESTING ICONS   289

13   EDITING ICONS   303

ICONS IN PERSPECTIVE

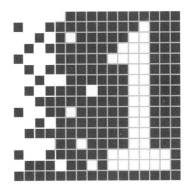

In the beginning was the image. Long before grunts and growls evolved into words, our ancestors communicated by facial expressions, postures, and pointing gestures. Cave paintings preceded written language by hundreds of centuries, and the alphabet evolved slowly from earlier pictographic scripts. Ironically, the development of computers has led to a rediscovery and redeployment of this prehistoric form of communication. The use of icons is both ancient and current.

People's reactions to icons are twofold: either they delight in clever helpful images, or they find them obscure enigmas, frustrating and pointless. Use the ideas in this book to increase the former and decrease the latter.

WHAT ARE ICONS?

The small pictorial symbols used on computer menus, windows, and screens are icons. They represent certain capabilities of the system and can be animated to bring forth these capabilities for use by the operator. In the computer industry, the term *icon* is often used as a synonym for any small visual symbol. Below you see an OS/2 screen on which is running Microsoft Word for Windows displaying a document containing a picture of an Apple Macintosh window.

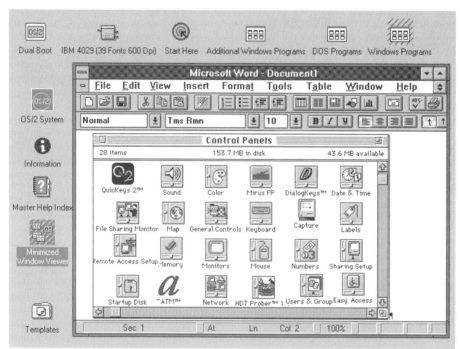

Screen images are used with permission from IBM Corporation, Microsoft Corporation, and Apple Computer, Inc.

How many different types of icons can you spot? On this screen, everything that is not a word label or a window border is an icon. All the visual symbols on this screen are, by this broad definition, icons.

Terminology wars

The whole world does not share our broad definition of icon. Academic researchers in the fields of semantics and semiology have evolved an extensive vocabulary to distinguish among visual items that represent meaning. They tend to use the term icon only for images that mimic or resemble the concept or object to which they refer. Other terms for simple visual images are symbol, sign, and signal. Sun Microsystems and some other companies distinguish between icons, which they say represent files, and glyphs, which are other visual symbols on the screen.

Although these terms add precision to the discussion, I have avoided using them for a couple of reasons. First, the use of the term icon to refer to visual symbols on the computer screen is so widespread as to be irreversible. Second, many of the distinctions made by scholarly researchers are almost impossible to apply in the real world, where the best designs mix, match, and overlap techniques with pragmatic abandon.

WHY USE ICONS?

You can use an icon anywhere you would use a word label. You can use icons to activate menus, to perform actions, to select tools, to toggle between modes, to manipulate windows, to point to items on the screen, to reveal the state of the data and allow it to be changed, to represent files and directories and disks, and to provide a way to delete unneeded items. You can also use them in publications: on the cover to represent the capabilities of the product, in the table of contents to represent the contents of each chapter, and in the chapter headings themselves.

To help users work smarter

When users must act quickly and surely, well-designed icons can help. They yield their meaning at a glance. We do not have to read, analyze, ponder, or translate them.

Well-formatted graphical displays improve the productivity and reliability of work, especially for impatient or harried users. Studies of road signs typically find that iconic signs can be read at twice the distance and in half the time as word signs.

To represent visual and spatial concepts

Words are not the natural language for describing visual appearances or spatial relationships. Graphics work better than words for representing subtle concepts of shape, color, position, angle, size, texture, and pattern. Engineers, scientists, architects, medical doctors, illustrators, and graphic designers work and think in images. Icons can speak their language.

To save space

A well-designed icon says much in few pixels. A concise icon can say more than an equally prominent word label or heading. Like monograms and trade-marks, icons replace wide rectangles of text with compact squares of meaning. Icons snuggle conveniently and legibly on computer menus, in window borders, on buttons and knobs, and other places where words would not.

See how much space these icons save?

Icon	Equivalent word label
⬇	Scroll down
🔋	Battery level is low
⊡	Adjust size

To speed search

Give an icon a distinctive shape and users will find it quickly and recognize it instantly, even on a crowded screen. However, word labels, especially ones in all capital letters, all have a rectangular shape. To find a word label we must read each of the labels in turn; to find an icon we merely scan for its distinctive shape. Notice the distinctive shape of each of these icons:

Access   Chart   Project   Alarm   Telephone

For immediate recognition

Icons are especially valuable in large complex products that test the user's ability to recognize and identify concepts. Once we have learned the unique shape of an icon, we remember it reliably and recognize it immediately.

Our ability to remember and recognize graphics seems almost unlimited.[1] In one experiment, test subjects were shown 2500 slides, each for only 10 seconds. They were then shown pairs of slides and asked which of the two they had already seen. They recognized 85 to 95 percent of the slides correctly, even when they saw the new slides for only a second or when the slides were mirror images of the original slides. When subjects were shown 32 slides at once, they could still pick out the one slide they had seen earlier 92 percent of the time. Slides that tended to show concrete objects in action resulted in 99.6 percent recognition.

For better recall

We remember visually encoded concepts better than those encoded verbally. Most of us remember faces better than names. We readily and easily learn icons. Well-designed icons are more memorable than text for three probable reasons:

- Icons are more visually distinct from one another than words are.

- When we encounter a visual symbol, we give it a name and remember that name along with the visual image. Thus icons are stored as visual and verbal memories, but word labels are retained only verbally.

- Not only are visual images stored in several forms, but the visual memories are tightly linked to one another and to other forms.

So users do not have to read

As computers have shrunk from house-sized behemoths to palm-sized appliances, the typical user has gone from a superbly educated scientist to a harried driver of a delivery van. Along the way, designers have met with the problems of illiteracy. Over one third of the people in the world—a billion adults—cannot read. About 15 percent of Americans are functionally illiterate.

---

[1]Standing, Lionel. "Learning 10,000 Pictures." *Quarterly Journal of Experimental Psychology*, (25 (2) May 1973. 207–222 (1973).

Until better education improves reading skills, clear and simple icons can give poor readers access to the computer systems they must use to earn a living. Icons can help by:

- Reducing absolute dependence on text

- Helping those with limited reading skills, for example, those who read English as a second language

- Adding another channel to overcome reading disabilities, such as dyslexia

Even those who can read text often won't read text. This voluntary illiteracy is as serious a problem as the involuntary kind. Take a stroll through a newsstand and notice the covers of magazines and books. Even stodgy literary magazines resort to graphics, color, and highly formatted text to liven up their covers and increase sales. Well-designed icons can make a product more visually appealing to users. They can interest potential users and seduce them into trying the system. They can reward continued use with visual variety and even beauty.

To help interfaces go global

Since medieval times, shopkeepers in Europe have hung three-dimensional signs to announce the goods and services they offer. The fishmonger uses a fish; the shoemaker, a boot; the optician, a pair of glasses; the watchmaker, a clock. More recent additions include a camera for photographic supplies. Such signs came about when illiteracy was common and continue today wherever tourists who do not speak the native language are common.

Except for "OK," no words are common to very many languages, but many visual symbols, such as those for no smoking, first aid, and no entry, are understood in almost any language.

Icons give a computer system an international look and reduce the need to translate every menu, message, and command each time you market the product in another country. Costs for translation are high, but not as high as the costs of confusion and failure. The attitude "if they can't read English, they shouldn't use our product" is a recipe for economic suicide in the global marketplace.

Even within the borders of your own country, you may have to accommodate recent immigrants and guest workers who read your language poorly or not at all.

THE ANCESTRY OF ICONS

The use of icon-like visual symbols is not new—it's among the oldest forms of communication. We have a rich heritage of visual symbology. This legacy benefits us in two ways. As designers, it provides us with thousands of tested examples to draw upon. We can observe what has and has not worked over the centuries. It also benefits us by ensuring us that the users of our systems have already had considerable experience interpreting visual symbols.

Cave drawings and petroglyphs

From the cave paintings of Lescaux and Altamira to the petroglyphs of the American Southwest, primitive peoples have used simple pictorial images to tell stories, record myths, and provide instruction.

Frijoles Canyon, Bandelier National Monument, New Mexico

Pictographic languages

All written languages evolved from pictographic images in which each idea was represented by a unique image, for example in these Mayan hieroglyphs:

The alphabet came about as visual symbols began to represent sounds rather than ideas:

Evolution of the alphabet

Ancient Egyptian hieroglyph	Sinai script	Moabite stone	Early Phoenician	Greek	Roman
☒	☒	☒	☒	A	A
∿	∿	☒	☒	Λ	M
☒	☒	○	○	○	O

In some written languages, such as Chinese, we can still see the original objects pictured in the streamlined and stylized symbols:

Pictorial basis of Chinese

Ancient Chinese	Modern Chinese	Meaning
☒	女	Woman
☒	口	Mouth
☒	日	Sun
☒	山	Mountains
☒	木	Tree

Folk art

Simple graphic symbols prevail in folk art. We find them decorating pottery, woven into fabrics, and carved into wood, stone, and precious metals. Consider these bird signs from pottery of the Pueblo people of the American Southwest:

Zuñi   **Acoma**

From Decorative Art of the Southwestern Indians, *by Dorothy Smith Sides.*

Esoteric and occult symbols

In the Middle Ages esoteric signs were developed by the practitioners of alchemy, astrology, and masonry. Christian sects likewise used symbols known to the initiated but indecipherable by outsiders. Notice the icon-like simplicity of these alchemical symbols:[2]

Antimony	Mercury	Tin	Nickel

Iron	Magnesia	Zinc	Steel

Bismuth	Iron filings	Copper splints	Brass

Marks of ownership

Cattle ranchers in the American Southwest found they needed simple, distinct symbols to mark their cattle. Much of the range was open and unfenced and cattle rustlers were not uncommon. They thus adopted the Spanish practice of

[2]Koch, Rudolf. *The Book of Signs.* New York: Dover, 1955.

branding cattle with a simple, robust mark. The mark of each ranch was distinct and readily recognized by neighbors and lawmen. Here are some examples of cattle brands from the American Southwest:[3]

Don José Tomas
Talamantes
California 1848

Lizard Ranch
Texas
1857

Laurel Leaf
Ranch
Texas 1868

Solomon Barron
Texas
1860

Don José Reyes
California 1855

Isaac & Squire
Williams
California 1847

Teodoso Yorba
California 1851

Almost all companies today have a distinctive visual symbol associated with their name and marked on their products. Many of these logos or trademarks are more familiar than the names of the companies themselves.

Travel signs

Probably the best known visual symbols are those we encounter along the roads and highways, especially those in Europe:

Some of the best I have seen occur in Quebec, where by law only the French language may be used on signs. This poses quite a problem for the many anglophone tourists. As a result, the province has developed a comprehensive series of visual road signs.

People from hundreds of different countries speaking dozens of different languages pass through a major international airport. Sign designers from the beginning developed a vocabulary of visual signs to direct travelers to their immediate and ultimate destinations and inform them of policies:

---

[3]Lehner, Ernst. *Symbols, Signs, & Signets.* New York: Dover, 1950.

Interstellar greetings

The first serious attempt to communicate with beings outside our solar system came when designers of the Pioneer 10 space probe attached a plaque using visual symbols to tell an intelligent being encountering the spacecraft where the probe came from and who sent it. It did so by using visual images of the few concepts and experiences an extraterrestrial being is likely to have in common with us: mathematics, physics, and basic chemistry.

Pioneer 10 spacecraft's interstellar greeting card

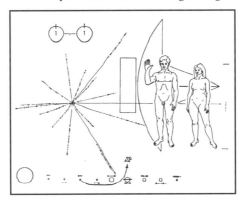

Designed iconic languages

The dream of a universal language has haunted linguists and philosophers for centuries. In the 1600s, the philosopher Leibnitz proposed creating such a language based on a set of simple visual symbols combined according to precise, logical rules. More recent attempts have included Yukio Ota's LoCos, Tom Zavalani's Jet Era Glyphs, and Jansen's Picto. Despite their clever design and noble intentions, these iconic languages have been used only in narrow disciplines for specific purposes.

Two iconic languages, however, have achieved somewhat wider use: Semantography and ISOTYPE. Neither is likely to replace words or even rival the most obscure written language. Nor does either seem likely to be adopted for computer interfaces. Yet they both offer icon designers examples of flexible, fully elaborated systems for representing concepts in visual symbols.

Semantography

Semantography is a system of visual writing developed by Charles Bliss. It consists of an "alphabet" of 100 fundamental symbols that are juxtaposed or superimposed to represent ever richer concepts. The fundamental set of symbols includes, besides numbers and mathematical symbols, simple geometric shapes. Many of these shapes are recognizable because they abstract familiar objects or are already used internationally.

Some basic symbols of Semantography

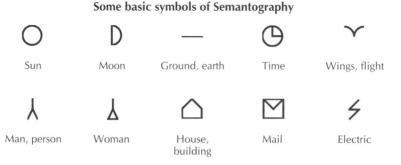

Sun	Moon	Ground, earth	Time	Wings, flight

Man, person	Woman	House, building	Mail	Electric

In the 882 pages of his book,[4] Bliss details how to combine these basic symbols to express thoughts that are more complex, more subtle, and more abstract:

Some combinational symbols

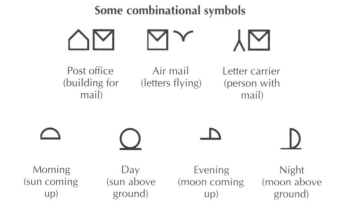

Post office (building for mail)	Air mail (letters flying)	Letter carrier (person with mail)

Morning (sun coming up)	Day (sun above ground)	Evening (moon coming up)	Night (moon above ground)

---

[4]Bliss, Charles K. *Semantography (Blissymbolics)*. Sydney: Semantography (Blissymbolics) Publications, 1963.

Semantography shows how to represent many varied ideas by combining a few simple symbols.

ISOTYPE

Otto Neurath (1882–1945), an Austrian teacher and social scientist, developed ISOTYPE (International System Of TYpographic Picture Education) to make complex statistical information understandable by everyone. ISOTYPE uses simplified pictographs to supplement words and to speed learning and understanding.

Examples of ISOTYPE symbols

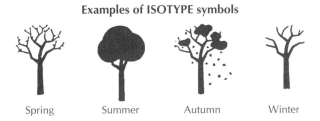

Spring   Summer   Autumn   Winter

The basic symbols can be combined to form a complete symbol language.

Combining ISOTYPE symbols

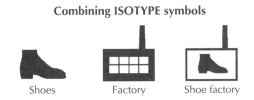

Shoes   Factory   Shoe factory

In their stark, simple design, ISOTYPE symbols presage computer icons. They can teach us much about how to make our symbols immediately recognizable by a large number of people.

COMMON NONSENSE ABOUT ICONS

Icons are controversial. If you spend much time talking to programmers, graphic designers, and computer users or you read the pontifical editorials in many of the computer magazines and newsletters, you will get many opinions about icons. Many of these ideas are wrong. Before we delve into how to design icons, perhaps we should clear away the poppycock, balderdash, and pure baloney that passes for proven fact.

Icons totally replace words

If you use icons in a user interface, you cannot and should not use words too.

Icons and words are not enemies. They are not mutually exclusive. In certain places each is needed. Most of the time, a careful combination of a well-designed icon and a succinctly phrased word label outperform either alone.

All-or-nothing designers miss opportunities to have the best of both words and icons. Word labels help users learn visual images initially, and the visual images help poor readers interpret word labels.

Icons are no better than words

Operating a computer by manipulating icons is so awkward and inefficient that iconic interfaces are just a fad.

Many computer users and programmers learned to operate a computer through a command-line interface that required remembering complex commands and typing them in. Often these users cannot imagine why others would rather do their work by pointing to silly little pictures. Such a response is natural. Once we have learned how to do something well, we find all alternative procedures awkward and inefficient. This is especially true if we have invested considerable time in acquiring knowledge and skills that do not transfer to the alternative procedure.

Another common objection to iconic interfaces is that they are hopelessly inefficient. Critics often point out how much more time it takes to shove icons around the screen than to press a function key. The problem with this analysis is that it ignores the time required to learn which function key to press, the time required to remember or look up which function key to press, and the time to correct a mistake made when the wrong key is pressed. When users have to learn a new program monthly and must use several different programs daily, iconic interfaces may be considerably more productive than remember-and-type interfaces.

Again it is not an either-or choice. Why not give users commands, menus, and icons and let them pick the style of interaction that best suits their needs?

Icons make products easier to use

To make a product easy to use, all you have to do is replace the words in commands and menus with icons.

Icons do not by themselves make a computer easier to use. Poorly designed or deployed icons may do just the opposite. Obscure icons make computer screens look like the control panel of an alien spaceship. Gaudy, garish icons make them look like a piece of "refrigerator art."

Icons do not make a product easier to use. Good design does.

Icons must be perfectly obvious

Reject any icon that is not immediately obvious to everyone everywhere every time.

Obvious icons are better than obscure ones, but there is more to good icons than instant recognition. In fact, making an icon immediately obvious to everyone may be such an elusive goal that by fixating on it, we obscure the system as a whole.

Some concepts are inherently difficult to understand—whether we represent them with icons or with words. For such concepts, the issue is not whether icons require study but whether they require less or more study than equivalent word labels.

An icon does not fail if it requires a few seconds of study the first time the user sees it. Provided users are not totally stumped by an icon, the process of figuring out its meaning adds an enjoyable challenge to learning the system. Watch users when they decode an icon. They smile.

This process of decoding an icon actively engages the user and helps the user remember the icon so that recognition is almost instant the next time. This instant recognition may be much more important than the initial delay, especially if the user will encounter the icon dozens or even hundreds of times.

Icons are pictures

The best icons are realistic, postage-stamp sized illustrations.

Icons are not pictures. We do not look at them to see what something looks like. In fact, if we have to look at them closely, they are probably not well designed. Icons are meant to be viewed entirely in a single glance and, once learned, recognized automatically. Overloading an icon with realistic detail may render it less rather than more recognizable.

Designing icons is pure art

Designing icons is a form of artistic self-expression. Beauty is in the eye of the artist.

No one would suggest using an ugly icon when an attractive one would work just as well. Many illustrators, however, compromise or even defeat the effectiveness of icons by considering only the aesthetics of the image. In technical icons, form must follow function, and when it does, the results are usually pleasing to the eye. When function is ignored and icons are used merely to decorate, viewers are frustrated, bored, or insulted.

FOR MORE INFORMATION

Aria, Barbara. *The Nature of the Chinese Character.* New York: Simon and Schuster, 1991.

Bliss, Charles K. *Semantography (Blissymbolics).* Sydney: Semantography (Blissymbolics) Publications, 1963.

Capitman, Barbara Baer. *American Trademark Designs.* Mineola, NY: Dover Publications, Inc., 1976.

Dreyfuss, Henry. *Symbol Sourcebook: An Authoritative Guide to International Graphic Symbols.* New York: Van Nostrand Reinhold, 1984.

Frutiger, Adrian. *Signs and Symbols: Their Design and Meaning.* New York: Van Nostrand Reinhold, 1989.

Jean, Georges. *Writing, the Story of Alphabets and Scripts.* New York, NY: Harry N. Abrams, Inc., 1992.

Koch, Rudolf. *The Book of Signs.* New York: Dover, 1955.

Lehner, Ernst. Symbols, Signs, & Signets. New York: Dover, 1950.

Modley, Rudolf. *Handbook of Pictorial Symbols.* New York: Dover, 1976.

Shelton, S. M. "The Eyes Have It." *Technical Communication*, 38 (2) Second Quarter 1991: 168-177 (1991).

Sides, Dorothy Smith. *Decorative Art of the Southwestern Indians.* New York: Dover, 1961.

How icons work

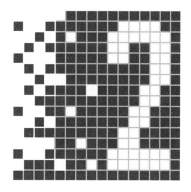

This chapter is about the ergonomics of icons. It concerns how people see, understand, and react to icons. If you are a harried designer with a deadline approaching at sixty seconds a minute, you may be tempted to skip this chapter, feeling it is too theoretical to be of much immediate use. You can skip this chapter for now, but please do not ignore it. A little theory can solve a lot of practical problems.

Misunderstanding leads to bad design. To make effective icons, you must understand how icons work. Understanding how people perceive, recognize, remember, and use icons guides our design efforts. It lets us apply what we know about other forms of visual design. Ignorance means starting from scratch. Knowledge lets us build on what we know and what we learn along the way.

WHAT PEOPLE DO WITH ICONS

All design is for a purpose. Whether you are designing sports cars, evening gowns, office buildings, or icons, you work for a purpose. That purpose may be artistic self-expression. It may be to win an award or to gain a promotion. Such designer-centered goals fail to deliver products that satisfy people's needs. Good design, on the other hand, focuses on the needs of the users of a product and what users do with the product.

For icons to succeed, users must be able to do four things with them: decode, recognize, find, and activate. Often icons fail because they enable only one or two of these functions. You may have to make tradeoffs among these four goals, but all are necessary to some extent.

Decode an icon

The first task confronting the user is to decode a new icon and to learn its meaning. This activity of making sense of what we see is nothing new. We do it thousands of times a day. Every time we encounter a visual image we have not seen before, we stop, however momentarily, until we can figure out what it is. We have gone through this process of puzzling out the meaning of practically every image we can now recognize. Newborn infants appear to recognize only three things: the color red, snakes, and human faces. Everything else has required decoding. We have performed this process so many millions of times that we hardly notice it at all—until it fails and we are stuck with an image or icon that remains a mystery.

Decoding an icon is basically a process of decomposing it into simpler and simpler graphic objects until we can recognize the separate pieces and combine their meanings to arrive at the meaning of the whole icon.

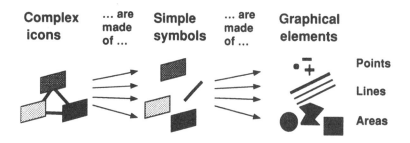

This decomposition is exactly how we recognize unfamiliar graphics. If we do not recognize the complex object, we try recognizing its separate parts. If we recognize the parts, we combine their separate meanings to infer the identity of the whole. If we do not recognize a part, we divide it and try to recognize its parts. This recursive, top-down process continues until we make sense of the object or are stumped and either give up or seek more information. As soon as we recognize an object, however, we rarely look more deeply into its parts.

The implication for designers is clear: **Draw a simple image already associated with the concept you wish to represent.**

If you cannot do this, then: **Represent the concept by combining familiar images in a simple way.**

Recognize an icon

Once we've learned an icon, we merely have to recognize it when we see it and we have to recall its meaning. Our ability to recognize large numbers of visual images is well documented. Even when the images are very similar, we can still recognize them. Consider how similar are the faces of all of your friends, yet you recognize them effortlessly. Recognition is especially quick and reliable when images are:

- Concrete, showing real-world objects
- Vivid, clearly depicted
- Conceptually distinct one from another

Superficial recognition is not enough. Not only must we sense that we have seen the icon before, we must also recall its meaning from memory. This deeper recognition means that the icon unambiguously implicates one of many possible meanings. This works best when the visual image of the icon is directly associated with other aspects of the concept it represents. The image should awaken memories of related sounds, words, and emotions.

To make this so: **Select a concrete, vivid image that is strongly associated with all aspects of the concept it represents.**

Search for an icon

The ability to quickly find the one icon we need on a cluttered screen is essential to productive use of a product. The process of visual search has undergone extensive study with some not too surprising results. The speed with which we can locate a visual object in a display depends on the degree to which:

- The searcher knows what the target looks like
- The target object is visually distinct from other objects

Thus, to make it easy for users to find the icon they seek: **Ensure that users can predict the distinctive visual characteristics, such as shape and color, of the icon they seek.**

Activate an icon

Once you find the icon, you may need to activate it. This in turn requires specifying which icon you want to interact with and then triggering the interaction. To designate which icon we want to activate we may:

- Point to it with a mouse pointer
- Point to it with a finger on a touch-sensitive screen
- Press a key to skip forward through the icons

We likewise have several choices for triggering interaction and signaling the kind of response we want. The response can vary depending on other input actions such as:

- Which mouse button was pressed
- How many times it was pressed
- Whether it was tapped or held down
- Other buttons or keys were held down at the same time

The number of possible combinations can explode to the point where users find the system impossible to learn and unpredictable to use. To avoid this confusion: **Establish, teach, and consistently follow a simple scheme for activating icons.**

HOW PEOPLE PROCESS VISUAL IMAGES

Understanding how people process visual images is important because icons demand more of our visual perception. It is also important because a naive understanding can lead to poor icons. Understanding visual perception enables us to design in such a way as to take advantage of how that perception system works.

And, if you understand how icons work, you understand how graphics work; if you understand how graphics work, you understand how we communicate—regardless of medium.

Naive model of visual processing

The naive designer conceives of human vision as something like a camera. Perception forms an interior image that replicates exactly the scene in front of the eyes. This scene is photographically recorded and filed in memory.

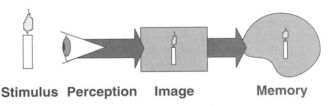

Stimulus Perception Image Memory

This is a simple, intuitive model, but it is wrong. If it were true, we could only recognize objects that look exactly the same as they did the first time we encountered them.

Richer model of visual processing

A more realistic model shows how everything in the visual system seems to affect everything else:

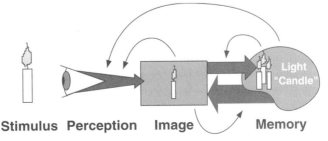

Stimulus Perception Image Memory

The differences between this and the naive model are important:

- Perception filters visual inputs. Less than 1/1000 of 1 percent of the information taken in by the retina makes it through short-term memory.

- We remember not just one visual image for the object but several.

- In additional to visual memories, we remember the name of the object and its characteristics. All these memories are linked so that recall of one triggers others.

- Much, perhaps most, of what we see comes not from the eyes but from memory. We see mostly what we already know and have seen before. Visual input seems designed more to trigger the correct memories than to tell us directly what something looks like.

- What we currently see and what we have seen affect how we interpret visual input and what we remember. We tend to seek out details that confirm our current interpretation of a scene.

It is a more complex model and it is messy. Everything affects everything else. This is why designing an effective icon is so difficult.

WHERE DOES MEANING COME FROM?

Icons alone are meaningless. An icon in a particular context, however, triggers memories and associations in a user's mind that produce what we refer to as the meaning of the icon. Only in a particular context and interpreted by a human mind does the icon have any meaning.

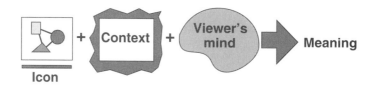

We are accustomed to thinking of the icon as the conveyor of an idea or concept. We talk as if meaning were inherent in the icon. The icon is more like a catalyst that releases meaning in the presence of a context and a human mind.

Context contributes to meaning

The context is the situation in which we view the icon. It consists of all the other things in the field of view that add to or interfere with the icon. We can think of context as all the hints that nudge us toward one particular interpretation of an icon.

Context includes:

- Adjacent icons
- Related labels or other text
- Other windows or displays
- Other objects in the environment

Let's see how context affects our interpretation of visual images. Quickly read the following two lines:

Most people read the top line as "eleven, twelve, thirteen, fourteen, fifteen" and the bottom one as "table," without noticing that the number "13" is identical to the letter "B."

In this example, notice how the following visual symbols achieve different meanings in different contexts:

Graphic	Context	Meaning
🚺	Hallway door	Women's restroom
	Hospital	Gynecology
🎥	Movie theater	Projection room
	Computer animation program	Show animation
☕	Highway sign	Restaurant
	Restaurant menu	Beverages
	Grocery store in the United States	Coffee
	Grocery store in the United Kingdom	Tea

Consider the different meanings of these common symbols often found in icons:

This symbol …	… in this context …	… means this
?	Menu bar	Help facility
	Data-entry form	Missing information
	Flowchart	To decide
	Equation	Variable to solve for
Arrow	Connecting blocks in a diagram	Movement in organizational structure
	Scroll bars	Direction the user's viewpoint will appear to move
	Flowchart	Flow of data or control
	Ruler of a word-processing program	Mark of a point, for example, a tab stop
Color red	Traffic light	Stop
	Weather map	Hot
	Anatomical diagram	Arterial blood flow
	Security	Danger

Often the strongest context is provided by adjacent icons. For example, the meaning of this icon:

In its most common pairing, it represents a gender:

In this group of icons, however, it represents a stage of life:

In this one, it represents one member of a traditional family:

Here it is merely a familiar object used to represent a size:

Without knowing the context in which an icon will be seen, we cannot say how users will interpret an icon. The context can reinforce or totally reverse our intended meaning.

The user's mind completes meaning

The icon in a particular context triggers mental processes that lead to the meaning. That meaning depends on the mental processes of the user.

- Perception filters inputs
- Interest and curiosity guide attention
- Memories and knowledge fill in blanks
- Reasoning interprets and infers
- Emotion motivates and energizes

Perception filters inputs

Human perception is a ruthless, purposeful filter. Only about 1/1000th of 1 percent of the information taken in by the eyes survives our short-term memory. This filtration not only saves us from being overwhelmed with raw data, it actively seeks out and presents simple patterns to us. Instead of 300 million dots of light, we see meaningful objects and patterns.

Do you see the white triangles, square, and circle in these figures?

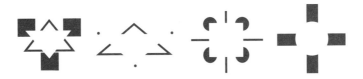

Interest and curiosity guide attention

We see what we notice and we notice what we are interested in. If you flip through the pages of a magazine, you are more likely to notice advertisements for food if you have not eaten in several hours than if you have just consumed a filling meal.

Memories and knowledge fill in blanks

We need little visual inputs to recognize familiar objects. For example, what are these two objects?

Even though you had only a few lines, you probably recognized a violin (or bass or cello) and a camel (or horse). Once you know what the object is, your memory can fill in all the necessary details.

Reasoning interprets and infers

Consciously and unconsciously we reason about what we see. Using visual input as a starting point we make inferences about what produced the input. Try this exercise:

Close your left eye and fixate your right eye on this point.

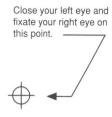

Adjust the distance of the page until the white circle at the right disappears.

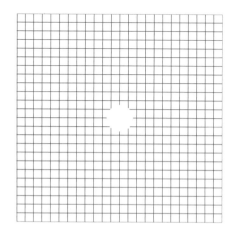

The white circle disappears because at a certain distance its image falls over the blind spot of the right eye, where the optic nerve joins the retina. When the white circle disappeared, what took its place? A continuous grid, right? Where did the rest of the grid come from? It came from a reasoning process that made the missing part of the image consistent with the rest of the image. Unconscious reasoning processes make the reasonable assumption that the missing part is just like the surrounding area.

One icon can have multiple meanings

Each icon has a matrix of possible meanings depending on contexts and users. The simple equation …

$$\textbf{icon}_i + \textbf{context}_j + \textbf{viewer}_k \Rightarrow \textbf{meaning}_{ijk}$$

… has great implications for us as designers.

An example of meaning depending on context and mind

What does this icon mean?

The answer depends on where it appears and on who is looking.

Shown alone, its meaning depends on the previous associations of the user. An electrical engineer is likely to interpret it as the symbol for battery. Someone familiar with word processors is likely to interpret it as centering lines of text. Others may be interpret it as an emblem for symmetry, elaborate sandwiches, or some other concept.

When shown in the company of related symbols, the meaning of centered lines becomes clear to most users, regardless of previous associations.

The effect of context overrides previously learned associations to suggest a new meaning.

Restrict the context

If the meaning varies with context, the symbol is context dependent. That is …

$$\text{meaning}_{i1k} \neq \text{meaning}_{i2k}$$

In this case we must control the context in which the icon appears. We must consider what other items are visible at the same time as the icon and what events lead up to its display. We must then control these so that the appearance of the icon suggests just the meaning intended.

Test with actual users

If the meaning varies with user, it is unclear. That is …

$$\text{meaning}_{ij1} \neq \text{meaning}_{ij2}$$

Icons that depend on specific professional or cultural knowledge are likely to fail for members of another profession or culture. The only way to know whether your icons are clear, is to test with actual users under realistic conditions.

Avoid ambiguous icons

If multiple meanings are possible in a single context by one user, the icon is ambiguous. That is …

$$\text{icon}_i + \text{context}_j + \text{viewer}_k \Rightarrow \text{meaning}_1 + \text{meaning}_2 + \text{meaning}_3$$

In this case, the user cannot figure out the meaning of the icon or is unsure about which of the possible meanings to believe.

Anticipate the mind of the user

Rather than starting with the design of the icon, we must start at the other end with the knowledge and mental processes of the user. We must ask ourselves what symbols, objects, and concepts are already familiar to the user. These may vary from one group of users to another:

Concept	For office workers	For engineers
Measure		
Draw		
Document		

Don't design standalone symbols

Conventional wisdom—or at least the user-interface style guides for several large computer manufacturers—insists that you should make icons completely meaningful regardless of context or user. Such a naive approach is both impossible and unwise.

Don't design icons to stand alone. An icon, like a word, achieves meaning only by its use in a particular context. Trying to make an icon completely unambiguous to everyone under all possible circumstances is usually impossible in most cases. Attempting such a feat leads to overly complex designs. Instead, design the icon so that under actual viewing conditions it combines with other information in the user's field of view and working memory to produce a clear meaning.

HOW DOES THE USER REACT TO THE ICON?

So far we have been looking from the inside out. We have been looking at what the designer does to encode meaning in the icon. We must now turn and look at the icon through the eyes of the user. We must turn from discussing what the designer puts into the icon to what the user gets out of it.

Every pixel contributes either message, enabler, or noise. The *message* is what you are trying to say. It is the concept you are trying to represent. The *enablers* help the user get the message reliably and accurately. *Noise* interferes with that process.

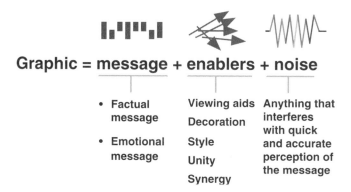

Graphic = message + enablers + noise

• **Factual message**	**Viewing aids**	**Anything that interferes with quick and accurate perception of the message**
• **Emotional message**	**Decoration**	
	Style	
	Unity	
	Synergy	

The message

The message is what the icon is all about. If the user recognizes the icon as representing the concept you intended, the message was understood.

There are two kinds of messages: factual and emotional. Factual messages represent specific information. They are ideas or concepts that we want the user to recognize intellectually. Emotional messages are feelings we want the user to recognize and perhaps experience. We want the user to feel motivated to use the product, concerned about dangers, and happy with results.

Messages may be communicated redundantly. That is, the same message may be encoded in two different ways in the same icon. Consider the stop sign, a red octagon labeled with the word "STOP." We could take away the word "STOP" and most people would still interpret the message in the same way. Thus we can say that the message was redundantly encoded with text, with color, and with shape. Redundant encoding is quite common where messages are critical or where conditions work against one encoding method. Those who cannot read the word "STOP" or those who are color blind could still get the message.

How do we know if something is part of the message? Take it out and test the icon. If nobody gets the same idea from the icon, then the thing removed was a non redundant message.

Enablers

Enablers are not part of the message but they may be essential to speedy, reliable delivery of the message. Enablers help the user interpret the message. The easiest way to think of enablers is to imagine what would happen if they were omitted. If you leave out enablers, users can still get the same message, but it will take them longer and they will make more mistakes. Enablers include:

- Backgrounds that make the subject stand out clearly
- Consistent style that highlights differences between the icons of a series
- Decorative touches that invite the user to notice and study the icon
- Borders, guidelines, and alignments of objects that guide the eye to the true subject of the icon

Anything that improves the efficiency and reliability of an icon is an enabler.

Noise

In any form of communication, noise is bad. Noise is anything that interferes with the sure delivery of the right message. Noise is simply poor design.

Anything that is not clearly enabler or message is probably noise. Noise is relatively easy to detect. If you suspect that something is noise, simply remove it and observe what happens. If users get the same message more quickly and reliably than before, then whatever you removed was noise.

Noise includes anything that distracts or misleads the user. It creeps in at every stage of design. Perhaps it is an irrelevant color or an object that triggers the wrong associations. Maybe it is a lack of foreground-to-background contrast. Often it is a decorative flourish that overwhelms the subtle message of the icon.

What are we designers to do?

As designers everything we do contributes to the message, to enablers, or to noise. Often it is not easy to know which. A choice of color or selection of an object can create message, enabler, or noise. The only way to be sure is to test with actual users under realistic circumstances.

Here is how you would analyze the test data:

If you take out the suspicious item and this happens ...	The thing you removed was this...
Users get the intended message more quickly and more reliably	Noise
Users get the message, but take longer and make more mistakes	Enabler
Some users get the message, others do not	Redundant message
No users get the message	Nonredundant message

As designers, our job is to convey messages. To do that we must encode the messages clearly, include enablers for reliability, and eliminate noise.

- Encode critical messages redundantly, that is, using more than one method to represent each idea.

- Add enablers only if testing shows that they improve the speed and reliability with which users interpret the message.

- Unless testing shows something is message or enabler, leave it out because it is noise.

FOR MORE INFORMATION

Arnheim, Rudolf. *Art and Visual Perception: A Psychology of the Creative Eye*. Berkeley, CA: University of California Press, 1974.

Baddeley, Alan. *Human Memory: Theory and Practice*. Boston: Allyn and Bacon, 1990.

Bloomer, Carolyn M. *Principles of Visual Perception*. New York: Design Press, 1990.

Bruce, Vicki and Patrick Green. *Visual Perception: Physiology, Psychology and Ecology*. Hove, UK: Lawrence Erlbaum Associates, 1990.

Horton, William. *Illustrating Computer Documentation*. New York: John Wiley, 1991.

Humphreys, Glyn and Vicki Bruce. *Visual Cognition: Computational Experimental and Neuropsychological Perspectives*. Hove, UK: Lawrence Erlbaum Associates, 1989.

Kosslyn, Stephen M. and Olivier Koenig. *Wet Mind: The New Cognitive Neuroscience*. New York: Free Press, 1992.

Marr, David. *Vision: A Computational Investigation into the Human Representation and Processing of Visual Information*. New York: Freeman, 1982.

Rock, Irvin. *The Logic of Perception*. Cambridge, MA: MIT Press, 1983.

REPRESENTING IDEAS GRAPHICALLY

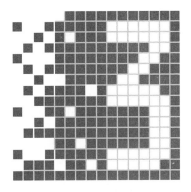

When we communicate, whether we are communicating facts, numbers, or pure emotions, we do so through symbols. They may be pictures, words, musical notes, a tone of voice, or a facial expression. Often they are subtle and other times, direct. Sometimes they are used so effortlessly that we would deny using symbols at all. Sometimes they work and sometimes they do not.

To communicate complex meanings in icons, you must expose the viewer to a collection of symbols. For the icon to evoke the desired meaning in the viewer's thought—conscious or sometimes unconscious—each symbol must trigger exactly the idea you intend. Each symbol must have a strong, direct association with the desired meaning, not just in your mind but in the mind of the viewer.

When selecting symbols, look for ones that naturally and directly suggest the idea you want to communicate. Start with symbols that show the subject itself or at least physically resemble it: These are easy to understand and recognize. Then consider ones that show a related object. These may take a little study and thought, but once understood, they are recognized reliably. If you cannot communicate the concept by showing a familiar object, only then consider more abstract symbologies, such as shapes, colors, position, pattern, and texture. Some of these symbologies may be well known, but most symbols based on abstract properties must be learned by the viewer.

This chapter provides a checklist of all the different ways of encoding meaning in icons. When you can't think of how to communicate an idea in icons, scan this list. Consider each technique in turn. Ask yourself, "How can I use this technique to communicate the idea?" Don't stop with your first idea. Continue through the whole list. Try to think of five or six different ways of communicating the concept. This way, you can combine the best techniques and throw away those that will not work in your user's situation or ones that you cannot draw recognizably.

THE SUBJECT DIRECTLY

Show the subject if you can. This is the most direct symbol and usually the best. The physical similarity between the real-world object and its graphical representation ensures that the subject is recognized reliably. Often when symbols mimic the subject, we forget that they are symbols at all and treat them as if they were the object being discussed.

Subject itself

If the subject is a familiar physical object, show that object. For example, to refer to a computer, show a recognizable view of that computer:

To refer to a diskette, show that diskette:

Use the image of an attachment to refer to that attachment:

Mouse   Printer   Disk drive   Microphone

Action being performed

When an activity involves manipulating a physical object, you can represent that activity by the image of the action being performed on the object. Show objects arranged the way they would appear to the user performing or observing the action. Here are some more examples of actions symbolized by the visual appearance of the act:

Making a   Pressing a button   Capturing a   Inserting a disk
phone call   screen

If the action requires a person to assume a distinctive posture, we can use that posture to represent the action:

Read   Exercise   Study   Teach   Wait

Person experiencing emotion

How can we represent something so intangible and ephemeral as an emotion or mental state? Artists and advertisers have been doing it for centuries. Let's see how we can borrow some of their techniques.

Human face

There is no more effective conveyor of emotion than the human face. It is so effective that the mere hint of facial expression suffices for simple emotions. Often senders of electronic mail messages indicate their feelings by including little sideways faces made of standard typewriter characters:

Happy	: -)	: - }
Sad	: - (	: - {
Wink	; - |	
Surprise	: - o	

Likewise, even a small icon can represent common emotions with a simple image of the face of a person experiencing that emotion.

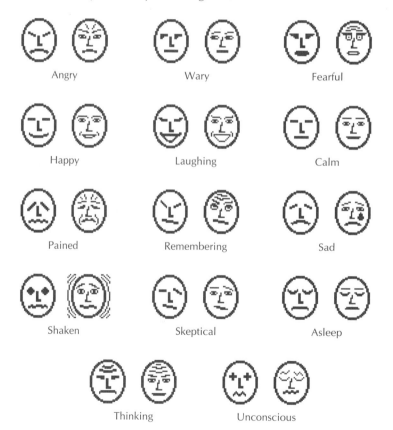

Angry   Wary   Fearful

Happy   Laughing   Calm

Pained   Remembering   Sad

Shaken   Skeptical   Asleep

Thinking   Unconscious

Spontaneous facial expressions, unlike conventional hand gestures, are generally universal and have the same meaning in all cultures. Some strict Islamic sects, however, forbid showing the human face at all.

Body language

Unconscious postures and poses can reveal the inner state of a human being. As such, they are good symbols of such states. Consider these emblems of mental states:

| Combative | Dejected | Perplexed | Joyful |

| Tired | Victorious | Surrendered | Unconscious |

These postures must be ones people spontaneously assume when experiencing the emotions. For good examples, watch the winning and losing athletes at the Olympic games.

A RELATED OR ASSOCIATED OBJECT

Designing icons would be easy indeed if all we had to do was hold up a picture of the subject. Alas, not all the concepts we must show are concrete objects. When we can't show the subject itself, often we can show another object that nonetheless calls the subject to mind. A concrete object can suggest, imply, or point to another idea. Each of these associations gives us another way to create an icon for a concept.

Logical analogies

When you can't show the idea directly, you can show an analogous object, one with recognizable parallels to the real idea.

Causal connection

Show the cause of the idea you want to convey. Icons for utility programs typically show an example of the problem the program is designed to overcome. For example, the Equation Solver program from Microsoft sports this icon that shows an equation with a missing value represented by the question mark:[1]

Utility programs for repairing damaged files could use an image that shows the kind of damage recovered:

Normal   Missing data   Inconsistent
database   data

Tool used to perform the action

If an operation requires a familiar tool, you can use the tool as a symbol for that activity. Consider these emblems for industrial activities:

Filmmaking   Photography   Drafting   Maintenance

Here the tool is one used in the actual activity. It may be the only tool used for the activity or it may be one of many tools. It must, however, be both familiar to the viewer and strongly associated with the activity:

Record video   Send a fax   Dine   Visit physician   Make a phone
                                                                      call

---

[1]Screen shot is reprinted with permission from Microsoft Corporation.

Functional analogy

If you can't show the object itself, you can show an object that performs an analogous function in a more familiar realm. Many computer programs automate processes that were once performed by people using physical tools. Often the icons for this software employ images of the tool, person, or body part used in the past to perform the software's functions.

Tools used for analogous activity

Computer programs often use physical tools and devices as emblems for the analogous functions provided by software. Electronic publishing systems typically use scissors, paste, pencils, and push pins for related functions:

Measure   Crop   Design   Attach

The desktop metaphors of various graphical user interfaces rely heavily on icons resembling analogous, real-world tools:

Clipboard   Clock   Notebook   Calculator   Names and addresses

Other examples of tools used as symbols include these:

Add color   Protect from viruses   Produce multimedia   Play back sounds   Unlock

Even general concepts can be represented by specific, familiar tools:

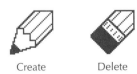

Create   Delete

Body part used in activity

If an activity is traditionally performed with a part of the body, you can show or feature that body part as a symbol for the activity. Consider the use of hands and fingers in these icons:

| Count | Cooperate | Press a button | Select | Handle with care |

Other parts of the body can represent activities commonly performed with these parts:

| Listen | Look | Speak |

Because we use each part of the body for many functions, body parts are seldom sufficient to unambiguously implicate one activity. They usually require labels or other objects to clarify the meaning. Remember also that standards of modesty vary from culture to culture; therefore, take care when showing body parts in icons for international users.

Results

People use computers to achieve results. They are inherently interested in the fruits of their efforts. Often the best way to communicate the function of a button or command is by showing its goal, effects, or consequences.

Many common symbols show the state or condition that will result from an action. The internationally recognizable emblem for poison shows a skull and crossbones, as if to say, "Drink this liquid and you'll wind up like this image."

Text formatting programs typically show individual characters or entire blocks of text as they will look after the user selects the icon:

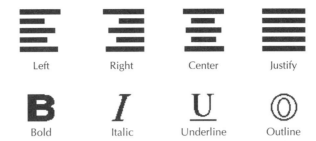

| Left | Right | Center | Justify |

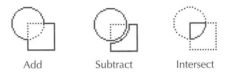

| Bold | Italic | Underline | Outline |

Likewise, drawing programs present the user with a menu of ways to combine shapes:

| Add | Subtract | Intersect |

Structural analogy

If the organization of the subject is important, you can often represent it by showing an object with an analogous structure. It can be one with corresponding parts:

Collection of
electronic
documents

Linkage among
programs

Or you can pick an object with a parallel organization, for example, to suggest modularity:

Structural analogy can be extended to portray a pattern of relationships, for instance, the file hierarchy of a computer system:

Disk   Directory   File

Metaphors and figures of image

Poetry and other forms of figurative language use figures of speech to express what cannot be said literally. We can use visual equivalents for some of these techniques when we cannot show the idea directly.

Synecdoche

In the figure of speech called *synecdoche,* we use a single, familiar part to stand for the whole object. This technique is widely used in road signs where a gas pump signifies a service station; a tent, an entire campground; a bed, a hotel; and a fork, knife, and spoon, a restaurant:

Restaurant

We see this technique in the tendency to represent entire cities or even countries by a single prominent building, such as the Eiffel Tower for Paris, Big Ben for London, the Space Needle for Seattle, and the Arch for St. Louis.

When the whole object is too complex or indistinct to represent a concept, pick a small, recognizable part:

Kerning   Games   Music   Electronics

This technique is often used on menus to present the user with a palette of simplest-case alternatives as in this example from Deneba's Canvas 3.0:

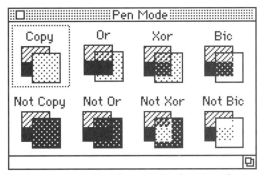

Pen Mode palette is reprinted with permission from Deneba Systems, Inc.

Litotes

When you cannot find a direct symbol for a concept, consider whether you can show it by the negation of its opposite, as in the figure of speech called *litotes*. We do this verbally when we show our approval by calling something "not bad." Although double negatives are generally discouraged in verbal languages ("Don't use no double negatives no time, no way"), they work well graphically:

 The pictographic language of the Kiowa Indians used the broken arrow as a symbol for peace.

 How do you show freedom? One way is to show release from its opposite, that is, imprisonment.

 The standard male symbol with a small piece snipped out represents the medical procedure of vasectomy.

This technique is particularly effective because we have several ways of reversing, limiting, thwarting, and denying concepts. For instance, to show negation or denial:

 Mark through it with an X or a slash

 Superimpose the standard circle with a diagonal slash

Include a minus sign

 Show an object used to block, thwart, or defend against
the concept

 Show a broken or distorted form of the object

 Reverse the normal action

Hyperbole

If the object you use to symbolize a concept is small, you may use *hyperbole*, or exaggeration, to make it more prominent. This technique is valuable when you must clearly distinguish among otherwise similar objects or concepts:

 We see hyperbole at work in the standard road sign for an incline. If the sign did not greatly exaggerate the slope, it would appear flat.

 Using the bomb as an icon for a system error certainly overstates the severity of the problem. This icon is the visual equivalent of phrases like "fatal error" and "catastrophic failure."

 When the user of a Macintosh drops the icon for a file into the trash can icon, the sides of the trash can seem to bulge.[2]

 By exaggerating the size and blackness of the plume of smoke from a factory smokestack, we create an emblem for air pollution.

Euphemism

Some concepts are too shocking or emotionally disturbing if shown directly. To represent them, we typically substitute a more acceptable object. This is akin to

---

[2]Screen shots are reprinted with permission from Apple Computer, Inc.

the verbal technique of *euphemism* whereby funeral directors refer to the body as *mortal remains of the beloved* rather than as the *corpse* or *food for worms*.

Human excrement   Injury   Bug

Synaesthetic analogy

Images in one sensory modality suggest images in another. Which of these two shapes is called *tukatee* and which is called *maluma*?

Most people label the one on the left as *maluma* and the one on the right as *tukatee*. Why? These are made-up shapes and names, yet people consistently feel one pairing of the names is more apt than the other. They cite the roundness of sounds in *maluma* and the sharpness of those in *tukatee*. Sounds do not have visible shape, so when we speak this way we are using *synaesthetic analogy*.

Synaesthetic analogy can apply to more subtle sensations as well. Which of these feels more soothing?

Conventions

Often we can borrow from another sign system that the viewer already understands. Sources of already learned symbols are all around us, on doors and walls, along highways, and in books and magazines we read.

Industrial and institutional symbols

Most technical and industrial activities have evolved their own system of visual symbols. In designing user interfaces for these disciplines, you should use the symbols that are already familiar to the reader.

These symbols tend to be quite simple and somewhat arbitrary. Electrical engineers, aerospace engineers, civil engineers, and computer scientists often deal with schematic diagrams of abstract relationships rather than realistic drawings of physical objects.

Consider these symbols for electrical engineers:

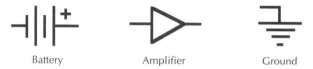

Battery   Amplifier   Ground

Symbols from many professional fields are familiar outside their narrow domain. Notice these familiar symbols:

Fragile   Atomic energy   Radioactive   Electrical
                                    hazard   safety

If a graphical form is widely practiced or well established in a field and your readers are familiar with it, think twice before you tinker with it. Unless your improvement is vast and obvious, it will confuse readers and probably be rejected by those comfortable with the familiar form.

Historical association

For a visual symbol, show not what something actually looks like but what users think or remember it looks like. Often this is an earlier, simpler version. Use this strategy when the current versions of an object are too diverse or have immediate associations that interfere with your use. A skeleton key is often used to represent "key" facts. On one project a deck of punched cards proved the best symbol for raw data more than a decade after punched cards were discontinued. One of the most common symbols for the oil pressure indicator in automobiles is a long-spouted oil can found only in antique shops. The most common icon for electronic mail is the rural mailbox, seldom seen in cities where most users live.

Education   Electronic mail   Document

Before using antiquated objects, make sure your users recognize the object. A factory-outlet shopping mall near where I lived used a factory steam whistle as its emblem. Most of the people I showed the emblem to thought it was a sky-rocket!

Public signs and symbols

Signs along the roadside and in public buildings provide a broad vocabulary of familiar symbols that many of your viewers will already know. Some are used directly as icons for analogous concepts:

Access denied   Difficult activity   Prohibited   Move this way   OK

Such signs suggest a simple, consistent way to use color and shape for meaning.

TEXTUAL IDENTIFIERS

Icons can contain letters, numbers, words, and mathematical symbols. Although including such textual identifiers may limit the number of viewers who can understand the icon, they may add critical information for those familiar with the included text.

Initials and punctuation marks

Public signs frequently use the initial letter of a word to represent that word. These signs are common throughout Europe:

Water closet,   Information   Parking
restroom

Initials are sometimes used in icons to represent the name of the product or its manufacturer, as in these icons for PageMaker:[3]

Program   Document

And this one for HiJaak:[4]

Though not as universal as mathematical symbols, punctuation symbols can be used for audiences whose written languages contain the symbols:

Help   Caution   Paragraph

For English and the Romance languages, the question mark and exclamation mark are safe when used for their conventional meanings. Avoid using periods, colons, and semicolons because they are too small, easily confused with other symbols, or not universally understood.

---

[3]Screen shots are reprinted with permission from Aldus Corporation.

[4]Screen shot is reprinted with permission from Inset Systems, Inc.

Math symbols

Common mathematical symbols are widely understood, especially in technical disciplines throughout the world. Even the general public understands the plus, minus, and equal signs:

| Increase | Zoom out, shrink | Battery | Formula |

Commonly used mathematical symbols include these:

Sign	Meaning	Advice
+	And, plus, more	OK for most users, provided it does not look too much like a cross hair.
-	Less, minus	OK for most users, but make it large enough that it is clearly visible. Use in a context that makes clear it is not a hyphen or a dash.
=	Equals	OK for most users, provided it is drawn legibly.
X	Multiply	Avoid unless the context makes clear it is the multiplication sign and not the letter X or the delete symbol.
/	Divide	Avoid unless the context makes clear it is the division symbol and not just a diagonal line.
>	Greater than	Nontechnical users will not recognize this symbol. It is often interpreted as an arrowhead.
<	Less than	Nontechnical users will not recognize this symbol. It is often interpreted as an arrowhead.
Σ	Add up, summation	OK for technical users only.
Δ	Change, degree of change	OK for technical users only.

Take care when using mathematical symbols with nontechnical users. I once overheard a group of accountants referring to the Σ (summation) icon in Microsoft Excel as the "funny E" icon. They did not recognize it as the Greek letter sigma. They were, however, able to use it successfully.

Labels

Sometimes, no matter how hard you try, you cannot find a graphical image more effective than a bit of text. Even if the text must be translated, it is better to use it if doing so makes an opaque icon communicate clearly. Text labels are often needed when the user must distinguish among items with no visible difference among them. Such labels are typically used to distinguish various file formats:

It is also used to specify the version number of a program as in these examples from PageMaker:[5]

Identifying trait

Sometimes a familiar word or phrase can unlock the meaning of an otherwise ambiguous image:

 The word *Extra* reminds us of the corner newsboy in the movies yelling, "Extra! Extra! Read all about it." That word confirms that this is a newspaper.

 The letters *ABC* identify this as a dictionary or glossary.

 Without the word *Prefs* the user would have no way of knowing this icon stands for a preferences file.

Remember that any text you include in the icon may have to be translated to other languages to remain meaningful.

---

[5]Screen shots are reprinted with permission from Aldus Corporation.

SPATIAL ARRANGEMENT

We can represent concepts by showing objects associated with those concepts. We can also represent some concepts in the way we arrange the objects we show.

Spatial mapping

By the technique of spatial mapping, we position objects in the image to communicate their spatial relationships. You see this simple technique in the airport signs for departing and arriving flights:

Departures   Arrivals

You can also see it in these icons for selecting how a word processor will print data on sheets of paper:

Portrait   Landscape

Spatial mapping is a direct method, since the visual image of the icon corresponds directly, though not exactly, to what the user sees in the real world.

Spatial analogy

Position also has a figurative meaning. Most religious art puts the more spiritual, godly things higher in the picture and more worldly and base objects lower. Things that are near seem immediate, primary, and intimate, while those farther away seem remote, secondary, and unfamiliar. Throughout Western art and literature, spatial positions and directions have consistent meanings.

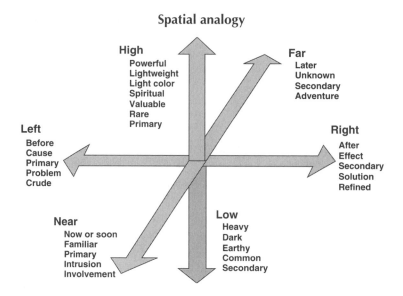

Spatial analogy

High
Powerful
Lightweight
Light color
Spiritual
Valuable
Rare
Primary

Far
Later
Unknown
Secondary
Adventure

Left
Before
Cause
Primary
Problem
Crude

Right
After
Effect
Secondary
Solution
Refined

Near
Now or soon
Familiar
Primary
Intrusion
Involvement

Low
Heavy
Dark
Earthy
Common
Secondary

Vertical position

Life is measured against a vertical scale. Decisions are made by the *high* and mighty, who eat *haute* cuisine and dress in *high* fashion. The *down*trodden eat *down*-home cooking and dress in hand-me-*downs*. If our status improves, we feel we have been *elevated* in our station in life. If our circumstances worsen, we feel de*based*. Ideals are *lofty*, but sometimes we have to get *down* to details.

The metaphor of vertical position shows up in the design of icons as well. Note the implications of vertical position or direction in these icons:

Organization chart   Increase   Sad (downcast)   Heavy   Sort in ascending order

This top-to-bottom orientation is almost universal. After all, we all live in a gravity field and we all read from the top of the page to the bottom.

Horizontal position

In Western art, time scurries from the left to the right. To show something moving horizontally, we best show it moving toward the right:

The same rule holds true for implied motion. Consider the directions of the standard controls for tape recorders and VCRs:

| Rewind | Play | Advance one frame | Fast forward |

Similarly, in icons depicting before-and-after conditions, the after condition is to the right:

| Combine | Enlarge | Copy to the clipboard | Format | Filter |

Anything pointing to the right implies motion. When we do not want to imply motion or change, we typically point to the left. Notice how arrows, hands, arms, and faces pointing to the left serve to arrest the rightward scanning eye and direct its attention to the interior of the icon:

Compare the effect of the left-pointing icons with their mirror images:

Although the meanings for vertical and depth position are consistent across most cultures, those for horizontal position are not. Arabic and Hebrew read from right to left, reversing the conventional horizontal flow of time. Chinese theater follows different conventions from the European theater for the movement of actors on the stage. For such users, you may need to add arrows to reinforce the left-to-right flow implied in your images.

Distance and depth

Things that come toward us or encroach into our personal space take on added importance. The nearness of an object affects how we interpret it and how we react to it. Consider the role of depth or distance in the meaning of icons. An object that blocks our view of another object draws attention to itself by the fact that it intrudes into our field of view. This effect can be used to focus attention on objects we might otherwise ignore or interpret as unimportant to the meaning of the icon:

Read
(attention focused
on the newspaper)

Microsoft Windows
(attention focused on
the mouse)

Engineering
drawing
(attention focused
on the compass)

Often icons must distinguish between things in the user's workspace or area of control. This is often done by showing things near or far:

Send   Receive

Depth can also heighten the emotional force of an icon by letting it point at the viewer or intrude into the user's personal space. This is sometimes called in-your-face design, and we see it in icons like this one:

Danger

Spatial grouping

A graphic arranges objects over an area. This selection and positioning of objects is called *layout* in graphic design, *composition* in painting and photography, and *mise en scéne* in film. How objects appear together tells us something about the objects and their interrelationships.

Grouping method	Example	How it works
Proximity		Objects close together seem related. Those farther apart seem unrelated.
Symmetry		Objects arranged in a symmetrical or regular pattern seem part of a group.
Alignment		Objects arranged in a line, or any regular pattern, appear part of a larger whole.
Boundary		Lines divide one side from another. They separate the graphic into two different areas. Objects in one area are clearly distinct from those across the line.
Enclosure		Enclosed items are part of a group. Everything within the border is somehow similar.
Connection		Objects connected by lines are seen as a whole.

If you want to see how to use spatial grouping, turn to Chapter 4, which contains several examples of icons that employ these techniques.

GEOMETRIC ELEMENTS AND PROPERTIES

Geometric elements and properties have associations we can use to communicate meaning in icons. Points, lines, and areas with their assigned color, pattern, texture, and size are useful in representing three kinds of concepts.

The three kinds of concepts are:

- **Geometric concepts and visual characteristics themselves**. Programs for graphic design, illustration, drafting, charting, and mapping often present the user with menus of geometric shapes and palettes of color and texture.

- **General and abstract concepts**. Using simple, regular, geometric shapes and characteristics can avoid the limitations of showing a particular instance. Since they do not look like a particular object, they can better represent a concept. For abstract concepts, simple squares, rectangles, circles, and ovals work best. More complex shapes carry more associations.

- **Emotional associations**. Many geometric elements and properties are associated with feelings and mental states. We can sometimes use them to trigger these emotions. They can alert, calm, arouse, reassure, or annoy the viewer.

Except for the first of these uses, the association between the geometric element or property and its referent is tenuous and probably has to be learned by the viewer. Geometric shapes, thus, work only in limited circumstances:

- You only have a few concepts to represent, typically no more than a dozen or two.

- Users will be taught the meaning of the icons before having to use the system.

- Users continually encounter the same set of icons.

- Users can easily look up the definition of any icon they do not recognize.

This suggests using geometric elements and properties to reinforce other methods of representing ideas.

Graphical elements

Ultimately all graphics can be divided into simple geometric elements, namely, points, lines, and areas.

Points

A point is any dot or other small mark that represents a location in space. In engineering and drawing programs, a point often represents a precise location or a vertex in a geometric element. In charting programs it may represent one observation or datum. When representing data, it may stand for an individual pixel or bit:

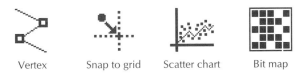

| Vertex | Snap to grid | Scatter chart | Bit map |

A point seldom has any meaning on its own. Instead it relates to some other object in the icon:

A point is too small to use graphical properties such as texture and pattern, but it can make limited use of blinking, color, size, and shape:

Property	Variations possible	Minimum size (pixels)	
Blinking	None, slow (2 Hz), and fast (5 Hz)	2 x 2	▪
Color	Black, white, red, blue, green, yellow	5 x 5	■
Size	Small, medium, large: · ▪ ■	3 x 3	▪
Shape	6 shapes: ■ ◆ ▮ ▬ ✦ ✎	4 x 4	■

Using properties in points is tricky. If we make the point large enough to clearly convey the property, we run the risk that the viewer will see it as an area and not a point.

Lines

Lines limit and divide objects. They typically represent edges, boundaries, or directions of motion or force. In icons, we use lines to represent:

- Boundaries and outlines of physical objects:

Edges and folds in a box	Edges and dimensions of an area	Edges of overlapping translucent squares

- Directions of force and action:

Projection of image	Line of sight	Movement to clipboard	Line slicing through object	Zigzag motion of double-tapping the mouse button

- Barriers or limits to action or movement:

Filter	Hide	Tab stop

- Paths of change or motion:

Jerky growth	Merge	Cycle	Rotate

- Discontinuities in texture, orientation, color, or value within an object:

Fragile	Corrupted data

- Long thin objects such as wires, cables, oscilloscope traces, lines of text:

| Lines of text | Noise | Paper clip | Earphones |

- Geometric lines:

| Align objects | Distance | Flip |

- Guides to the eye:

| Cross hair | Snap to grid |

- Connections between objects:

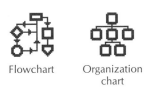

| Flowchart | Organization chart |

Lines can take on several graphical properties to represent more complex meanings:

Property	Variations	Limitations
Blinking	None, slow (2 Hz), and fast (5 Hz)	Blinking may distract or annoy the viewer. Use it with restraint.
Curvature	Straight, jagged, and curving	Smooth, tight curves are difficult to show in pixels.
Orientation	Vertical, horizontal, and diagonal	Diagonals at angles other than 30, 45, and 60 degrees become jagged.
Direction		Arrowhead requires at least 3 x 5 pixels.
Color	Black, white, red, green, blue, yellow	Line must be at least 2 pixels wide, and the color of the line must contrast with the background color.
Pattern and texture		Dotted lines suggest imaginary lines and edges. In science and engineering, many line patterns have conventional meanings.
Thickness		Short lines wider than 3 pixels can appear as rectangles, not lines.

Areas

Areas are two-dimensional forms that represent two- and three-dimensional objects. In icons, we often use areas to represent:

- **Geometric shapes themselves**. Areas can represent geometric shapes directly:

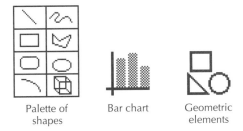

Palette of shapes   Bar chart   Geometric elements

- **Surfaces of solid objects**. Often the simplest way to draw an object is to depict it as a combination of simple geometric shapes:

Battery   Bookmark   Exit   Film   Calculator

- **Abstract symbols**. Many shapes have conventional meanings that we can borrow to represent general concepts:

Caution   Contrast   Fast forward   Full

Areas can convey a full range of graphical properties, such as shape, color, texture, and pattern.

Graphical properties

Geometric shapes communicate meaning through the graphical properties they display. Such graphical properties can be applied to the icon as a whole, to groups of related icons, or to objects within the icon. Graphical properties can represent several kinds of information.

- **The property itself**. Visual design requires selecting the visual properties of the objects we are designing. Such programs often present the user with a sampler of available visual properties:

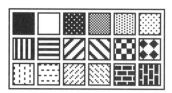

- **An object associated with the property**. In the figure of speech called *metonymy*, a characteristic stands for an object. For example, IBM is frequently referred to as "Big Blue" after the color of its logo. The building housing U.S. military headquarters is referred to as "The Pentagon" because of its shape. In geology, the symbols for various types of rock resemble the pattern of actual rocks. Notice the concepts associated with each of these visual properties:

| Calendar | Data port | Unformatted text | Noise | Printout |

- **Emotions triggered by the property**. Colors, patterns, orientations, and shapes all have emotional associations. What kinds of feeling do you have as you look at these shapes? Which shape seems soothing? Which is most disturbing?

Value

Value is the lightness or darkness of an image relative to its background. Seeing requires just such contrast between foreground and background:

The degree of contrast affects the visual prominence of an object. Objects that stand in high contrast to their backgrounds appear powerful and important:

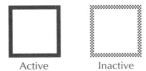

Active   Inactive

This is why we draw ghost images and imaginary lines in lower contrast than primary edges and shapes:

Add to   Filter   Hide   Replace

The general lightness of the icon affects its overall tone. A light tone suggests a friendly, playful mood. A dark tone suggests a somber, serious, or ominous mood.

Often we reverse light and dark in an icon (reverse video) to highlight an icon or to show that it is active:

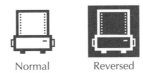

Normal   Reversed

In most cases this causes no problems. There are two exceptions, though:

- On some CRT displays light flows from the bright to the dark areas, causing small light items to bloom or smear and small dark ones to fill in. This means that icons may be less legible when reversed.

- Some objects have such a strong concept of lightness that we cannot reverse them without causing confusion or ambiguity:

Value also affects the legibility of icons and text. Without adequate foreground/background contrast, the icon disappears into the screen. Without adequate value contrast, we can see few sizes, colors, shapes, orientations, and textures.

Size

The size of an object affects its prominence in our field of view and its perceived importance. Consider these phrases indicating the importance of size: *bigger is better, the big picture, large-minded, big deal, big business, Mr. Big, Big Daddy, Big Mama, big cheese, big wheel, big league, big top, big shot, big man on campus, the Big Ten, small potatoes, small-fry, small change, small-minded, small-time,* and *small talk.*

Size is relative, and without a frame of reference, we cannot say whether something is small or large. Without the surrounding border, the inner square would have no clear size:

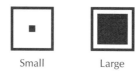

Small   Large

Viewers can readily distinguish about four different sizes in an icon, provided each is at least 30 percent larger than the previous:

Color

Color, or more properly, hue, offers a rich set of overlapping meanings:

- **Importance**. Brighter colors seem more powerful and important.
- **Mood**. Light and warm colors produce a festive, cheerful feeling. Dark and cool colors produce a more restrained mood.
- **Temperature**. Reds, oranges, and yellows suggest warmth and activity. Blues and greens suggest cool and calm.
- **Mimicry**. Water is blue, grass is green, fire is red.
- **Safety**. Red is a warning, yellow is a caution, and green means OK.

These meanings and other uses of color are covered in detail in Chapter 7.

Pattern

Pattern is any visual property repeated over an area or along a line. Pattern is analogous to tactile sensation. It often represents something of the characteristic of a surface:

A pattern of light and dark squares could represent a game board, and wavy lines have been used to stand for water and smoke:

Game board   Water   Smoke

The distinctive pattern of cells in a spreadsheet or text on a page provides clues to the identity of different kinds of data:

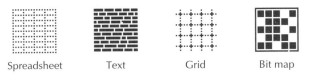

Spreadsheet   Text   Grid   Bit map

A distinctive patterned background can identify the separate icons of a single application, for example, these for HiJaak for Windows:[6]

Some patterns have conventional meanings in science and engineering. These hatch patterns represent different materials shown on cross sections:

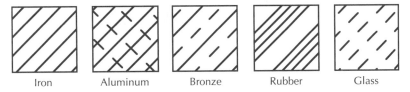

Iron   Aluminum   Bronze   Rubber   Glass

---

[6]Screen shots are reprinted with permission from Inset Systems, Inc.

Patterns can also have an abstract, symbolic meaning. For example, regular patterns suggest uniformity and order, while irregular patterns suggest coarseness, crudeness, vulgarity, turmoil, and violence:

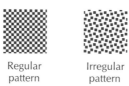

Regular
pattern

Irregular
pattern

Texture

Texture is closely related to and often confused with pattern. Whereas pattern concerns the way in which visual figures repeat themselves, texture concerns the frequency or scale at which the pattern repeats. Texture is usually described in terms of the number of lines or marks for a given area. It results from varying the scale of a pattern of marks, but not the pattern of marks itself. Varying texture does not change the overall balance of light and dark (the value) of an area:

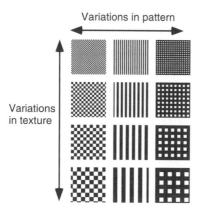

A sudden change of texture can indicate an edge, a fold, or a crease within an object:

In drawing, a gradual change of texture indicates changes in the angle of the surface relative to the source of light or to the viewer. However, when we must work with units of screen pixels, it is difficult to make a gradual change in texture. The result usually shows distinct bands rather than a smooth transition:

Texture can also contribute a symbolic meaning. Coarse textures suggest strength and crudeness. Fine textures appear more precise and refined.

To use texture in icons, we must avoid a couple of problems:

- The relatively large size of screen pixels makes it hard for us to use many different variations of texture. The finest textures may appear more as a continuous tone than as a repeated pattern. As we make the texture coarser, the pattern may fragment as the viewer begins to perceive separate objects rather than a repeated pattern.

- Some textures appear to shimmer or vibrate. This effect is worst for a 1-mm texture of 50 percent value. This shimmering effect draws undue attention to the texture and annoys many viewers:

Shape

The outline of any object gives it a shape. That shape may be regular or irregular, straight edged or rounded, concave or convex.

Straight edged shapes occur most frequently in man-made objects. In abstract shapes, they suggest a mechanical or rigid quality:

| Computer | Mechanical design | Battery | File cabinet | Chart |

Rounded shapes occur in nature and living organisms. We associate them with organic, fluid concepts:

| Vegetation | Globe | Bug | Laughter | Night |

Regular edges make a shape predictable, but less exciting. Simple, regular shapes can represent abstract categories and concepts better than irregular shapes, which tend to draw attention to their irregularity. All road signs are shaped as simple, regular geometric shapes:

| Stop | Permission | Caution | Activity | Information |

Irregular shapes call attention to themselves. They may appear spontaneous and unplanned. They may be used to represent objects that are unique or are exceptions to the rule:

| Electric | Missing data | Module |

Concave shapes draw the eye into the enclosed space, focusing attention on whatever resides there. They present a void and invite the eye and mind to fill it:

| Enter | Insert | Handle with care | In basket | Package |

Convex shapes push the eye outward and onward. They seem to radiate or broadcast:

Fire

Light

Speech

Alarm

Brightness

The effects of shape are subtle but real. Consider the meaning conveyed by the shape of speech balloons in cartoons. What kind of message would you expect each of these speech balloons to deliver?

Angle or orientation

The orientation or angle of an object relative to the viewer and to the horizon contributes to a feeling of action or stability. Compare these shapes. Which appear stable and which unstable? Which appear to be in motion and which are still?

Usually we are vertical when awake, horizontal when sleeping, and diagonal when falling or running. Therefore, a horizontal orientation of a figure suggests stability and repose, a vertical orientation offers energetic potential, and a diagonal orientation conveys instability and excitement:

Orientation also affects how well we recognize an object. The more the orientation of an object or text differs from its most common form, the more slowly and less accurately we recognize it.

Dynamic characteristics

Most icons are static. They do not move or change before our eyes. We can be thankful. A screen of tumbling, blinking, squirming icons might amuse us for a few seconds. However, if we had to use it to do real work, we would find the cavorting, caroming, flashing cacophony of shapes annoying to the extreme.

We can, though, use the ability of the computer to vary its display to help icons communicate simple messages. By changing the display of an icon over time, we can focus the user's attention and communicate specific messages about dynamic subjects. Dynamics are helpful to:

- **Represent dynamic concepts** such as change and motion. Any static icon that does this with arrows or multiple views is a candidate for animation.

- **Focus attention on a single icon or object**. In a basically static display, the eye is reliably drawn to any moving, blinking, or changing object.

- **Represent concepts** or emotions associated with a pattern of change or motion.

Blinking

Blinking compels attention. Blinking an object draws the eye to the blinking object. It is effective to call attention to emergency conditions and special exceptions.

We blink an object by alternating its display characteristics. We can alternate between:

- Displayed and hidden

- Bright and dim

- Two contrasting colors

Blinking is the strongest way of emphasizing a visual object and is the only emphasis method effective in peripheral vision. It is so powerful that it is easily overdone. Never blink more than one icon at a time. Let users turn off blinking once they have acknowledged the message conveyed by blinking.

For a single blinking rate use 3 Hz. For two rates use 2 Hz and 5 Hz and use no more than two blinking rates. Make on-times equal to or longer than off-times.

Vibration

Icons and objects in them can shake, jiggle, and bounce around to suggest vibration that we might otherwise show with edge lines, like these:

To make an object appear to vibrate, we must continually shift its size or position slightly. The vibration should be enough for the user to notice but not so much as to distract or alarm the viewer. The movement should be about 2 to 5 pixels per shake. It should shift at a rate between 3 and 10 Hz. If the rate is too slow, the motions will seem unconnected. If it is too fast, the eye cannot form the separate images and the object will seem to blur rather than vibrate.

Motion

An object or icon may move about the display. It may move smoothly along a curve or zigzag erratically. The motion may be controlled by the computer or the user. Motion is most effective in animating dynamic concepts:

The pattern and style of motion suggest characteristics of the object in motion. Straight movement suggests control and constraint. Motion along a curve has a more natural, fluid quality. Steady movement can seem mechanical and may suggest that the object is not moving under its own power. Accelerating or decelerating movement makes the object seem to propel itself across the screen. Smooth movements make the display more predictable, whereas erratic movements add a spontaneous, lively character to the object—if not overdone.

Change

Even icons that stay in one place can use dynamics. Such animated icons are especially effective in expressing concepts of variation and change. These techniques work best for representing concepts that have similar patterns of change. Here are just a few of the ways of arranging objects in sequence:

Montage

In montage, we jump quickly from object to object. Rock-music videos and early films both rely heavily on montage for excitement.

In icons, we can use montage to quickly show a range of possibilities. For example, we might cause a category icon, when activated, to flip through all the members of that category.

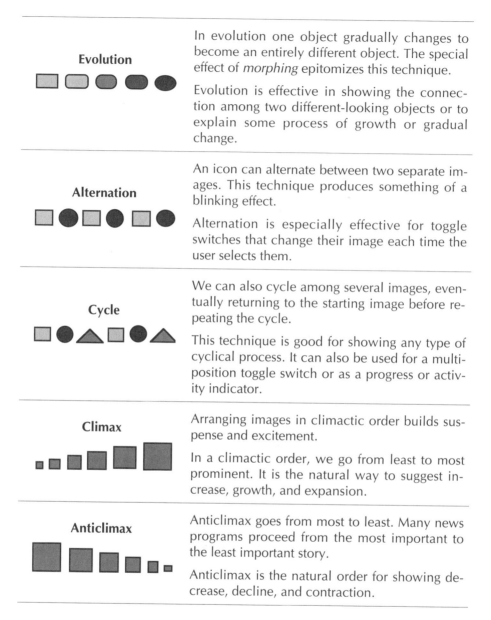

Evolution

In evolution one object gradually changes to become an entirely different object. The special effect of *morphing* epitomizes this technique.

Evolution is effective in showing the connection among two different-looking objects or to explain some process of growth or gradual change.

Alternation

An icon can alternate between two separate images. This technique produces something of a blinking effect.

Alternation is especially effective for toggle switches that change their image each time the user selects them.

Cycle

We can also cycle among several images, eventually returning to the starting image before repeating the cycle.

This technique is good for showing any type of cyclical process. It can also be used for a multi-position toggle switch or as a progress or activity indicator.

Climax

Arranging images in climactic order builds suspense and excitement.

In a climactic order, we go from least to most prominent. It is the natural way to suggest increase, growth, and expansion.

Anticlimax

Anticlimax goes from most to least. Many news programs proceed from the most important to the least important story.

Anticlimax is the natural order for showing decrease, decline, and contraction.

ARBITRARY OBJECT

One last possibility exists for representing ideas. Select an arbitrary object, unassociated with the concept, and use that object as a symbol for the concept. The best advice I can offer for using arbitrary objects as symbols is this:

Don't do it!

When you think of Marlboro cigarettes, what visual image pops into your mind? Around the world, even in areas where people have never seen American Western movies, the Marlboro cowboy is a fixture of the visual language. Yet during the 1940s and 1950s Marlboro was marketed as a woman's luxury cigarette. How then did Marlboro become so firmly associated with the image of the rugged cowboy? Through the expenditure of millions of dollars of advertising over decades.

The lesson is this: If you have enough time and money, you can teach people to associate any concept with any visual image. If your resources are more limited, you should seek images the user already associates with the concept. Avoid using arbitrary objects unless you have a large budget and a long time to teach the meaning of the object. Instead, use objects and properties that rely on the meanings users have already learned for them.

FOR MORE INFORMATION

Capitman, Barbara Baer. *American Trademark Designs*. Mineola, NY: Dover Publications, Inc., 1976.

Dreyfuss, Henry. *Symbol Sourcebook: An Authoritative Guide to International Graphic Symbols*. New York: Van Nostrand Reinhold, 1984.

Frutiger, Adrian. *Signs and Symbols: Their Design and Meaning*. New York: Van Nostrand Reinhold, 1989.

Holmes, Nigel. *Designing Pictorial Symbols*. New York: Watson-Guptill, 1990.

Modley, Rudolf. *Handbook of Pictorial Symbols*. New York: Dover, 1976.

Murphy, John and Michael Rowe. *How to Design Trademarks and Logos*. Cincinnati: Nforth Light Books, 1988.

Thompson, Philip and Peter Davenport. *The Dictionary of Graphic Images*. New York: St. Martin's Press, 1981.

SHOWING RELATIONSHIPS

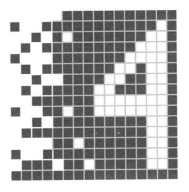

It is difficult to communicate complex messages within the confines of the 32 x 32-bit canvas of an icon. How can we express any but the simplest messages? This chapter shows you how to apply the principles of the previous two chapters to group and categorize, to rate and rank, and to show depth and change and motion. It will present examples of how icons can show similarity and difference, importance, motion, emotion and states of mind, and quantity. Let's explore these common relationships and look at how we can represent them in icons.

SHOWING SIMILARITY

One of the simplest concepts in any language is identity, the expression of the similarities linking two ideas or objects. Often we need to say that two things are equal or similar, that they belong to the same category, or that they should be thought of as a group. To communicate these messages with icons, we must visually associate separate visual objects.

Cluster the objects

Proximity links objects to each other and blank space distinguishes them from unrelated objects:

Objects close together seem related. Those farther apart seem unrelated. Notice how proximity helps group the separate visual elements of each of these icons into a few simple objects:

| Separate | Sort in descending order | Paragraphs of text | Checklist |

Connect the objects

Just as lines can separate and divide, they can also join and unite objects. Objects connected by lines are seen as a whole. The eye naturally follows the lines and will shuttle among objects thus connected:

When the subject of the icon is the pattern of interrelationships among objects rather than the objects themselves, you can design an icon that shows interconnections among separate items. Here, the vertical and horizontal position of an item is not as important as which objects are connected to other objects. Notice how the style of the connecting line helps indicate the nature of the relationship:

Hierarchy   Swap   Combine   Network

Box the objects

To single out a group of objects in a crowded icon, you can draw a box or border around the group of related objects:

Enclosed items are part of a group. Everything within the border is somehow similar. In fact, surrounding objects with a border symbolizes the act of grouping or categorizing itself:

Group, bind
together

If the frame is formed by the outlines of an object, the enclosed objects are seen as part of the enclosing object or as subordinate to it. Notice how a distinctive outline identifies and claims the inner objects in these icons:

Telephone   Bright idea
book

Use similar graphical properties

Display related objects using similar visual characteristics, such as color, texture, shape, or orientation. Color is especially effective in showing relationships among distant objects. Notice how quickly you can group all the solid black objects:

In each of these icons, notice how all the objects of a particular type have the same size, shape, line weight, and value:

| Scatter diagram | Checklist | Organization chart | Filter | Group |

Arrange in a pattern

We can group items merely by arranging them in a simple pattern, such as evenly spaced along a straight line:

Or, arranged in a symmetrical or regular pattern:

Notice how arranging objects along a line or in a grid ties them together into one perceptual unit:

Format	Reproduce	Number	Ungroup	Users

In these examples symmetry simplifies the visual image of regular objects emphasizing their abstract and general meaning:

Handbook	Handle with care	Global	Hierarchy	Process

Symmetry is most effective when icons for opposite concepts are mirror-images of each other:

Page header	Page footer	or	Minimum	Maximum

Even when the symmetry is not total, the effect is still strong:

Combine	Separate	or	Sort in ascending order	Sort in descending order

Show, make visible	Hide, make invisible

Summary: Showing similarity

Cluster the objects

Place related objects close to one another. Leave more space between unrelated objects

Connect the objects

Use lines to connect objects, arranging lines and objects to reveal the pattern of relationships among objects.

Box the objects

Draw a box or border around related objects, shutting them off from other unrelated objects.

Use similar graphical properties

Make related objects look alike. Give them the same color, size, shape, or value.

Arrange in a pattern

Arrange the objects in a simple, regular pattern. For example, evenly space them along a straight line.

Arrange symmetrically

Arrange analogous objects in mirror-image positions.

SHOWING DIFFERENCE

Like the concept of identity, the expression of difference is basic to any language. Whenever you combine objects in an icon you must take care that they maintain their distinct identities. Viewers may fail to notice subtle differences between small objects within the confines of an icon. There are several techniques we can use to separate and categorize individual objects.

Separate by blank space

Just as proximity associates two objects, distance separates them. In page design, typographers often use blank space to separate different pieces of information. In designing icons we leave more space between groups of objects than between the members of a group:

In these icons, notice how the spacing of objects groups them and controls what we see as a single unit and what we read as rows or columns:

Merge   Binary data   Format   Numbered list

Separate with rules and lines

Rules and lines can provide fences for the wandering eye, keeping it from inadvertently straying into unrelated information:

Lines divide one side from another. They separate the icon into two different areas. Objects in one area are clearly distinct from those across the line. For instance, a boundary can separate two states of a toggle switch:

A line can also represent the act of dividing some other object as well as hiding an object:

Split   Hide

Vary more graphical properties

Items that differ in only one way are harder to distinguish than those that differ in several ways. Objects that differ by shape, for example, are less distinct than those that differ in size, value, and color:

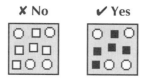

For a more powerful icon, make two objects differ in more than one visual characteristic. Notice how the icons below distinguish one object from another by differences of size, shape, orientation, line thickness, and value:

Chart   Command   Books   Graphical user   Pollution
                                           interface

Increase the difference

Do not depend on small, subtle differences of shape, color, or value to stand out clearly in a small icon on a crowded screen. To be sure you are understood, increase the contrast among the different objects:

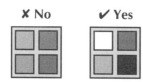

To fully distinguish objects, make them truly opposite. Choose graphical characteristics from opposite ends of the scale such as black with white:

Contrast   Harmony   Modularity   Read

Juxtapose opposites

One way to highlight differences is to place them side by side so that they are obvious in a single glance. For instance, the light-dark extremes of this icon are made more obvious by juxtaposing the shades with the greatest difference:

✗ No   ✔ Yes

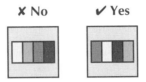

To apply this technique, put distinctly different, contrasting images close together:

Shapes   Swap   Marriage   Currency   Text style

We apply this technique when we arrange the icons of a menu. Often we can make the meaning of icons clearer by putting icons for related but different concepts in a single eye glance:

✗ No   ✔ Yes

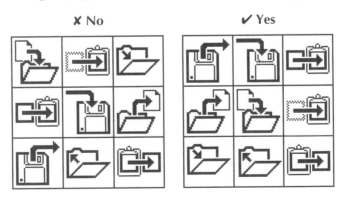

Summary: Showing difference

Separate by blank space		Cluster together the objects of a group. Put more space between the groups than between members of a group.
Separate with rules and lines		Put borders between unrelated groups of objects.
Vary more graphical properties		Make different objects differ by more than a single, subtle visual characteristic.
Increase the difference		Draw differing objects in a clearly contrasting style. Exaggerate the degree of difference.
Juxtapose opposites		Place clearly different objects close to one another so that their differences can be seen at a glance.

SHOWING IMPORTANCE

Not every item in an icon is equally important. When all objects are equally emphatic, viewers often overlook small, critical details or fail to notice the true subject of an icon. Often we must vary the emphasis of objects in an icon to:

- Say that an object is the most important or powerful
- Show varying levels of importance or power
- Ensure that the user does not overlook a small detail crucial to under-standing the icon
- Show a small object that is recognizable only in the context of other, larger objects

We have several techniques to control the emphasis given to individual objects in an icon.

Show the object in motion

Movement and change compel attention. Viewers attend longer and more deeply to objects in action:

Any dynamic characteristic draws attention. We naturally notice any object that is:

- Blinking
- Vibrating
- Moving
- Changing

We can suggest urgency by the rate of movement or blinking, but don't expect viewers to be able to distinguish more than 2 or 3 different rates. Also, don't expect them to attend to more than one moving or blinking object at a time.

Heighten contrast

Give the primary object the highest degree of contrast with its background. If the background is light, make it the darkest object in the icon. If the background is dark, make it the lightest:

In these icons, notice how the use of high contrast helps us spot small but critical details, identify the true subject of the icon, and tell which object is more important:

Double tap the
left mouse
button   Make visible   Heavy   Measure
precisely

If we cannot fill the interior of an object with a high-contrast value or pattern, we can often give it a thicker border. The object with the thickest border will appear most prominent:

This technique is often necessary when designing icons for display in black and white where filling a shape with black or white would offer too much or too little contrast. Notice how these icons indicate the primary object by outlining it with thick lines while using thinner lines for secondary objects or interior details:

Reminder   Put in folder   Keyboard   Clipboard   Select user

Use brighter colors

Paint the object in a bright, saturated, warm color. Brighter, warmer, and higher-contrast colors emphasize an object. Warm colors appear more aggressive than cool colors. For example, red and yellow are used for warning or caution signs whereas blue and green are used for messages of approval or acceptance.

Color figure 1: Color draws attention

Chapter 7 contains the color plates with the color figures. It also provides advice and examples of using color in icons.

Enlarge the object

Larger objects appear more powerful and important. For similar objects next to one another, a 10 to 15 percent difference is noticeable. However, if the objects differ in color, shape, or other properties, or if they are not close together, you may need a 30 percent difference in size:

Good designers often emphasize crucial concepts by making them larger or more imposing than they appear in real life. They also do this to make a small object noticeable and recognizable. In these icons, objects are not drawn to the same scale. Notice which objects are drawn larger:

Pollution   Page number   MS-DOS

Give the object a distinctive shape

Jagged, irregular shapes are more eye catching than smooth, regular ones. In a design where verticals and horizontals predominate, a diagonal line will stand out:

Notice how the eye reliably finds the irregular shapes and diagonal lines in these icons:

Incomplete   Fragile   Chart   Magnetic   Slice

Point to the object

Use elements in the icon to direct the viewer's eyes to the object you want noticed first. You can simply show an arrow or hand pointing to the object:

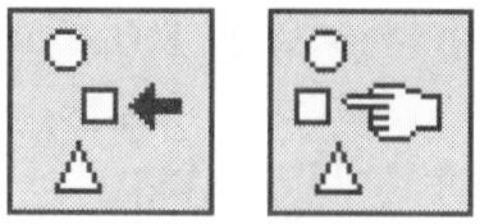

If the icon includes people, you can show them looking or pointing at the object:

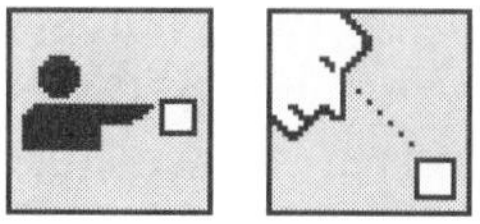

Notice how these icons direct your eye to the critical object in each design:

Hide Center Maximum Paragraph Subtotal

Frame the object

We frame pictures before hanging them on our walls and we circle classified ads that are of interest. A box or border around an object focuses attention on that object:

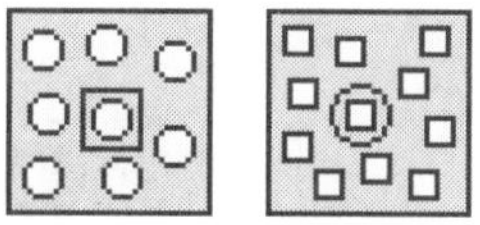

This is a difficult technique to use directly. Often the icon does not allow room for a border around an object. Further, the border itself is easily misinterpreted as an object rather than a way of emphasizing an object. One place where it does work well is where one object in the icon naturally encloses or encircles another. In this case, attention flows to the smaller item:

Menus

Time

Phone book

Zoom in

Design

You can also surround the object with blank space:

In small icons, however, there is seldom enough blank space to clearly single out any individual object.

Put the object in front

Things that are nearby seem more immediate. This immediacy gives weight and importance to graphical objects. To emphasize one object, make it appear closer by having it overlap other objects in the icon:

Notice the role of overlap in giving emphasis to the smaller objects in these icons:

Family

Bulletin board

Read

Graphical user interface

Application program

In addition to expressing importance, overlap is one of the ways we can show depth in flat icons. Overlap and other depth cues are discussed later in this chapter.

Increase detail in the object

The eye in its quest for information scans the icon seeking every clue provided by the designer. The more information an object promises, the sooner and longer the eye examines it. We can reliably draw the eye to an object by drawing it in more detail or depicting it as a solid object:

Notice how the eye gravitates to the small details in these icons:

Project   Audio tape   Newspaper   Safe   Scatter chart

Put the object in a position of power

Position, as we discussed in Chapter 3, has a figurative meaning. Objects in the center, top, or upper-left corner of the scene appear the most powerful or important:

In these icons, note the importance given to the object at the top, center, or upper-left corner:

Snap to grid   Handle with   Double tap   Add to series
point   care   mouse button

Summary: Showing importance

All emphasis depends on contrast. In an icon filled with large, red, diagonal objects, a single small, blue, horizontal object will dominate. This principle is the visual equivalent of whispering to be heard in a noisy room. The goal is to make the emphasized object visibly unique. Limit the amount you emphasize. Any emphasis device loses its effectiveness if overused.

In emphasizing objects, use these techniques:

Show the
object in
action

Blink, vibrate, move, or change the object.

Heighten
contrast

Increase the contrast between the primary object
and its background.

Use brighter
colors

Show the primary object in bright, saturated, warm
colors.

Enlarge the
object

Draw the primary object larger than other objects.

Give the
object a
distinctive
shape

Give the object a shape that contrasts with other
shapes in the icon. Irregular shapes and diagonal
lines are especially eye catching.

Point to the
object

Direct the viewer's gaze to the object. Point to it
with an arrow. Or show a person pointing to or
looking at the object.

Frame the
object

Draw a box or border around the object. Or leave
extra blank space around it.

Put the object
in front

Let the primary object overlap other objects, thus
implying that it is nearer.

Increase
detail in the
object

Show finer details in the primary object. Or draw
it as a solid object and other objects as flat shapes.

Put the object
in a position
of power

Put the primary object at the top, center, or upper-
left of the icon.

SHOWING DEPTH

Icons can create the illusion of depth. Since men first drew bison on the walls of their caves at Altamira, artists have invented and honed techniques to capture the illusion of depth on flat surfaces. And in the last century psychologists have verified the potency of these *monocular cues* in conveying a feeling of depth. Just as these cues are used to infer the distance of an object without the use of stereoscopic effects, so too can they be used to imply depth on the flat surface of the computer screen or printed page. We can use these monocular cues to:

- Show distance
- Depict solid objects
- Highlight important objects and make them stand out
- Add interest

What are the techniques and how do they work?

Overlap

Allowing one object to block our view of another tells us strongly which is nearer. Nearer objects eclipse or obscure farther ones:

We see this technique used to help us tell which objects are in front of other objects in these icons:

| Bulletin board | Write a computer program | Character-based user interface | Family | Read |

Overlap involves more than one technique. Let's look at each of them in turn.

Blocking

Blocking occurs whenever the lines of one object stop at the outline of another object:

The most regular shape will appear in front of less regular ones. In the figure above, the square in the center appears to be atop the other squares simply by the fact that it looks like a square and they do not. Notice how the more complete shapes appear closer:

Undo   Truck   Tools   Clipboard

Hidden lines

Edges of obscured objects are omitted or conventionally drawn with dotted or dashed lines:

Notice the use of hidden lines in these icons for the concept of layers:

Aura of blank space

Obstructed edges typically stop short of the intersection:

By artistic convention, the lines of more distant objects do not actually touch the outlines of nearer objects. Instead, these lines stop short as if the nearer object were surrounded by a thin aura of blank space.

| Attach | Engineering drawing | Bookmark | Crop | Teach |

Translucency

Sometimes the nearer object is translucent and therefore does not completely block our view of the farther object:

The color in the area of overlap is a blend of the color (or gray level) of both objects. The amount each object contributes to the overlap depends on the translucency of the top object. The more translucent it is, the more of the color of the overlapped object or background shows through. See "Calculating Translucency" in Chapter 14 for instructions on how to assign colors in the area of overlap.

Scale

The size of a familiar image indicates its distance. Larger images seem closer; smaller ones farther away:

Scale only works when the object is one we readily recognize and whose size is constant and well known to us. With an abstract geometric shape, scale conveys variations in size rather than depth:

We can restore the effect by combining the technique of scale with another depth cue, such as elevation:

Use scale when the scene contains several instances of a familiar object at various distances from the viewer:

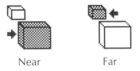

Near   Far

Elevation

Objects higher in our field of view normally appear farther away than those lower:

As with scale, this technique works best when combined with other cues, such as overlap and scale:

✗ No   **✔ Yes**

Notice how these icons put farther objects higher than nearer ones:

Addresses   Reproduce   Users

Use elevation when several instances of the same familiar object appear at various distances from the viewer. Elevate each object in proportion to its distance from the viewer.

Shade and shadow

Light reflected from a surface gives clues to its orientation and position relative to the light source. Shading and shadows aid our perception of volume, shape, and texture.

Surfaces of an object facing a source of illumination are light. Those facing away from the light source are shaded with what is called *attached shadow*. The shading shown on a the background on the opposite side of the object from the light source is called a *cast shadow*. Often attached and cast shadows are combined. A third kind of shadow arises more from artistic conventions than from an attempt to mimic nature. Called a *drop shadow*, it creates the illusion of a flat object hovering just above the surface of the screen or paper by casting a shadow backward onto the surface:

Attached   Cast   Attached and   Drop
                              cast

Notice the use of shadows to add depth to these icons:

Send   Button   Mail   Pull-down menus

Highlights, glints, and reflections also suggest depth:

Hot	System error	Dark	Weight

Chapter 6 on how to draw icons explains shadows in more detail and gives advice on how to use them wisely.

Linear perspective

During the Renaissance, artists such as Leonardo da Vinci and Albrecht Dürer formulated rules on when and how parallel lines and repeated forms converge toward vanishing points on the horizon. Their several mathematical systems enable us to produce optically correct images of three-dimensional objects, for example:

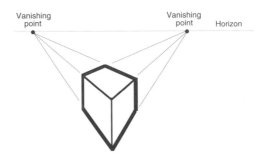

An object drawn in true perspective resembles the retinal image of that object as seen from a particular viewpoint in space.

There are several different perspective schemes involving different angles of view and different numbers of vanishing points. For designing low-resolution, small icons, only the simplest schemes are practical. Usually this involves nothing more complex than showing the object from a viewpoint in front of the object, slightly above it, and slightly to one side. Parallel edges may or may not converge. By exposing the top and sides of a regular geometric solid, we create a strong impression of depth:

Send	Computer	Package	Disk	Filing cabinet

Perspective can prove confusing unless the objects shown are recognizable solid objects. A simple, flat geometric shape can be interpreted several ways. An ellipse can be simply an ellipse; or, it can be interpreted as a circle turned at an angle relative to the viewer. Likewise, a trapezoid may be seen as a rectangle or square turned at an angle. To avoid ambiguity, give the flat object thickness:

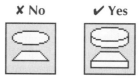

Chapter 6 on how to draw icons gives more advice on using perspective.

Aerial perspective

Distant objects appear less colorful, less sharp, and less detailed than nearby objects. These three effects, which were described by Leonardo da Vinci, are grouped together under the term aerial perspective since they are caused by the visual effects of the air between the observer and the distant object:

On a hazy day, objects seen across an expanse of space appear paler, bluer, and grayer than nearby objects. Accordingly, the mind perceives paler and bluer or grayer objects as more distant (color figures are found in the color plates in Chapter 7):

Color figure 2: Aerial perspective

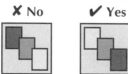

Color perspective

When you look at swatches or patches of various colors, do some of the colors seem to project toward you and others to recede? Generally warmer colors—

reds and oranges—will seem to advance while cooler colors—blues and greens—will seem to recede:

Color figure 3: Color-depth effect

There seem to be two causes for color perspective: One is the psychological association of aggression with warm colors and regression and calm with cool colors. Another is the physiological fact that different wavelengths of light are refracted to different degrees by the lenses of our eyes. These different colors come into focus at different planes and the eye cannot focus them at the same time. The mind concludes, incorrectly, that they come from objects at different distances. This three-dimensional effect of color is called *chromostereopsis.* It encourages us to use of intense warm colors for nearby objects and cooler, less saturated or darker colors for more distant objects:

Color figure 4: Color suggests distance

✘ No   ✔ Yes

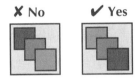

Summary: Showing depth

Overlap

Let nearer objects eclipse or obscure more distant objects.

Scale

Make the image of nearer objects larger than the image of more distant ones.

Elevation

Draw farther objects higher in the frame of the icon. Put nearer objects lower.

Shade and shadow		Draw the object as if illuminated by a light source. Make surfaces toward the light brighter than those away from the light.
Linear perspective		Show more than one face or side of the object. Foreshorten surfaces at an angle to the viewpoint and let parallel lines converge.
Aerial perspective		Draw more distant objects in a paler, cooler color than that for nearby objects.
Color perspective		Use bright, warm colors for nearby objects and dim or pale cool colors for more distant ones.

SHOWING CHANGES OR MOTION

Animation is the natural language for showing change or motion. If we can show dynamic concepts dynamically, we should. But how do we convey change and movement on the static, unchanging screen or page? How can we represent more than a frozen instant, a mere snapshot? The answer is that we must plant clues from which the reader can infer motion and change. These clues are called *graphical dynamics*, and we can use them to:

- Suggest movement
- Show change
- Direct the reader's eye
- Draw attention

Arrows

Arrows are universal symbols of movement. They can represent or suggest many kinds of action, motion, or change:

Arrows alone can show motion in a pure or abstract sense:

Fast forward   Mix   Repeat   Receive   Undo

Arrows can be combined with an object to show a movement of that object:

Close file   Rotate   Insert   Add to   Snap to grid

Arrows can show the change from one state or condition to another:

Format   Filter   Combine   Hide   Sort
descending

Arrows can show flow of data, activity, or control:

Read from disk   Exit   Swap   Program   Package

They can indicate motions the user is to make or actions the user should take:

Press left   Tap left mouse   Double-tap left
mouse button   button   mouse button

Arrows can direct the viewer's gaze to a particular object:

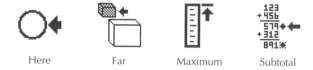

Here   Far   Maximum   Subtotal

We can draw them in many ways:

There are no universal standards for the meanings of different styles of arrows. A few conventions are worth following:

- For change or motion, show the arrow going from left to right (the normal direction of reading). For pointing out an object or directing attention, reverse the direction:

- For movements of solid objects, draw arrows as solid or draw them in perspective with the movement of the object:

Speed lines

In cartoons, speed lines trail behind a moving object like contrails from a speeding jet or the tail of a shooting star:

Speed lines imply the velocity of an object. The number, length and direction of the lines indicate the speed, angle, rate, and curvature of the motion:

Notice the use of speed lines in these icons:

Fast disk   Falling rocks   Speedy mail   Rapid recharge   Go fast

Shake lines

Shake lines parallel the edge of an object to suggest vibration, turbulence, or nervousness:

Use shake lines to:

- Show vibration in an object:

- Make invisible sound waves visible:

• Suggest turmoil, turbulence, or agitation. To convey a nervous, stressful state:

Ghost images

In many forms of art, ghost images trail behind an object to indicate its rapid movement. We can use ghost images to show motion along a simple path:

In order to use this technique effectively, start with an object having a simple, strong outline and an uncluttered background. Use no more than three to five ghost images and make them progressively lighter and fainter as they proceed away from the object. Be sure the ghost images reinforce the illusion of movement by proceeding from the object to the left or to the top:

A simple version of this technique shows up in before-and-after icons. These icons indicate the "before" position or condition displayed as a fainter version of the image as it appears in the "after" state:

Move   Flip   Enlarge   Cut to
                                        clipboard

Sometimes, however, you have to reverse this convention. This occurs when drawing the "after" image as a solid would not sufficiently distinguish it from adjacent objects:

Insert   Make invisible   Add to

In these cases, you may need to use an arrow to make the direction of change completely clear. Or, if you are designing in color, you can avoid this problem by making the moving or changing object a different color from any of the unchanging objects. Then, make the ghost image a paler shade of the color of the moving or changing object.

Sequence of snapshots

A series of illustrations can show the object at the various stages of change. Our habit of reading a page from top to bottom, for example, supplies the notion of time passing when objects are arranged one on top of the other:

Use a sequence of snapshots to show a single, steady change in a familiar scene or object. This technique works best when change takes place against a fixed background or from a fixed viewpoint:

The most common use of this technique is in before-and-after icons that show snapshots of both conditions. They are usually arranged left to right with an arrow connecting the two views:

Combine   Make invisible   Summarize   Unformat   Sort

Posture of action

Even in a static graphics, we can often tell which objects are moving and which are still. An object in motion has a different posture or orientation than one that is static:

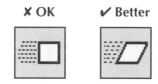

Cartoonists often suggest the forward rush of a car or bicycle by showing it leaning forward, its wheels distorted into ellipses with their major axes tilted toward the direction of movement:

This is a quaint artifact of photography. The earliest cameras fast enough to photograph a speeding race car used a shutter that exposed the film through a narrow horizontal slit that traveled vertically over the film, exposing it from the bottom to the top of the image. The speeding car moved even as the picture was being exposed. By the time the shutter got to the top of the image, the car had advanced. The resulting distortion tilted vertical lines and squeezed circular wheels into ellipses to make the car appear to be leaning into the charge.

Cartoonists use a similar technique when depicting someone walking or running:

Walk   Run

To start walking we lean slightly forward to shift the body's center of gravity off the stable base of our feet. Before we can fall, however, we move a foot forward to restore stability. The process of walking is nothing more than controlled falling. When running, we lean even farther forward. We associate this leaning with forward motion and vice versa.

Show a posture of action whenever you want to show an object clearly in motion or an action as it occurs. The effect is heightened if the object is in an unstable position:

| Fill | Launch | Conflict | Exercise |

Pregnant moment

Artists often produce an inferred perception of motion by creating images that play on the viewer's imagination. This technique gives certain works special vitality and energy. By depicting an action, not at its climax but a few moments earlier, the implied climax is like a magnet that pulls the action forward:

This depicted state is called the *pregnant moment.* The gap between the pregnant moment and the climax produces a directed tension that the viewer can relieve only by achieving closure. This closure comes when, in the viewer's imagination, the action proceeds to its climax.

The pregnant moment is often used in warning signs that show an impending disaster rather than the consequences of the disaster. Such signs let the viewer play out the scene in the imagination, thus heightening its emotional impact and its effectiveness as a warning:

We can use this technique by showing a picture that clearly says, "Something is about to happen." We imply the action by showing its potential:

| Fragile | Activate | System error | Multimedia | Threat |

Summary: Showing changes or motion

Arrows		Use an arrow to point in the direction of movement or change. Style the arrow to reflect the kind of motion or change.
Speed lines		Show faint lines trailing after the moving object like the tail of a comet.
Shake lines		Show faint lines parallel to the edges of a shaking, vibrating, or trembling object.
Ghost images		Show fainter images of a moving object trailing behind it.
Sequence of snapshots		Show static images of the object at key phases of the change or at regular points along its path of movement.
Posture of action		Draw the object the way it looks (or we think it looks) in motion.
Pregnant moment		Show an impending action and let the viewer's imagination carry through the action.

FOR MORE INFORMATION

Arnheim, Rudolf. *Visual Thinking.* Berkeley, CA: University of California Press, 1969.

Barratt, Krome. *Logic and Design in Art, Science, and Mathematics.* New York: Design Press, 1980.

Bertin, Jacques. *Semiology of Graphics.* Green Bay, WI: University of Wisconsin, 1983.

Dondis, D. *A Primer of Visual Literacy.* Cambridge, MA: MIT Press, 1973.

Gombrich, E. H. *Art and Illusion: A Study in the Psychology of Pictorial Representation.* Princeton: Princeton University Press, 1969.

DESIGNING AN ICONIC LANGUAGE

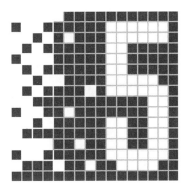

What would you do if you were asked to create dozens of icons? Hundreds? Thousands? Inexperienced designers, faced with such a task, gauge the distance to the deadline and start designing individual icons as fast as they can. Seasoned professionals, however, know the folly of designing large sets of symbols one at a time. They create an iconic language from which they can assemble most of the icons needed.

An iconic language is a systematic way to combine elementary symbols to represent more complex concepts. This chapter guides you through the process of creating a vocabulary of basic symbols that you can combine according to a few simple rules to produce the icons you need.

WHY A LANGUAGE?

Designing symbols one at a time can waste your time and lead to sprawling, inconsistent sets of icons. On the other hand, designing a coordinated set of icons:

- Reduces the effort required to design, draw, test, and revise the icons. It lets less skilled designers prepare first-draft versions of icons.

- Ensures and enforces fundamental consistency.

- Makes icons self-explanatory and deducible. Lets users predict what an icon will look like.

- Helps users get started more quickly and master advanced features sooner. It also helps them learn additional programs based on the same iconic language.

- Gives your product or product line a distinct style.

WHAT IS AN ICONIC LANGUAGE?

A language is a symbol system that two people use to communicate with one another. English is a language. So are French, Chinese, Swahili, and pig Latin. By my broad definition, mathematics is a language too. Charts and graphs form yet another family of languages. The international travel signs common in airports and rail stations make up still another language. Our icons are a language too.

Every language has two parts: a vocabulary and a grammar. The *vocabulary* is the collection of elementary symbols that are combined according to the rules of the *grammar* to form units of expression. For a language like English, the vocabulary consists of the words we can use. The grammar records rules for how putting words together into sequences changes their individual meanings. Grammar tells us what combinations have meaning and which do not. In such verbal languages, a sentence is the unit of expression.

Mathematics, as we said, is a language too. Its vocabulary consists of simple symbols for mathematical operations $(+, -, \div, =, \neq, \Sigma, \Delta)$, for variables (X, Y, Z, μ, Ω), and constant values $(7.0, \Omega, \pi)$. The grammar of mathematics provides rules such as those you learned in algebra class. For example, a number appearing as a superscript tells how many times the variable to its left is multiplied by itself. The unit of expression for mathematics is the equation:

$$E=mc^2 \qquad A=\pi r^2 \qquad F=ma$$

An iconic language combines elementary symbols (its vocabulary) by a systematic formula (its grammar) to produce an understandable icon (the unit of expression). To set up an iconic language, we must design the elementary symbols and lay down rules for combining them.

What makes a language easy to design and to use? If you have studied a foreign language, you spent a lot of time learning the words of the language and the rules of how to combine them. If the words were consistent in spelling and easy to pronounce and the rules of combining them were few and simple, you probably had a relatively easy time of it. The same principles apply to designing and using iconic languages—consistency and simplicity.

CASE STUDY: LANGUAGE FOR ILLUSTRATING SOFTWARE

Large, complex systems benefit most from a simple, consistent iconic language. Imagine that you are charged with developing an iconic language for a computer program used by draftsmen, engineers, architects, technical illustrators, and other design professionals to make precision engineering drawings. You might invent a language with a grammar like this:

Command = Action on Object by Method

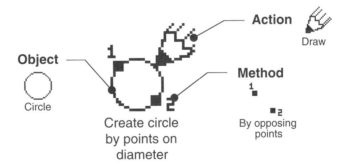

Actions are what the user does to or with elements. These include primitives like the following:

| Draw | Erase | Measure | Paint | Find |

Objects are the geometric figures being created and manipulated. These include such items as:

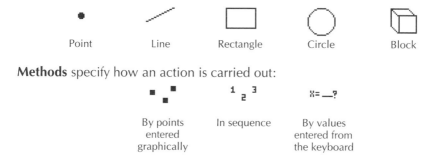

| Point | Line | Rectangle | Circle | Block |

Methods specify how an action is carried out:

By points
entered
graphically   In sequence   By values
entered from
the keyboard

With a clearly defined language, a new icon is generated by stating its concept in terms of the grammar and vocabulary of the language. For example, we can make a slight variation on the initial example by changing just the method by which the circle is defined:

Draw circle by
center and
edge point

The icon for a different object using the same action and method can be created by simply changing the object part of the icon:

Draw rectangle
by corners

The icon for a different action is consistent with earlier designs because it relies on the same design grammar and vocabulary:

Erase object

LIST CONCEPTS

The first step in designing an iconic language is to list all the things for which you will eventually need icons. Include all:

- Programs
- Files
  - Data created or used by the program
  - Preferences and other utility files
- Commands
- Prompts
- Messages
  - Status messages
  - Error messages
- Data the user creates, imports, or manipulates

List both generic and specific concepts. Don't forget to consider current and future versions of the product. A clear, consistent list of concepts is necessary for naming components as well.

Once you have compiled the list, edit it for consistency and clarity. Limit and simplify your vocabulary by expressing similar concepts in the same words. Use terms that are understandable and meaningful to users, and avoid terms that merely describe the internal workings of the product.

DESIGN BASIC SYMBOLS FOR VOCABULARY

The next step in creating the iconic language is to build a collection of basic visual symbols that will appear in the icons. Design these basic symbols for combining. Such symbols should be:

- Simple
- Small
- Flexible: easily resized and reshaped
- Easy to combine
- Thoroughly tested

Parts of speech for icons are similar to those for verbal languages but not exactly the same. Parts of speech for an individual iconic language may be *ad hoc*, but will tend to use different combinations of a few basic categories. Look for recurring categories throughout your list of concepts. Some categories are especially common. They are described in the sections that follow.

Actions

Actions are the verbs of the language. Action symbols reveal the changes that occur and the forces that act on objects. Actions include movement, transformation, and creation. Here are some common kinds of actions to consider in your language:

- **Creation**. Many commands in computer programs cause new data to come into existence. We typically represent these actions by showing the tool used to create an analogous object:

Measure   Draw   Erase   Paint   Record

- **Change of state**. Many actions transform something from one condition to another. These actions are typically represented by showing the before-and-after states connected by an arrow. If the before state is well known, the image may show only the destination state (note the Align example):

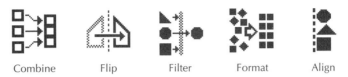

| Combine | Flip | Filter | Format | Align |

- **Manipulation of data**. Actions that modify, delete, or rearrange data are typically shown by a concrete action upon an image of the data:

| Cut | Fill | Erase | Measure | Open a file |

- **Physical or conceptual movement**. Changes in physical space or data space are typically shown by arrows:

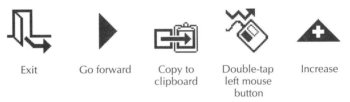

| Exit | Go forward | Copy to clipboard | Double-tap left mouse button | Increase |

- **Activity**. An activity is shown by an image of the activity being performed or of the tool used to perform an analogous activity:

| Read | Access | Activate | Diagnose | Inspect |

Objects

Objects are the nouns of the language. They are the things acted upon. Grammatically, objects are most like the subject or direct object of an active verb. Objects can be concrete or abstract. For concrete objects, we typically show a picture of the object:

| Telephone | Film | Video camera | Battery | Report |

For conceptual or abstract objects, we show an analogous or associated object:

| Sound | Weight | Atomic energy | Color | Speech |

Qualifiers of actions

Qualifiers are the adverbs of the language. They limit and sharpen actions. They tell how, when, where, and to what degree. Use qualifiers to distinguish similar forms of an action or to add shades of meaning. Qualifiers can specify several characteristics of an action.

- **Where**. In what location, to what destination, in which direction:

| Here | There | Copy to disk | Add to package | Press left mouse button |

- **Sequence**. In what order:

- **Negation**. The action is avoided, thwarted, or reversed:

No   No   Stop

- **How much**. To what degree, how urgently, at what speed:

Slow   Fast   Fast   Fast

- **How**. In what manner, in which direction:

Handle with   Zoom out   Sort in
care   descending
order

Limiters of objects

Limiters are the adjectives of the language. They sharpen the reference to an object. Limiters are especially helpful when we must show the subject of an icon in the context of other objects to make it more recognizable. Limiters specify:

- **Type or kind**. If several versions exist, the limiter specifies which one:

Electrical   Mechanical   Bullet list   Checklist

- **How different from generic form**. How does the subject of the icon differ from the norm or stereotype for its type or kind?

Corrupted   Incomplete   Underlined   Unformatted   Formatted text
data   data   text

- **Which one, what part**. If only part of the image is the subject of the icon, we must tell the viewer which part that is. Usually we do this by pointing to the item or making it more emphatic than its neighbors:

| Paragraph | Subtotal | Maximum | Height | Bookmark |

Relationships among objects

Often the meaning of an icon is not in the objects or actions shown but in the relationship among the objects in the image. We need an extensive vocabulary of visual techniques to show relationships among concepts. Some common relationships are:

- **Ownership**. One object may possess or control another. Some objects may depend on or support other objects:

| Ownership | Support | Data on system clipboard |

- **Inclusion**. Some objects include other objects:

| Page number | Grouped data |

- **Equality**. We often need to show that two objects are equivalent:

| Equal | Balanced | Swap |

- **Connection**. If there are physical or metaphorical connections among objects, the icon must show them:

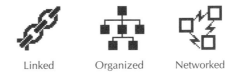

Linked   Organized   Networked

- **Position**. Icons are often called on to show physical or spatial relationships among objects:

Far   Right-aligned   Distance
            text

- **Consistency and compatibility**. Icons show whether two items work together or not:

Compatible   Inconsistent   In conflict

Chapter 4 includes many techniques for showing common relationships.

States of being

Objects can exist in various states or conditions. Showing this state or condition is important in icons used for status and error messages.

Often the state or condition of interest concerns whether something is active or inactive or whether some resource is available or not:

On   Off

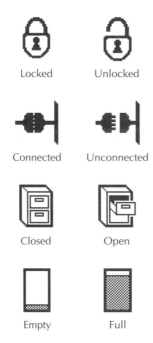

Other states concern the availability of the system or product:

Icons may also represent human emotions, either as the subject of the icon or as an analogy to the condition of a system:

Identifiers

Icons must often identify particular people, places, or things. Such icons are like proper nouns. Often identifiers are combined with other classes of icons to associate them with a particular manufacturer or product line of which they are a part.

Here's how you might use an identifier. Imagine that you are designing icons for a program used to create multimedia presentations. You want to give your icons for the various media a thematic unity and you want to clearly associate them with your program and your company. You start with your company trademark:

And you simply incorporate that emblem into the icons for the various media handled by your product:

| Animation | Slides | Video | Audio | Printouts |

CASE STUDY: COMPUSERVE INFORMATION MANAGER

Many programs use and create multiple files. Some of these hold data for the user while others contain reference information for the application itself. The CompuServe Information Manager is one such program that uses a consistent iconic language.[1]

The grammar of this language looks like this:

File = Trademark + Data type + File type

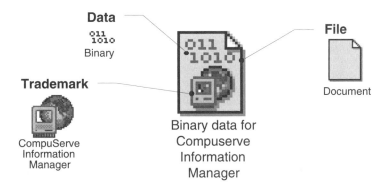

---

[1]Screen shots are reprinted with permission from CompuServe, Inc.

The **trademark** is always the same. It is the program emblem for the CompuServe Information Manager program. On the Macintosh it looks like this:

The **file type** is indicated by a border or shape. Most of the icons in this series use the border for regular documents:

The **data type** is shown by a small, self-contained symbol, usually in the upper left of the icon:

  Text   Binary   Phone   Users   Computers   Modems   Folders
                          numbers

The scheme is simple and regular enough that even the exceptions are easy to interpret:

  Generic data   Address book   Help file
     file

SET UP RULES FOR COMBINING SYMBOLS

A language must have a grammar. A grammar is the set of rules for combining symbols, whether the symbols are words or pictures. Such a grammar ensures that basic symbols are combined in simple, predictable ways that users readily understand. It is like a chemical formula relating elements to the compound formed of them.

A graphical grammar should specify:

- Which elements are required and which are optional.
- How elements may be graphically combined, for instance, by antithesis, addition, and intersection.
- How elements are arranged left to right, top to bottom, and front to back.
- How each element is represented, for example, as a border, as an object within the border, as an attachment, or as a modification of a standard element.
- Which elements are the same for all icons in the series and which vary from icon to icon within the series.
- How many elements may be combined before the resulting symbol is too complex.

Just as words can be combined into verbal statements, questions, and commands, there are four basic ways of combining iconic elements. These methods are antithesis, addition, overlap, and specification.

Antithesis

In *antithesis*, we combine two sharply contrasting objects or characteristics to suggest a richer idea than is conveyed by either alone. We see this technique used in an emblem for classical theater:

Superimposing the smiling mask of comedy and the frowning mask of tragedy reminds us of the breadth and depth of theater.

Antithesis is most useful where the symbol represents some aspect of an extreme difference or the range of concepts between two extremes:

| Contrast control | Racial harmony | Modularity | Undo | Unformat |

By combining inconsistent parts into a single figure, we can produce a graphical form known as a paradoxical figure. We can use such self-contradictory images to force the viewer to rethink an accepted idea—or just for fun:

Devil's tuning
fork

Software
square

Addition

In the technique of *addition*, we create a compound symbol by adding the independent meanings of separate objects

This technique works well where a concept can be represented as the sum of its parts. One test is whether you can express the icon with a formula like this:

$$\textbf{Whole} = \textbf{Part}_1 + \textbf{Part}_2 + \dots \textbf{Part}_n$$

 Traditional family = Mother + Father + Child1 + Child2

 Application program = disk + manual

 Windows GUI = screen + window + pull-down menu + two-button mouse

 Library = book + book + ... + book

CASE STUDY: HELIX EXPRESS RELATIONAL DATABASE

The icon for the Double Helix relational database manager combines images from the icons for the various parts of the data base.[2]

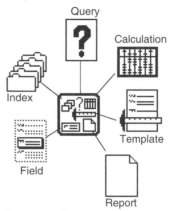

Notice how the images included in the composite icon differ from those of the separate icons:

- They are reduced in size (index, report, query).
- They are simplified (index, calculation).
- Only an especially important part is included (field, template).

Overlap

By the technique of overlap, we signify an abstract or general concept by combining objects that have only this concept in common. In decoding the icon, the user asks, "What are all of these images examples of?"

| Tools | Type styles | Currencies | Formulas | Religions |

For the overlap technique, we can express the grammar this way:

Meaning = Overlap (Object₁, Object₂, ... Objectₙ)

---

[2]Screen shots are reprinted with permission from Helix Technologies, Inc.

The technique of overlap is superb for representing abstraction and general categories. Consider an abstract concept like *technology.* Any concrete instance of technology has many associations.

 Electronics, circuit, diagram, technology, energy

$e=mc^2$ Physics, relativity, formula, technology, energy

 Benzene, molecule, chemistry, diagram, formula, technology

However, when we combine them in a single icon …

… the result is a symbol of the intersection or overlap of their meanings:

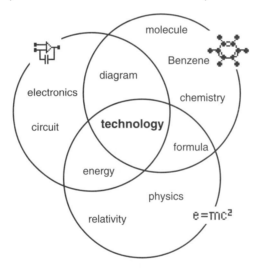

Specification

Often an icon must refer to one specific item or category. Specification combines separate images so that each restricts the reference of the others. It is like the practice of stacking up adjectives in front of a noun to sharpen its reference. A "big, blue ball" is more specific than "a ball" or even "a blue ball."

The grammar of the technique can be expressed:

$$\textbf{Meaning} = \textbf{Object}_1 \bullet \textbf{Object}_2 \bullet \ldots \bullet \textbf{Object}_n$$

Where • means restriction of meaning, much like the AND operation in querying a database or in Boolean logic.

These control panels illustrate specification:

Control panel for sound   Control panel for recording volume   Control panel for brightness   Control panel for contrast

You are probably familiar with one famous symbol that uses this technique. Have you ever wondered where the Peace sign came from? No, it has nothing to do with the Mercedes-Benz trademark. Supposedly designed by philosopher Bertrand Russell, it made its debut at a march held Easter weekend in 1958 in London to advocate total nuclear disarmament. It combines a circle, representing the globe or the idea of totality, with the semaphores for N and D, the first letters of "nuclear disarmament." (Note: *Semaphore* is a system for signaling using two flags that are held one in each hand.)

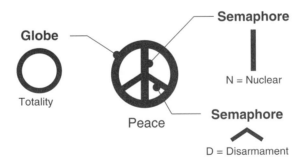

Only later during the Vietnam war did the sign achieve its broader meaning of peace.

CASE STUDY: MICROSOFT EXCEL AND WORD FILES

How do you help users recognize all the files created and used by a family of applications that can manipulate different forms of data? This was the problem confronting the icon designers for Microsoft Excel and Word. They created a powerful language by consistently following a few simple principles. The grammar of their language uses the technique of specification and can be expressed like this:[3]

File = Application ● Type file ● Type data

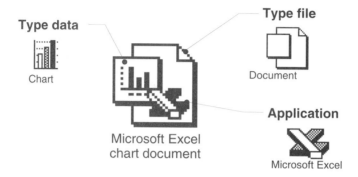

The **application** specifies which product was used to create the file or which application uses it. The **type data** represents the kind of information stored in the file. The **type file** tells the format in which the data is stored.

The vocabulary is likewise simple. It consists of just a few possibilities for each category:

Application	Type data		Type file
Microsoft Word	Text	Help	Document
Microsoft Excel	Worksheet	Glossary	Template
	Chart	Preferences	Published edition
	Macro	Startup	

---

[3]Screen shots are reprinted with permission from Microsoft Corporation.

We can appreciate the power of this language by looking at the many ways components can be combined while still maintaining a high degree of consistency.

Look at these icons for text documents, each created with a different application:

Excel text
document

Word text
document

Notice the similarity and differences among all the icons for the different types of data created and used by Excel:

Text   Worksheet   Chart   Macro   Startup   Help file   Preferences
                                                  document   file

And these for the same data in different formats:

Regular
document

Template

Published
edition

The scheme readily accommodates the special case of a Microsoft Excel workbook which includes more than one type of data.

ARRANGE THE DISPLAY

The icon must speak for itself. But what it says depends on where it is. The context of an icon affects our interpretation. The same is true of words. The word *set* has different meanings when uttered by the starter at a track meet, a sports reporter at a tennis tournament, or a buyer of fine china. For icons, the context consists of how the icons are positioned, grouped, and labeled.

Group icons

There are few more daunting sights to a novice than a screen filled with randomly arranged icons. Often when performing usability tests, I have noticed test subjects sorting icons into groups and arranging the groups as an aid to figuring out their meaning. After alternately pondering and shuffling, they exclaim, "Oh, now I get it."

The first step to bringing order to the chaos is to group the icons into meaningful categories and subcategories. There is no magic recipe for doing this, but experience provides some guidelines:

- **Involve users from the start**. Let users help you pick the categories and subcategories and have them suggest names for the them.

- **Group by task**. Strive for categories based on tasks the user performs rather than based on the architecture of the software. I have, alas, seen icons grouped on menus according to the internal algorithm, the command used, or by which department wrote the command.

- **Balance groups**. For a first attempt, try for no more than 3 levels of categories and about 5 to 10 items per group.

- **Stay practical**. Avoid pedantic or fanatical organizational schemes. If an icon appears to fit in more than one group, duplicate it.

Position icons

The next step is to position the icons to reveal relationships and categories. Put related icons close together, especially those that are almost the same and those that are opposites. Never arrange icons randomly or (I have actually seen this) alphabetically by the undisplayed name of the icon.

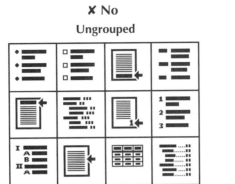

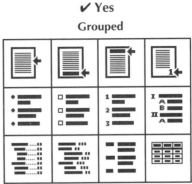

Make organization clear

Merely grouping icons may not be enough. You must make the organizational scheme crystal clear.

- To show grouping and relative importance, put groups into separate windows and palettes.

- Label windows, palettes, and groups of icons especially if the individual icons are not labeled.

- Put thicker borders or more space between separate categories or sub-categories of icons.

- Use a different color or background pattern for different categories of icons.

CASE STUDY: FILES IN APPLE'S SYSTEM 7

When Apple introduced its System 7 operating system for the Macintosh, users were suddenly exposed to new layers of complexity. System 7's modular architecture, built-in networking, and security features meant that users needed to be able to distinguish many more types of files than before. To help, Apple designed a simple but rich language for desktop icons.[4]

---

[4]Screen shots are reprinted with permission from Apple Computer, Inc.

The grammar of the language has three parts:

File = Contents + Container + Modifiers

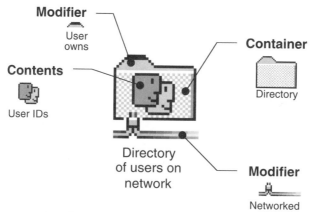

The **container** specifies the type of file and the **contents** show what it contains. The optional **modifiers** specify special characteristics of the file or distinguish between similar files.

Containers are typically shown as a distinctive border or background object. Containers represent generic types of files. Some common containers for data are these:

Besides these containers, which might be created by a user, there are other containers for software and resources:

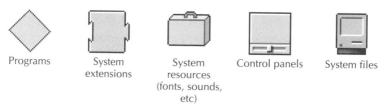

The symbol for the **contents** indicates what the file contains. There are many of these and their designs vary considerably from application to application. Apple provided a consistent set for helping users distinguish the different directories needed by the system.

| System extensions | Control panels | Printers | Preferences | Fonts | Apple menu items | Start-up items |

Modifiers inform the user of special characteristics of files. These modifiers are specific to a single type of container. For example, for directories, these modifiers are available:

Modifier	Image	Example
Available over a network		
Locked, cannot be opened		
Owned by the user		
Write only, the user can add to this container but cannot take from it		

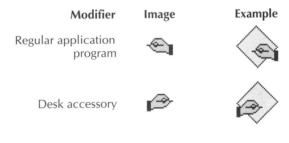

Apple uses a similar scheme to distinguish between two types of programs.

Modifier	Image	Example
Regular application program		
Desk accessory		

FOR MORE INFORMATION

Bodmer, Frederick. *The Loom of Language: An Approach to the Mastery of Many Languages*. New York: W.W. Norton, 1944.

Dondis, D. A *Primer of Visual Literacy*. Cambridge, MA: MIT Press, 1973.

Dreyfuss, Henry. *Symbol Sourcebook: An Authoritative Guide to International Graphic Symbols*. New York: Van Nostrand Reinhold, 1984.

DRAWING ICONS

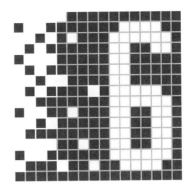

Once you have decided what to draw as an icon, you need to decide how to draw it. How big should it be? Should you make it realistic or simplified? Or should you style it as a caricature? Should you draw the object as solid or flat? If solid, how do you make it recognizable? How will you compensate for the coarse-grained texture of the computer screen? Most important, how will you ensure unity among all the icons of a set? This chapter helps you answer these questions.

DRAW WITH APPROPRIATE REALISM AND DETAIL

After you have decided what objects to include in your icon, decide how to draw the objects. Should you draw them in a detailed, realistic style or a simplified, minimalist one?

Appropriate details make objects easier to recognize. Our eyes seek out detail in a scene and detail can draw our eye to an image. However, detail can distract and clutter. Excessive detail makes it harder to see a pattern of relationships.

Which is best? The rule is simple: Include just those details necessary for the icon to accomplish its purpose. Often a less detailed image makes a better emblem, especially for general or abstract concepts.

We can draw icons in five different degrees of detail and realism:

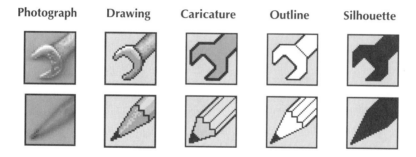

Although each of these styles has its place, it is difficult to mix radically different styles in a set of icons. The best approach is to select a primary style and use it for most of the icons of a set. When you encounter images that cannot be rendered in the primary style, consider as an alternative a style similar to the primary one. For instance, you might select the caricature style as your primary style and use the drawing and outline styles as alternates. The caricature style would not mix well with the photographic or silhouette style.

Photographic realism

Photographs and photo-realistic drawings can serve as icons. Typically this technique is used for complex objects that require a uniformly high level of detail to make them recognizable. One common use of photographic icons is to represent specific people, buildings, or works of art. Information about history, art, and current events often features recognizable images. Consider this example showing famous landmarks.

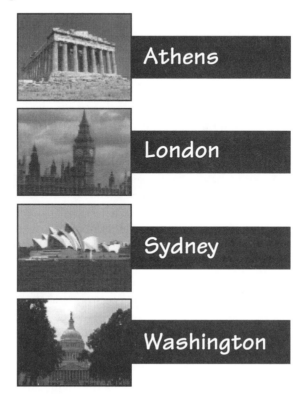

Another common use of photographic images is to represent visual images themselves. For instance, some multimedia authoring tools capture a frame of video or animation and use that frame as an icon for the actual clip or sequence:

Photographic icons are not practical in all circumstances. For photographic icons to work, you need three things:

- **Large area**. It takes space to represent a complex object realistically. The typical 32 x 32-pixel area available for icons is seldom enough for anything but the simplest objects.

- **Color or gray-scale display**. For manmade objects, 16 colors or levels of gray will suffice. For human faces, 256 colors are often required to avoid unsightly banding and blotches in skin tones.

- **Familiar object**. Unfamiliar objects, even when depicted in detail, are not likely to be recognized at a small size.

Simplified drawing

Probably the most common icon drawing style is that of a simplified drawing. The hallmark of this style is a clear outline contour and distinctive interior details. Details may be omitted for simplicity, but features are not deliberately exaggerated.

This style works well for complex objects that require specific details to be recognized. We often use it for mechanical and electronic devices:

This style is especially useful when objects contain small, significant parts like the vernier wheel in a drafting compass or the spiral binding of a notebook:

The simplified drawing style helps us distinguish among objects that share a common profile. Many man-made objects share a basically rectangular or circular profile; therefore, interior details are necessary to identify these objects. It would be difficult to identify any of these objects without their interior details:

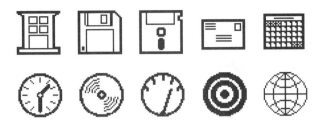

Such interior details are necessary to distinguish closely related objects with similar overall appearance:

Video tape   Audio tape

Caricature

The caricature style departs from the simplified drawing style by deliberately exaggerating critical details. Though often used for humor, more often caricature calls attention to a small, crucial feature of the icon.

In caricature we distort a part of the image to emphasize that part. For instance, we make the part larger than it would be in a realistic drawing:

Caricature is also useful to simplify complex detail. Here we enlarge small components or reduce the number of repeated ones:

Caricature can add a whimsical tone to what might otherwise seem cold or menacing. One of the most effective uses of this tone is Apple's icon and visual symbol for the Macintosh:[1]

---

[1]Screen shot is reprinted with permission from Apple Computer, Inc.

We can use this same technique to take the hard mechanical edge off a control panel, soften the impact of bugs in a computer program, or just make a clever icon for sounds:

If an object is familiar, we need few details to make it recognizable. Users seldom notice details in icons for familiar objects. Hardly one user in a thousand has noticed that the floppy disk icon in the toolbar for Microsoft Word and Excel (for Macintosh and Windows) is a mirror image of an actual disk. The image is close enough for them to recognize it as a disk.

Outline

The outline style is the next degree of simplicity. Objects are drawn as an outline contour with only the most prominent internal details are shown. This technique is good for small icons that represent a familiar object having a distinct profile. Many objects fit this category, such as:

By omitting internal details and simplifying outline contours, we imply that the icon represents an abstract category or class:

Games   Macintosh   Industry   Exit
             computers

The outline style may be the only style practical when the object consists of just edges and lines:

The outline style can be used to reduce the prominence of an icon. By giving the icon a thin outline contour rather than filling it with an emphatic color, we make it visible without letting it dominate other icons:

Overly emphatic   **Less emphatic**

Silhouette

The silhouette style is the maximum in simplicity. Here we show a shape filled with a solid color contrasting with its background. By obscuring irrelevant details, such as skin color, this style makes icons more generic:

Silhouettes are used in common road and packaging signs. They are also used in the icons derived from those signs:

Fragile   Restaurant   Danger

The silhouette style results naturally from objects too thin to have a separate outline contour:

Filling a shape gives it a visual mass that makes it stand out from a plain background and from unfilled objects. By combining filled and unfilled shapes, you can control the relative emphasis given to different icons or different objects within an icon:

The silhouette style does not work for objects that lack a distinctive profile. Can you identify these icons without their interior detail?[2]

MAKE OBJECTS RECOGNIZABLE

Each icon should answer these questions: What is this? What is most important about it? How do I use this icon? How is it related to the rest of the program, especially to other icons? Communicating these messages requires making the objects shown in the icon as easy to recognize as we can.

Use characteristic viewpoint

For every object there is one viewpoint that makes the object most recognizable. The image of the object from this viewpoint is called the *characteristic view* or the *canonical view.*

We have several choices for which viewpoint to use:

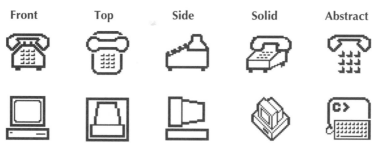

The characteristic view of an object depends on the object and the viewer. For most common objects, the characteristic viewpoint is the one we assume most often when seeing the object. This is usually the solid view from the front, slightly above, and slightly to one side. If this is difficult to draw, we can often substitute the front view.

Keep in mind, however, that the best view is the one that most clearly reveals the object. For a desktop computer, the frontal view may be the most recogniz-

---

[2] From left to right, they are an audio cassette, a CD-ROM, floppy disk, small diskette, window.

able; but, for a laptop computer, the side view may better reveal its distinct profile:

Exaggerate crucial concepts

An icon is not a drawing. The purpose of an icon is not to tell someone what something looks like, but to remind them of something they already know. For this reason, we often must exaggerate the size of important but small items in an icon:

Page header   Page footer   Page number

This exaggeration is part of the caricature drawing style and the representation scheme known as *hyperbole*. With exaggeration we can distill the meaning of an icon to its essence:

Left   Right   Center   Justify

Use depth effects consistently

Unless all your images are strictly flat, you must take care to use depth effects consistently. Layering flat objects or rendering solid objects requires care to maintain a credible illusion of depth.

Two- or three-dimensional images?

Three-dimensional images are easier to recognize but harder to draw:

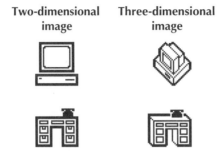

Two-dimensional
image

Three-dimensional
image

We live in a three-dimensional world and our perceptions are accustomed to recognizing three-dimensional images. Showing an image from a viewpoint that robs it of depth usually makes it harder to recognize. Three-dimensional images, however, require more space and can be hard to manage given the small size of most icons.

Viewpoint

When showing three-dimensional objects, we have three choices for viewpoint—the position of the viewer in relation to the object:

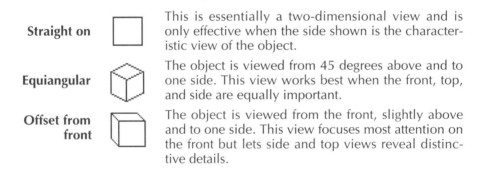

Straight on
This is essentially a two-dimensional view and is only effective when the side shown is the characteristic view of the object.

Equiangular
The object is viewed from 45 degrees above and to one side. This view works best when the front, top, and side are equally important.

Offset from front
The object is viewed from the front, slightly above and to one side. This view focuses most attention on the front but lets side and top views reveal distinctive details.

True perspective vs. paraline view

After deciding on the viewpoint to take, there are basically two ways of drawing solid three-dimensional objects. In true perspective schemes, parallel edges of solid objects seem to converge toward vanishing points, typically on the horizon. In paraline drawing, these same parallel edges are drawn with parallel lines:

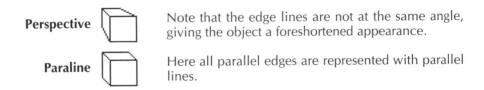

Perspective   Note that the edge lines are not at the same angle, giving the object a foreshortened appearance.

Paraline   Here all parallel edges are represented with parallel lines.

In general, perspective drawings are more interesting and can appear more realistic. However, paraline is easier to draw, especially at the small size of an icon. Most objects can be drawn with combinations of vertical, horizontal, 45-degree, and 30-degree lines, thus minimizing jaggedness. Paraline offers one other practical advantage: Objects drawn in true perspective cannot be combined or moved in the image without redrawing their edge lines. Objects in paraline can be combined and rearranged freely:

✗ No   **✔ Yes**

Objects in perspective are harder to combine   **Objects in paraline combine readily**

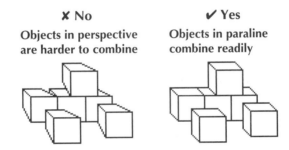

Axis of depth

When showing three-dimensional objects or overlapping flat ones, we must chose whether we view the objects from the left, from the right, or straight ahead:

Left   Straight   Right

Left or right views work equally well, provided there is consistency among all icons. Looking straight down the axis of depth, however, causes smaller objects to appear stacked atop nearer ones.

Layering

When showing flat objects, we can overlap them. This overlapping gives the icon a layered appearance. For clarity and consistency, decide how many layers to allow and how far to separate each layer.

Number of layers

The maximum number of layers will be controlled by the relative size of objects in the icon and by the minimum separation between objects:

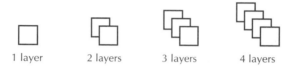

1 layer   2 layers   3 layers   4 layers

For most schemes, flat objects can be shown in two or three layers. With more layers, the clarity of the layering begins to break down and the illusion of depth is reduced.

Spacing of layers

When layering flat objects, we must decide the separation between layers. This spacing should be adequate to visually distinguish the objects:

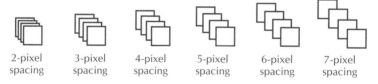

2-pixel   3-pixel   4-pixel   5-pixel   6-pixel   7-pixel
spacing   spacing   spacing   spacing   spacing   spacing

If the separation is too little, the edges of stacked objects resemble the side or top face of a solid object. If the separation is too much, objects become separated and, again, the illusion of depth is lessened.

Cast consistent shadows

Shadows can help depict the shape of objects, reinforce a three-dimensional metaphor, and add interest to the interface. Whether drawn with two-dimensional or three-dimensional shapes , shadows must be used consistently if these benefits are to be realized:

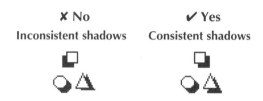

✗ No   **✔ Yes**

Inconsistent shadows   **Consistent shadows**

Drop or cast shadows?

In icons, we have a choice of what kind of shadow to use with flat objects:

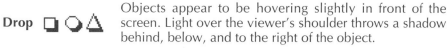

Drop   Objects appear to be hovering slightly in front of the screen. Light over the viewer's shoulder throws a shadow behind, below, and to the right of the object.

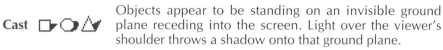

Cast   Objects appear to be standing on an invisible ground plane receding into the screen. Light over the viewer's shoulder throws a shadow onto that ground plane.

Cast shadows are perhaps more interesting, but they are harder to draw.

Direction of shadow

Our world is illuminated from above. This is not a metaphor but a simple observation. In icons, therefore, draw the shadow as if cast by a light source above the plane of the viewer's eyes:

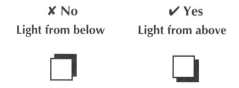

✗ No   **✔ Yes**

Light from below   **Light from above**

Three-dimensional objects illuminated from below appear to reverse near and far dimensions. Reversing the shading of a three-dimensional button makes it appear indented rather than raised:

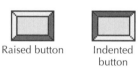

Raised button   Indented button

Shadows should be cast by a light from above, but should that light come from the left or right?

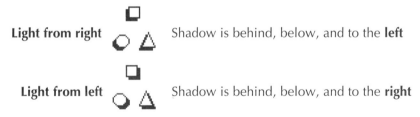

Light from right   Shadow is behind, below, and to the **left**

Light from left   Shadow is behind, below, and to the **right**

About four times as many icons cast their shadows to the right as to the left. This appears to be a convention that goes back to pen-and-ink, when right-handed draftsmen put their lights to the left to avoid shadows cast by their drawing hand. Either side works, but be consistent.

Distance of shadow

If you are using drop shadows, you must decide how far behind the object its shadow falls:

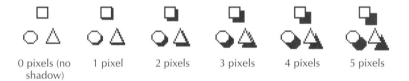

0 pixels (no   1 pixel   2 pixels   3 pixels   4 pixels   5 pixels
shadow)

If this distance is too little, the shadow may be ignored or may appear to be part of the border. If it is too large, the shadow becomes a separate object in its own right. On a black-and-white system, such black shadows may be more prominent that the object casting them, as in the example with 5 pixels of separation.

Shadow consistency

Drop shadows should consistently reinforce the illusion of flat objects hovering above the surface of the screen. Drawing drop shadows is usually quite simple. The shadow is a filled outline of the object behind the object itself. The shadow is simply offset a certain number of pixels below and to one side. When over-lapping objects occur, however, the situation is a bit more complex. In this case, we must take care to let the shadow of the nearer object fall onto the far-ther one. Where the shadow falls on the farther object, however, it is not offset as much as where it falls all the way to the imaginary surface of the screen:

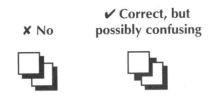

Merely offsetting the shadow of each object produces the illusion of a black object hovering between the two original objects.

Shadows falling onto shadows or onto foreground objects add complexity beyond what many viewers can handle. If you have objects on different layers, you may want to avoid shadows altogether.

Use gradations for smooth surfaces

The gradient of illumination across a subject reveals the object's shape. Use gradual transitions from light to dark to suggest a gently curving surface. Use sudden changes in brightness to suggest a sudden change of slope or a sharp edge:

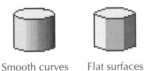

Smooth curves   Flat surfaces

DESIGN FOR THE SCREEN

All media limit the symbols they can convey. Cuneiform writing was styled by the requirements of clay and styli. Roman typefaces were shaped by the need to carve in stone. Oriental scripts are based on brush strokes. Our designs for icons must be tempered by the technology of the computer screen.

Icons for the screen are not the same as printed visual symbols. Icons must be designed to accommodate the limitations of the display screen and to take advantage of its display characteristics.

Beware of jaggies

Icons displayed on high-resolution computer screens seem coarse and blocky compared to visual symbols printed or hand drawn on paper. The requirement to draw icons in pixels can produce jagged images, especially for lines at angles almost vertical or horizontal. This jaggedness is referred to as *aliasing* or just *jaggies*.

Avoid oblique angles

To minimize jaggies, avoid oblique angles, those that are nearly horizontal or nearly vertical. Draw as much as possible with vertical and horizontal lines, which are not jagged at all. Try to draw diagonals with 45-degree lines. If this is not possible, then use 30- and 60-degree lines.

Notice in the diagram below how exaggerated jaggies become as the angle decreases:

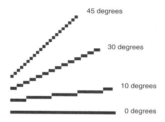

Avoid circles and arcs

Rectangles and other shapes made entirely of vertical and horizontal lines draw smoothly at even the smallest size:

Circles and curves, however, become distorted at small sizes. It takes an area of about 8 x 8 pixels (64 pixels) to draw a clear circle, but only a 3 x 3 area (9 pixels) to make a square:

When drawing small objects, try to avoid arcs or else substitute straight-edged shapes.

Antialiasing

Icons displayed on a color or gray-scale monitor can reduce jaggies by taking advantage of a technique called *antialiasing*. In this technique, each pixel varies its color or value to reflect the amount of its space occupied by objects and background. The effect is to fill in jagged edges somewhat:

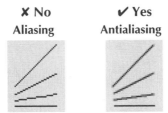

An enlargement clearly shows the averaging effect in smoothing out the jagged edges of diagonal lines:

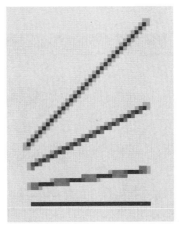

Antialiasing is not without costs. First, it only works on color or gray-scale monitors. Second, it reduces jagginess but lowers effective resolution. Images appear slightly out of focus and may lack crisp edges.

Fatten diagonal lines

Which of the diagonal lines is the same thickness as the vertical and horizontal lines?

Unless you have astigmatism, you will see the upper-left to lower-right diagonal as the same thickness as the vertical and horizontal lines. As a general rule, make 45-degree diagonals about one and a half times as thick as verticals and horizontals. The result is that the thickness across the diagonal is the same as across vertical and horizontal lines.

Positive or negative contrast?

Do you draw your icons lighter or darker than the background?

Negative   Positive
contrast   contrast

Research on legibility has found that users can read text slightly quicker and more accurately when the text is displayed dark on a light background. Further, there was a strong preference among test subjects for the dark-on-light display. Such findings, if extended to icons, would recommend negative-contrast displays. Life is never so simple.

Most of the research on the legibility of text was done in typical office settings. Most people in office settings handle paper—white paper with words and numbers printed in black. They perform tasks that required them to read from paper source documents, enter the information they read into a computer system, and then print it out to paper again. They do all this in offices with lighting designed to optimize reading printed paper documents. No surprise they preferred and performed better with displays that looked like paper.

In different situations, a positive-contrast display may work better. In work, such as air-traffic control, which is not tied to paper documents, the performance advantages of "artificial paper" are questionable. In other tasks, such as engineering design, the ability to show many small color-coded objects against a dark background may outweigh the advantages of negative-contrast legibility.

No hard-and-fast rule is possible. If users are accustomed to negative-contrast displays and must consult paper documents frequently, use negative-contrast icons. If their jobs involve tracking small objects, especially those with color codes, try positive-contrast display. If in doubt, use a negative contrast display. It is more common today.

In either case, take steps to ensure the legibility of icons. Watch out for the blooming effect: the tendency of light to flow from the light pixels into the dark ones. A light background will fill in thin lines and small areas. Bright lines and objects will tend to expand on a dark background.

Also take care to maintain sufficient contrast between foreground and background, regardless of which is light and which is dark.

Flat or 3D ink?

On color and gray-scale monitors you can display icons in three-dimensional relief:

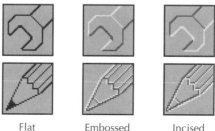

Flat   Embossed   Incised

Although the effect is at times striking, three-dimensional relief is something of a novelty whose appeal may fade if it becomes more commonplace. The lower contrast of gray-on-gray display can pose problems of legibility, especially when the icons are small or the user's eyesight is less than perfect. This three-dimensional effect works best for simple shapes with distinct outline contours and few interior lines.

ARRANGING THE OBJECTS

The way we arrange the various parts of the icon establishes a tone and affects the relative emphasis given the parts. Whether accidental or intentional, the arrangement of components is a potent element in the design of an icon. In arranging the parts of an icon, we must first consider what that arrangement communicates to the viewer about the balance, symmetry, and stability of the image.

Balance

Balance affects the formality and dynamism of an image. A balanced image appears more formal and static than an unbalanced one. A graphic image is balanced if its visual center is near its geometric center:

Unbalanced   Balanced

The visual center of an image is its center of visual mass. This is usually located at the intersection of the horizontal and vertical axes of the main objects in the image. The closer the visual center corresponds to the physical center, the more balanced the icon appears.

Notice the importance of balance in these before-and-after icons. By ensuring balance between the before-and-after images, we direct attention to the sometimes subtle difference between them:

Ungroup   Format   Sort

For other messages, however, imbalance may better direct attention to the critical matter of the icon. Imbalance occurs when visual mass is not evenly distributed about the geometric center:

 Here, imbalance emphasizes the screening effect of a filter.

Here, it provides a thwarted momentum consistent with the effect of a tab stop.

And here, imbalance draws attention to the person teaching.

Visual mass and its effect on balance depend on several factors:

Number

The visual mass depends on the number of objects. When more objects are on one side than the other, imbalance occurs.

Size

Larger objects have more visual mass. A small object does not counterbalance a larger object.

Prominence

The more prominent an object, the greater its visual mass. An object that contrasts with the background will have more mass than one that fades into the background. Bright colors have more mass than drab ones.

Leverage

The effect of a visual mass depends on its distance from the center. Objects farther from the center have more leverage than those near the center.

These effects do not operate independently. You can readily combine them to add counterbalancing effects:

Prominence
balances number

Size balances
prominence

Prominence
balances leverage

Symmetry

Symmetry is the correspondence of parts across a boundary or a point. It strongly binds separate objects together into a single image and affects the formality, coherence, and balance of the icon:

None The lack of symmetry gives the icon a lively appearance and helps objects maintain their separate identities.

Vertical Symmetry about a vertical line strongly links objects. It gives a formal, static balance.

Point Symmetry about the center is less formal but still balanced.

Notice the varying degree of symmetry in these three icons for communications media:

Book   Newspaper   Bulletin board

The strict symmetry of a book reinforces its formal authority while the asymmetrical arrangement of messages on a bulletin board gives it a lively informality. The newspaper seems midway between these two extremes.

Stability

Stability determines whether an icon seems ready to topple over or is likely to stand for years. Stability affects whether the effect of the icon is dynamic or static, urgent or calming. Stability depends on two factors: top-heaviness and orientation. For a stable icon, lower the center of mass; for an unstable one, raise it. Top-heavy icons appear less stable than bottom-heavy ones:

Unstable   Stable

Bottom-heavy or vertically balanced images are the rule. We should reserve top-heavy images for exceptions where the imbalance serves a purpose:

 In this icon for industrial pollution, top-heaviness makes the black smoke more ominous than it would otherwise appear.

 The Undo command reverses normal forward progress. Its icon, therefore, uses a top-heavy image to emphasize this reversal.

Icons with a strong diagonal appear less stable. The viewer sees a leaning stack of blocks:

Unstable   Stable

Notice how the diagonal arrangement of objects, gives these icons a sense of motion that would be missing in a vertical or horizontal arrangement:

Launch   Write   Heavy

Stability and instability can both be used to reinforce a message. Here are two icons with very similar messages:

Handle with care   The bottom-heavy, perfectly symmetrical icon produces an ultra-stable image.

Fragile   The top-heaviness of the image and its use of diagonals for the crack and stem reinforce the message of risk and concern.

VARY THE IMAGE

Each icon may require several different versions. You should plan for these from the beginning.

Various numbers of colors

To ensure the legibility of your icons, you may have to design versions that use different numbers of colors. Consider all the different ways your icons will appear:

- **Unlimited number of colors**

- **256 colors**

- **16 colors**. Usually available on most color monitors.

- **8 levels of gray**. Even though some laptops display 16 levels of gray, users often find it hard to discern more than half that number in realistic work conditions.

- **Black and white only**. Many users have only monochrome displays, some are color blind, and some will need to read black-and-white print-outs of icons.

Various sizes

We often abbreviate a long label or complex name. How do we abbreviate an icon? We can show a simpler, smaller version. Besides the main version of an icon, we may need a smaller version for inclusion in lists and on brief menus. We may also need a larger version for use as an emblem on the product's box or in its manual. Here are some variations on the standard 32 x 32-pixel size:

Normal	32 x 32 pixels
Condensed	16 x 16 pixels
Print emblem	25 mm x 25 mm (1 in x 1 in)

Different styles

Although we want to consistently use the same object to represent a concept, we may want to vary how we draw that object. Once Macintosh users learned that the trash can icon deleted files, they had little difficulty when encountering different forms of the image:

Similarly, users of HyperCard readily recognized many variations of the Home icon.

Once users have learned the association between the object and concept, we can vary our drawing style. We should not do this frivolously or simply for self-expression. There are some good reasons to vary our style:

- **To establish and maintain a product- or corporate-identity scheme**. You may want your company's icons to have a distinctive look.

- **To avoid violating someone else's copyright**. Copying pixel-for-pixel another company's icons without its permission is seldom a good idea. To ensure ownership of your own designs, create a unique image.

- **For fun**. Products used by children and products used for entertainment, demand more variety and tolerate a more whimsical approach than those used strictly for business.

DRAW ON A GRID-TEMPLATE

Many icon designers say they find it helps to draw icons, or at least preliminary sketches, on a grid background. Here is the grid on which many of the icons in this book were drawn:

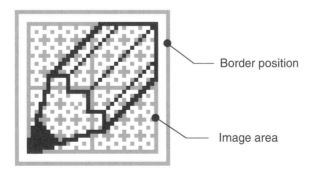

Border position

Image area

One of the paradoxes of icon design is that design is easier if the grid has an odd number of pixels along each side. This is because an odd number provides a center pixel around which to focus the design:

✘ No   ✔ Yes

Even-numbered grid   **Odd-numbered grid**

FOR MORE INFORMATION

Hambridge, Jay. *The Elements of Dynamic Symmetry.* New York: Dover, 1967.

Hamm, Jack. *Cartooning the Head and Figure.* New York: Grosset & Dunlap, 1967.

Hanks, Kurt and Larry Belliston. *Draw! A Visual Approach to Thinking, Learning, and Communicating.* Los Altos, CA: William Kaufmann, 1977.

Hodges, Elaine R. S. *The Guild Handbook of Scientific Illustration.* New York: Van Nostrand Reinhold, 1989.

Huntley, H. E. *The Divine Proportion: A Study in Mathematical Beauty.* New York: Dover, 1970.

Muse, Ken. *The Secrets of Professional Cartooning.* Englewood Cliffs, NJ: Prentice Hall, 1981.

Nelms, Henning. *Thinking with a Pencil.* Berkeley, CA: Ten Speed Press, 1981.

COLOR IN ICONS

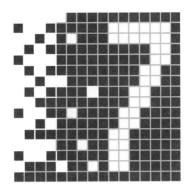

In the design of icons, color plays a somewhat ambiguous role. Used properly, color can communicate. Used carelessly, it can confuse. Color can make the message clear or hopelessly opaque. It can delight and entertain, or distract and annoy. Color can make the most important information pop out, or it can make everything illegible. The effect of color depends entirely on where and how you use it. Let's see how to use color effectively in icons.

Note: In this book I use the word *color* in its everyday sense, that is, a difference in hue (green vs. red vs. yellow) or a noticeable difference in a combination of hue, lightness, and saturation. Technically this is called *chromatic color.*

RULE ONE: DESIGN IN BLACK AND WHITE FIRST

It is ironic but usually the best way to use color is first to avoid it. Icon designers could bypass 95 percent of the problems of using color and reap 95 percent of its benefits by following this simple rule:

> **First, make your icon work in black and white.**
> **Then, add color to make it work better.**

When I asked designers of successful icons what advice they would offer their less experienced colleagues, almost all of them included some variation of this rule.

This rule leads us to express the primary message of the icon in light-dark contrast and reserve variations in hue and saturation for amplifying the primary message or expressing secondary messages.

Icons in black and white overcome several common problems caused by color:

- **Color blindness**. If you can see, you can see black and white. Yet 5 to 10 percent of men and 0.25 to 0.5 percent of women are red-green color blind.

- **Low quality display**. Poorly calibrated display monitors make viewing and recognizing color icons difficult. Poor convergence blurs images and adds color fringes. Low contrast clouds the image.

- **Small images**. Tiny icons or those read at a distance require high contrast. The part of the human eye that perceives details is most sensitive to differences in lightness.

- **Imperfect viewing conditions**. Icons viewed obliquely, as when users share a screen, are harder to recognize. Screen glare robs the screen of contrast and compounds all the other problems of legibility.

Use color redundantly

The color figures can be found on the color plate in this chapter. The images within the text are just placeholders.

Never use color as the only means to convey a critical or primary message. Without color, can you reliably tell which of these is which?

Color Figure 5: Color as sole identifier

Blood   Water

Or, could you pick the correct season from these leaves?

Color Figure 6: Color as sole identifier

Spring   Summer   Autumn   Winter

Say it in black and white and then use color to reinforce, amplify, and support the original message. If color is the only distinguishing characteristic for an icon, give the icon an unmistakable text label.

Select robust color combinations

As you incorporate colors into your design, you must select colors that maintain the light-dark contrast of the original black-and-white design. These high-contrast designs work well over a wide range of colors and gray levels. Icons designed without sufficient contrast lose legibility when displayed on systems with fewer colors or gray levels than intended. This problem often occurs when icons are designed on one system and then converted for use on another one that defines colors differently.

Notice what happens when these two icons for books are designed with different color schemes:

Color Figure 8: Depend on contrast not color

✘ No   ✔ Yes

High contrast   Low contrast

See how they appear when displayed on screens with different numbers of colors:

Color figure 9: Different display levels

Levels	Color	Gray
256	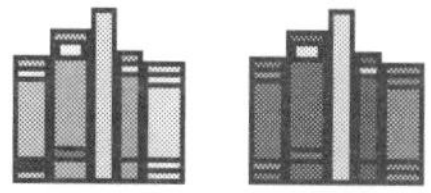	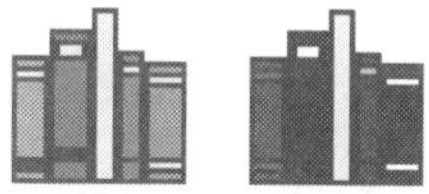
16	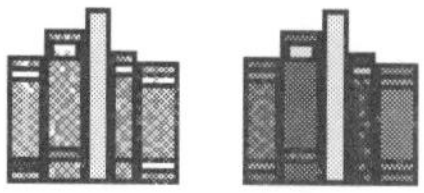	
4	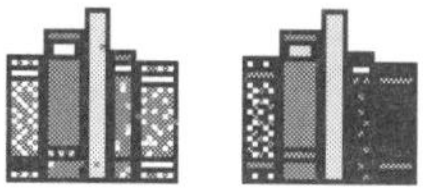	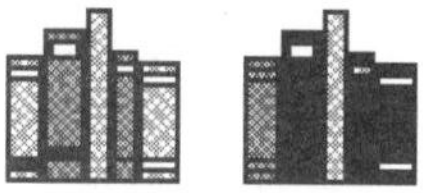
2	Black and white only	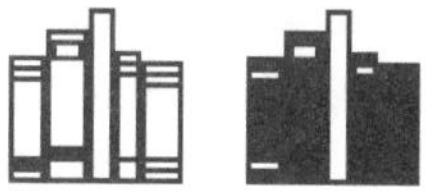

The icon with high foreground-background contrast remains legible under all conditions. The same is not true of the low-contrast icon.

DECIDE WHY YOU ARE USING COLOR

In designing computer displays, there are several good reasons to use color. Users can find and extract information quicker from colored displays. Color can add excitement and fun to an otherwise drab display. However, the way we use color to liven up a display can conflict with the ways we use it to speed up search.

In general, you can use color for one purpose in an icon and for only one or two purposes in a group of icons displayed together. Your first step in incorporating color into your icons is to decide why you want to use color. Be careful not to have conflicting purposes. Study this list and pick the one or two most important reasons for using color:

- **To direct attention**. Color can ensure that users notice and attend to critical icons or small details within an icon.

- **To speed search**. Color helps users find information quickly. Color coding can reduce the time required to find an item in a complex display. Color coding is more effective than coding by shape, brightness, or other techniques.

- **To aid recognition**. Realistic colors help users recognize an icon. Colors can also reduce the jagged edges which interfere with recognizing small images.

- **To show organization**. Color helps users distinguish and understand items in a complex display. Users can then make decisions faster and more accurately.

- **To rate or quantify**. Color can express numerical relationships. It can rank items in order and can express a value along a scale, though not precisely.

- **To represent color itself**. When users must apply, define, or edit a color, they want to see the color. The words *pale aquamarine* are no substitute for a swatch of the color.

- **To attract and please users**. Users prefer color displays. In survey after survey users say color displays improve their performance and confidence and reduces eye strain and discomfort.

- **To reinforce or arouse an emotion**. Color can shape our feelings toward an idea and can represent emotions directly.

The rest of this section suggests ways to use color for each of these purposes.

To direct attention

Color can direct the user's gaze to specific icons or specific objects within the icon. It can change the apparent importance of icons and objects.

To call attention to a small item

To make a small item stand out, give it a conspicuous color. Pick a color that contrasts with the background and is distinctive from the color of other objects:

Color figure 7: Color focuses attention

Press **this**
button

Book **mark**,
not the book

Ensure a foreground-to-background contrast ratio of at least 7 to 1. Use a bright, saturated color for the object you want to emphasize and display everything else in neutral colors. Draw the emphasized object as large as possible. Otherwise, users may not notice the colors. Try to make the object at least 5 x 5 pixels in size.

To emphasize an area or group of icons

When emphasizing a larger area of the display or when showing an ongoing theme or general category, use paler or darker colors. Large areas of pure, saturated color overwhelm and tire users. For small items, such as individual icons, use bright, pure, high-contrast colors. For larger areas, use lower-contrast, more neutral colors.

To deemphasize an object

To deemphasize, hide, or camouflage an object. Fade it into the background. Give it a color close to that of the background. Select a similar hue and lower the lightness difference between the object and its background.

To speed search

Color can greatly reduce the time required to find an item in a complex display:

Color figure 24: Color aids search

Find the square
here

Find the yellow
circle here

For the quickest search:

- Display the icon you want the user to notice in a unique color. Minimize the number of other icons and objects in that color.

- Use as few colors as possible. If icons are close together, you can use about 7 colors. If not, limit yourself to 4 colors.

- Teach or tell the user what color to search for.

- Select color codes that represent characteristics of the icons. Make sure these characteristics are meaningful to the user.

Color coding can fail if you use too many colors, or if there are too many items in each color.

To aid recognition

Color helps us recognize objects. Objects displayed in familiar colors are recognized more quickly than those without color, and much better than those in unexpected colors. Color must be plausible, but it need not be highly accurate. Only images of foods and faces require high-fidelity color. Most other objects remain recognizable provided we maintain the relative color differences among their parts.

For quickest recognition display the icon in sterotypical colors. Show an object the way users expect the object to be colored—even if the expectation is unrealistic. Remember:

Roses are red.
Violets are blue
At least on maps,
Rivers are too.

Here are some examples of the use of expected colors in icons:

Color figure 15: Expected colors

Printout   First aid   Fire   Faucet   Road

Use colors traditionally associated with an object. Show the color of the most common, most widely used, and best established version of an object:

Color figure 16: Color identifies object

Pencil   Eraser   Flashlight   Highlighter   Palette

Use conventional colors for established symbols. Whenever you use traffic or safety signs in icons, show them in their conventional colors:

Color figure 17: Conventional colors in signs

Caution   No   Stop   Radioactive   Electrical   First aid
                                                    hazzard

To show organization

Color can be effectively used to categorize and group. It can show which icons are similar and which are different. We naturally see items of the same color as a group. To show that separate icons are of the same type, class, or category, display them with the same color. You can show up to 6 or 7 categories provided you use a distinct color for each. Display similar icons in similar but distinguishable colors. Use very different colors to represent dissimilar concepts. For mutually exclusive categories, use complementary colors.

Color effectively shows which objects are the same or similar and which are different:

Color figure 18: Color categorizes

Retouch   Design   Paint   Repair   Measure   Attach

To rate or quantify

Color can suggest a ranking or sequential order among separate items and can represent a numerical value within a range.

To rank items

To imply an order or ranking among a group of icons, assign them colors varying in lightness, not just hue. One of the most common mistakes in color coding is to use the color spectrum to imply an order. This scale, which arranges colors as they occur in a rainbow, is not immediately recognized. Users must memorize it:

Color figure 10: Spectral order

The color scale also progresses from dark colors to light and back to dark again, providing conflicting clues. Fortunately, there are three scales that avoid these problems. One is the scale of lightness. Select a single hue and vary its lightness:

Color figure 11: Lightness scale

The other scales rely on the subjective "temperature" of different hues. They arrange colors in order from cold to hot. One temperature scale spans the cool colors from violet to yellow:

Color figure 12: Cool scale

The other spans the warm colors from yellow to red:

Color figure 13: Warm scale

The entire hot-cold range is split into two scales since each half is also a scale of lightness.

To express a range of values

Color can express a numerical value within a range—but only approximately. Use a continuous mixture of colors between two extremes. For example, to represent temperature, use a range of colors from deep blue to bright red. Notice how the shape reinforces the color, and that the icon works in both black and white as well:

Color figure 25: Color as secondary cue

Cold   Moderate   Hot

If the range spans both positive and negative numbers, use a cool color for negative values, a warm color for the positive values, and a neutral color for the zero point.

Although users can infer the general value from a color, do not rely on color alone to express a value. Color is best used to reinforce a value expressed more precisely by some other means:

Color figure 19: Color reflects sound level

Off   1   2   3   4   5

To represent color itself

The most direct, most obvious, most natural use of color is to represent color it-self. Applications for mapping, illustration, photo retouching, presentation graphics, and other business activities often require users to select, apply, and edit colors. These applications must show the colors the user is working with. Phrases such as *deep red* and *bluish green* are too vague.

Icons can include swatches of color to show the currently active or selected color. For example, these drawing tools each show the color applied by each tool. If the color assigned to a tool changes, the color in its icon changes:

Color figure 20: Color represents color

Changing the color of parts of an icon to show color assignments takes some programming finesse and on some systems may prove impossible. In most cases, however, the background color of icons can be changed to reflect color assignments.

For the most accurate perception, display the sample color against a black, white, or gray background. Also, make the area of color large enough that the user can see it clearly, at least a 5 x 5-pixel area. Otherwise display a separate swatch of the color elsewhere on the display and use color in the icon only as a reminder for the user.

To attract and please users

We all like some colors better than others. Designers who ignore the subjective and aesthetic effects of color are as remiss as those who consider only their own tastes in color.

Reactions to color are so subjective and personal that we may never have exact rules for selecting colors. The best we can strive for are guidelines for using colors in ways that offend few people and unify rather than disrupt the design.

Balance colors

Staring at a large area of one color for long periods of time dulls the user's ability to perceive that color. Most people, thus, find balanced color combinations more comfortable. Screen colors are balanced if the red-green-blue values of pixels throughout the screen average out to a neutral gray. To balance colors:

- **Mix colors with different characteristics**. Use warm colors to balance cool colors and dark colors to offset bright colors.

- **Select colors equally spaced around a common color harmony wheel**:

Color figure 22: Distinct colors

- **Use pure, bright colors only over small areas**. An icon is a small area. Cover large areas, such as the surface of a menu, with a neutral color like gray or white. If you must use color over a large area, use a pale or a dark hue.

Avoid garish colors

You cannot please everyone—at least in your choice of colors. You can, however, avoid offending many. Put your own subjective preferences aside and select colors based on research and common sense:

- **Limit use of bright, primary colors** unless your program is used by children. Reserve these colors for accenting and highlighting small objects or individual icons.

- **Pick colors that most users like**. Western adult viewers prefer colors in this order: blue, red, green, purple, orange, and yellow.

- **Use colors found in nature**. They seldom offend.

- **Select proven colors and combinations**. Pick colors that have been popular for many years and in different cultures.

- **Avoid trendy, vogue color schemes** unless you plan to redesign your icons every year or so.

Avoid conflicting colors

Unless designers create icons and screens with a simple, consistent color scheme, the screen becomes a babbling riot of contending colors:

- **Do not overwhelm subtle color icons** with bright borders and brilliant backgrounds.

- **Avoid juxtaposing spectrally distant colors** like red and blue.

- **Limit your use of opponent color combinations**, such as blue and yellow, green and red, and green and blue. Such combinations produce afterimages and indistinct edges.

To reinforce or arouse emotions

The ability of color to arouse emotions has long been documented. Color affects blood circulation and pressure, respiration rate, muscular strength, brainwave activity, and electrical conductance of the skin. The strength and direction of the effect vary with the different colors. We can use colors to moderate the emotional state of the user:

People's reactions to colors have been studied since cave dwellers first decorated their walls with images of bison and hunters. Some common emotional associations have been observed:

Color	Associations
Red	Aggression, impulsiveness, warmth, extroversion, crudeness, optimism, danger, shame
Orange	Friendliness, congeniality, deference, warmth, pride, gregariousness
Yellow	Novelty, idealism, introspection, warmth, caution, betrayal, cowardice
Green	Freshness, hope, health, prosperity, envy, jealousy, madness, nausea, approval
Blue	Cold, calm, truth, innocence, precision, doubt, depression, hopelessness
Purple	Vanity, wit, nostalgia, spirituality, resignation, regret
Brown	Duty, parsimony, reliability, earthiness, barrenness, poverty
Gold	Richness, wisdom, honor, high quality, haughtiness, vainglory, power
White	Lightness, innocence, purity, wisdom, truth, cold, ghostliness, void
Gray	Restraint, neutrality, barrenness, grief, indifference, inertia, maturity
Black	Death, grief, morbidity, gloom, despair, dignity, solemnity, sin, negation

CHOOSING COLORS

Once you have decided why to use color and have considered the requirements of color for that purpose, you must select the actual colors to use. In some cases the choice is obvious: If you are using color to represent colors, you simply make your colors the same as those they represent. For making objects recognizable, you pick realistic colors consistent with the user's expectations. For other purposes, especially those involving color coding, you must often balance conflicting requirements.

Use as few colors as you can

Computers can display millions of colors, but how many should we use in icons? Only as many as we need. As we use more colors, each color becomes less distinct. The more colors we put in a display, the slower and less certainly the user reacts to each.

So, how many colors do we need? The number varies with the reasons for using color. Here are some general guidelines:

Reason for using color		Number of colors
Best legibility		black and white
Fastest search	Over entire display	3 to 4
	Close together	6 to 7
Recognizable images	Faces and foods	100+
	Other objects	20-50

Rely on learned associations

Select colors whose meanings users have already learned. Avoid using colors in ways that conflict with common associations for colors.

Color associations learned from nature are reliably understood worldwide. Consider these common meanings for color:

Color	Meaning	Associated with
Red	Danger	Blood
	Heat	Fire
Yellow	Warmth	Sun
Blue	Cool	Water
Green	Life, youth	Young leaves
Brown	Age, death, earth, soil	Dying vegetation
Paler colors	Distance	Atmospheric haze

Consistently warm colors suggest activity and excitement, and cool colors suggest quiet and calm.

Where natural associations do not apply, we can draw on broadly followed conventions for color meanings. Safety warnings and road signs provide a consistent model to follow:

Color	Safety signs	Traffic signs
Red	Danger, stop	Danger, warning, no
Orange	Dangerous parts of equipment	Cautionary
Yellow	Cautions	Cautionary, important
Blue	Non-safety messages	Information, yes
Green	Safety	Go
Black on yellow	Radiation	
Black on white	Traffic markings	

Notice how analogous colors are used to show the remaining charge in a battery:

Color figure 26: Color represents range of values

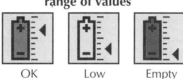

OK   Low   Empty

If no general conventions apply, we may look for associations prevalent in the discipline or business of users. An accounting program could, for example, use red as a symbol for financial loss.

Pick harmonious colors

There is no magic recipe for picking harmonious color combinations. Yet a simple technique combined with a selective eye yields usable combinations.

For distinct hues

To pick a few, distinct, harmonious colors, select colors from symmetrical positions around a traditional color harmony wheel. For two colors, this procedure yields complementary colors. For any number of colors it ensures that the colors are distinct from one another.

Color figure 22: Distinct colors

For similar hues

For similar hues, pick colors from adjacent slots on the color wheel, for instance:

Color figure 23: Similar colors

Varying lightness

Instead of picking harmonious hues, you can pick a single hue, such as green, and vary the lightness of that hue:

Color figure 11: Lightness scale

Color figure 1: Color draws attention

Color figure 2: Aerial perspective

✗ No   ✔ Yes

Color figure 3: Color-depth effect

Color figure 4: Color suggests distance

✗ No   ✔ Yes

Color Figure 5: Color as sole identifier

Blood   Water

Color Figure 6: Color as sole identifier

Spring   Summer   Autumn   Winter

Color figure 7: Color focuses attention

Press **this** button   Book **mark**, not the book

Color Figure 8: Depend on contrast not color

✗ No   ✔ Yes

High contrast   Low contrast

Color figure 9: Different display levels

Levels	Color	Gray
256		
16		
4		
2	Black and white only	

Color figure 10: Spectral order

Color figure 11: Lightness scale

Color figure 12: Cool scale

Color figure 13: Warm scale

Color figure 14: Saturation scale

Color figure 15: Expected colors

   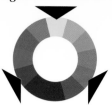

Printout   First aid   Fire   Faucet   Road

Color figure 16: Color identifies object

Pencil   Eraser   Flashlight   Highlighter   Palette

Color figure 17: Conventional colors in signs

Caution   No   Stop   Radioactive   Electrical hazzard   First aid

Color figure 18: Color categorizes

Retouch   Design   Paint   Repair   Measure   Attach

Color figure 19: Color reflects sound level

Off   1   2   3   4   5

Color figure 20: Color represents color

Color figure 21: Lightness contrast improves legibility

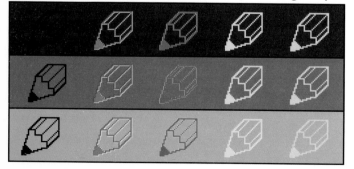

Color figure 22: Distinct colors

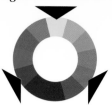

Color figure 23: Similar colors

Color figure 24: Color aids search

Find the square here   Find the yellow circle here

Color figure 25: Color as secondary cue

Cold   Moderate   Hot

Color figure 26: Color represents range of values

OK   Low   Empty

Varying saturation

Another set of harmonious colors results from varying the saturation or purity of a color:

Color figure 14: Saturation scale

Because such colors do not vary in lightness, they will be impossible to distinguish on gray-scale monitors and can pose problems for color-blind users.

Pick colors systematically

Assign colors in a meaningful way. First decide why to use color, then how to, and which colors. Here is an example of the process of selecting colors for an application.

Step	Action	Example
1	Decide why you are using colors. Select one primary purpose.	The application controls flow through the pipes of a computer-controlled refinery. We want to color code icons to reflect the function they trigger.
2	Specify the categories you need to represent. This lets you know how many colors you need.	Commands perform four kinds of functions: (1) open valves, (2) close valves, (3) restrict the flow through pipes, and (4) label pipes and valves with descriptive information.
3	Select candidate colors.	We pick red, green, blue, and yellow.
4	Make tentative assignments based on common associations of the colors.	On traffic signs these colors have these meanings: red = stop green = go yellow = slow blue = information
5	Fix specific assignments in the context of the assignment.	By analogy we use red for icons that close pipes, green for icons that open pipes, yellow for icons that restrict flow, and blue for icons that annotate the display.

AVOID COMMON PROBLEMS

Careless or haphazard use of color leads to problems. We can overcome these problems by understanding them and taking steps to avoid them.

Ensure legibility

Color can reduce legibility. Color-on-color displays lacking lightness contrast make icons, thin lines, and text hard to see. Because of misregistration, color can also produce fuzzy edges, especially at the edges and corners of the screen. If you must use color for icons, follow these guidelines:

- **Maintain a high tonal contrast between foreground and background**. Avoid low-contrast color combinations such as dark blue on black and yellow on white. On a light background, use a dark color, such as red or blue. For a dark background either use a light color like yellow or green or else use a pale tint of a color:

Color figure 21: Lightness contrast improves legibility

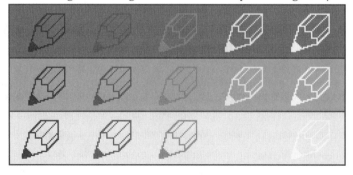

- **Lighten dark pure colors like red and blue when they appear on a dark background**. Likewise darken light colors, such as yellow and green, when they occur on a light background.

- **Use pure blue as a background only** since many people cannot focus clearly on small blue objects.

- **Do not put pure red and blue side by side**. Red objects appear nearer than blue ones. Using red and blue together creates an illusion of depth.

Do not distract viewers

Excessive and irrelevant color distracts users and makes finding information on the screen harder and less reliable. The distraction of meaningless color disrupts the user's visual scanning patterns. To avoid the disruptive effects of color:

- **Use few colors**. The more colors you use, the longer the user takes to respond to each and the greater the confusion between colors.

- **Use bright, conspicuous colors only for icons that need extra attention**.

- **Use color only where its meaning is clear to the user**.

Compensate for color blindness

Although only one person in 30,000 is totally color blind, many do have problems with certain colors. About 8 percent of men and 0.4 percent of women have trouble distinguishing red and green. Most of us are blue-blind in the very center of our field of vision where we perceive fine details such as icons. Because of yellowing of the lens of the eye, this difficulty seeing pure blue increases as we age.

To overcome the problems caused by color blindness:

- **Use color redundantly**. Use color only to repeat or reinforce messages expressed in black and white.

- **Take care with problem colors**. Avoid using red vs. green for any critical distinction. Use pure blue as a background only.

- **Vary lightness contrast.** Use color combinations that differ in value, not just in hue. Consider a bright yellow, a medium green, and a dark red.

- **Pick colors most can distinguish**. Distinctive combinations include red and blue, red and cyan, blue and yellow.

- **Use just a few colors**. Limit how many colors users must distinguish.

- **Keep colors to be compared near one another**. Locate color legends near the colors they decode.

FOR MORE INFORMATION

De Grandis, Luigina. *Theory and Use of Color.* New York: Abrams, 1986.

Durrett, H. John, ed. *Color and the Computer.* Boston: Academic Press, 1987.

Itten, Joseph. *The Elements of Color.* New York: Van Nostrand Reinhold, 1970.

Thorell, Lisa G. and Wanda J. Smith. *Using Computer Color Effectively: An Illustrated Reference.* Englewood Cliffs, NJ: Prentice Hall, 1990.

White, Jan V. *Color for the Electronic Age.* New York: Watson–Guptill Publications, 1990.

Wong, Wucius. *Principles of Color Design.* New York: Van Nostrand Reinhold, 1987.

STANDARD PARTS OF THE ICON

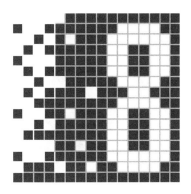

An icon may contain more than an image of some recognizable object. The image may appear with a border around it, a background surface behind it, and a label that identifies it.

In this chapter we consider the design issues raised by these optional components. When do we include them in the design? What can each communicate about the icon? How should they appear?

Keep in mind that many of these design issues may be settled by the style guide for the graphical user interface or by the software that displays the icon on the screen. In these cases, you need to understand the restrictions these factors place on your design and how to take advantage of the uniformity they promote.

Standard parts of the icon

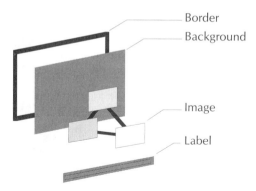

Border

Background

Image

Label

<hr />

BORDERS

Borders limit and define. The border of an icon, or any graphic, limits the extent of the image. Whether visible or just implied, the border is an active element of the design.

Should you use a border?

Should you put explicit borders around icons? The decision is an important one because the border affects the way we see and use icons:

No border   Border

Borders show extent of the icon

A border provides reassuring closure for the image. The border shows the extent of the visual symbology. The border tells us unmistakably where one icon ends and another begins.

In interactive systems, a border makes clear where to point the cursor or finger to select the icon. Showing the target area is critical when the image of the icon does not fill the selection area and when icons are closely spaced.

Borders increase uniformity

Consistent borders give all the icons a uniform shape and size their individual images may lack. Compare the ragtag appearance of these images …

with the military precision of these uniformly bordered ones:

Borders make icons less distinctive

The uniformity provided by borders robs the icon of a unique outline. Visual perception relies on such distinctive outlines to rapidly identify objects. The penalty is even greater when scanning for a recognizable shape. We must force ourselves to ignore the uniform border and consciously probe for the contents.

Borders can clarify meaning

The shape and style of the border can designate the type of information contained in the graphic. The border can specify the general class or type of information represented. Within that border an image makes the icon more specific.

Borders are not limited to rectangular shapes. By varying the shape of the outline, we can represent characteristics of the object contained by the border. We can even make the border resemble the outline of a familiar object. What would you expect to find inside each of these borders?

Borders compete with the image

As a visual object, the border competes with its contents for attention. A visible border alters the balance of prominence among objects within the image and serves to impose its own organization them.

Borders require smaller images

For the image to fit legibly within a border, you must draw it smaller than when it can use the full space of the icon. Because the subject cannot extend all the way to the border, borders waste space. For example, a 32 x 32-pixel icon gives us a drawing space of 1024 pixels. If we allow a 1-pixel border with a margin of 2 pixels between the image and the border, our drawing space is reduced to 26 x 26 pixels. This gives us an area of only 676 pixels—a reduction of 34 percent in image area.

Drawing the border

Make the border a meaningful part of the icon by using it to reinforce and clarify the message of the image it contains.

Pick the shape

One strategy is to use the outline of a familiar object as the border. This border suggests the general category of the concept represented by the icon. The image within the border then indicates the specific instance of the concept represented by the icon:

Book   Telephone   Phone book

Here are some examples of objects used as borders and what each might signify:

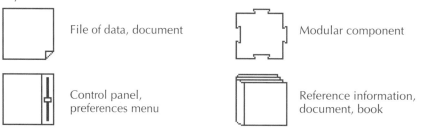

File of data, document

Modular component

Control panel, preferences menu

Reference information, document, book

Portable items or resources

Collection of items selected by the user

Command, button

Home. For use in the home

Industry. For use in business settings

Directory or collection

Caution

Component of reference information

Template or stationery pad

Photograph

Slide

Document, book

Telephone, communication over telephone lines

Movie, film, animation

Screen, display

Window

Printout, report

Direction, movement, activity

Stop, stopping point

Words, speech, quotation

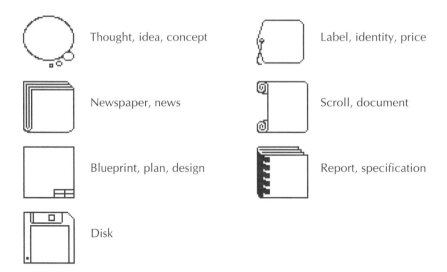

Thought, idea, concept	Label, identity, price
Newspaper, news	Scroll, document
Blueprint, plan, design	Report, specification
Disk	

To use an object as a border, you should select an object recognizable by its outline or edge details. Objects recognized from their interior details cannot serve as borders.

We must also draw the object in a special way. Our goal is not to render it realistically but to make it recognizable with its details squeezed into a zone a few pixels thick. For example, compare these icons with the borders derived from them:

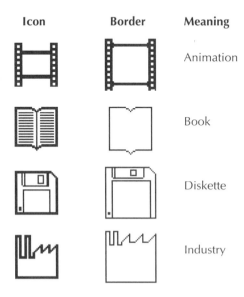

Icon	Border	Meaning
		Animation
		Book
		Diskette
		Industry

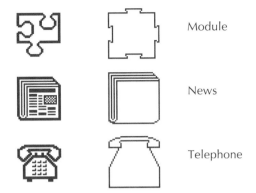

Module

News

Telephone

Vary shape to modify meaning

You can also alter the meaning of an icon by making slight changes to the shape of the border. Any deviation from a standard rectangular shape can represent a secondary concept. You can cut one of the corners:

You can also cut a pronounced notch in the rectangular shape:

These corner details offer a clever way to amend the primary meaning of the image. Unfortunately, such notches have no established or standardized meanings. Don't use them unless you plan to teach users their meanings. Also, don't use them for any critical message.

Vary border style to reinforce meaning

Borders can be drawn in several different styles. Some merely mark the extent of the icon but others can represent attributes of the icon or give it a three-dimensional appearance.

Implied

Many icons lack a full border enclosing the entire image. They may, however, imply the extent of the icon by how they cut off an obviously continuous image:

Plain

A plain border is a simple rectangular shape surrounding the image. It provides an unadorned frame for the image:

Incised and embossed

We can give the border a three-dimensional appearance by drawing it as if incised into the background surface or as if embossed on top of it:

Incised   Embossed

The effect is achieved by simulating the highlights and shadows that an overhead light would produce. For an incised border, pixels on the top and left sides of lines are drawn darker than those on the bottom and right. For embossed borders, we just reverse these conventions.

Raised and sunken

We can also make the entire area of the icon appear raised above the surrounding surface or sunken into it:

Raised   Sunken

The effect results from simulating a light source above and usually to the left of the surface. Thus the top and left edges of raised icons are lighter than the right and bottom edges. The opposite is true of the sunken icons.

In some user interfaces, such as Hewlett-Packard's NewWave, the raised icons represent sources of data or activity and the sunken ones represent destinations for generated data.

This effect is most commonly used to simulate the appearance of push buttons. Often the edge-shading effect is augmented by darkening the surface of the icon when it is pushed in. To further indicate that this is the ON state, the image is often reversed or drawn in a bright color, as if it were lighting up:

Button up   Button down

Vary characteristics to show status

The thickness of the border influences the attention we give to the border and how it relates to the image within, as well as how it relates to the borders of other icons. The thicker the border, the more attention we will give it:

none   1 pixel   2 pixels   3 pixels

To show changes in status of an individual icon, you can vary the width, color, value, pattern, texture, or other visual characteristics of the border. Making the border thicker and darker draws more attention to the icon, for instance, to single it out as the one currently active.

For example:

Available   Active   Not available

Unless the border is a simple rectangle, it may prove difficult to make the border thicker without altering its shape. Curving borders usually require thin lines.

Controlling interaction between image and border

If the image extends to the border, it is perceived as continuing beyond the border. Notice how by extending the image to the border we imply a larger object than we can show:

Search   Highlight   Paint   Erase   Write

You can enhance the three-dimensionality of an object by letting it protrude over the border of the icon. If the image naturally extends outside the border, you can let it eat into the thickness of the border:

You can also draw the border so that it lets a significant part of the image stick out:

BACKGROUND

It is easy to think of the background as just the empty space left over after the image is drawn. Many designers do not even think about the background. They pass up the opportunity to use the background to represent concepts, to control emphasis, and to separate and organize the parts of the image:

No background   Background   Background
or border   but not border   and border

Putting a border around the image, implicitly defines a background for the image. Even if the background is the same as the surrounding space, it seems a separate background for the objects of the icon.

Emphasize the image

The prominence and legibility of an icon depend on contrast between the foreground image and the background surface. Unless the image differs strongly from the background, the background swallows up the image:

✗ No   **✔ Yes**

Background   **Subject**
overwhelms image   **stands out**

The more similar the image and background, the harder we must strain to see the image:

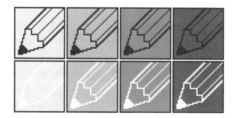

The background of any graphic image sets the basis for all comparisons. A gray icon on a darker background will appear light. The same icon on a lighter background will appear dark.

The primary rule in designing the background is this: **Ensure sufficient light-dark contrast between the image and the background**. Books universally print small text in black ink on white paper. Although bleached paper and opaque inks cost more, we use them because high contrast is necessary to make small type legible.

Other than maintaining high light-dark contrast, there are no absolute rules for how to render the background to make the object stand out. Some general suggestions to consider are:

- **Don't cover more than half the available area with objects**.

- **Draw the background as a smooth continuous surface.** Draw the image as a discrete object. Avoid patterns in the background.

- **Render the background as if farther away**. Put the image clearly in front of the background.

- **Let the background surround the image**. Place objects in the center and the background around the periphery.

- **Use unsaturated, cool colors for the background and saturated, warm colors for the foreground image.**

- **Keep the background static.** If anything blinks or moves, the viewer perceives it as foreground image.

- **Make the image a simple rendition of a recognizable, concrete object**.

Sometimes one object in the image serves as background for another object. If this happens, make sure the nearer object does not obscure the farther object and that they contrast sufficiently:

An irregularly shaped background can give an icon a distinctive shape. Used to highlight an important icon, this is effective. Overused, it gives icons a tawdry uneven appearance.

Express a message

A distinctive color or pattern in the background can help us identify an icon. This technique works best when the background pattern reminds us of a simple, flat object. For example, we can make the background resemble a distinctive type of paper. What would you expect to find on each of these backgrounds?

Group and classify

Viewers can easily categorize icons by the colors or patterns of their backgrounds:

We can unite the separate icons of a family of products by giving them a distinctive background. For example, imagine a set of programs for designing and maintaining brick structures:

BrickPlan　　　BrickMeasure　　　BrickPlumb

Show status

We can vary the background to show the status or condition of an icon. Lowering the contrast between the object and its background can indicate that the icon is not available. Making one background different from the others can indicate which icon is currently active:

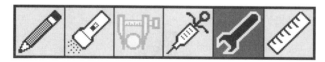

One innovative way to use the background is to progressively fill it to indicate progress toward some goal:

0% done   25% done   50% done   75% done   100% done

LABELS

Should you label your icons? Emphatically, yes. If the symbol is not obvious or known to all your readers, you must label it, at least the first time the reader encounters it. Few symbols are so unambiguous that first-time readers do not benefit from word labels. Almost all research comparing the use of visual symbols and word labels has found that the combination of the two works better than either alone.

In some icons the label tells the type of concept represented by the image. Such a label is redundant. In others, it is designed to clarify the image, especially for the novice. In many others, it merely specifies the particular item of a type represented by the image. For example, the image represents the type of data and the label the name of the file containing that data.

Typography

Our first concern must be the legibility of the label. Making labels legible is not difficult if we follow a few simple guidelines:

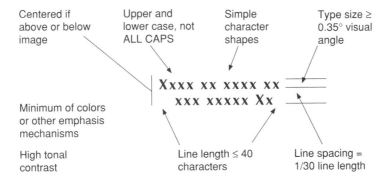

- **Display the label in high contrast to its background**. Take special care with color-on-color display. Human visual perception depends on differences of light and dark to read best. A difference in hue, between green and blue for instance, is seldom sufficient.

- **Display the text in a simple text font and style.** Use a simple sans serif typeface, such as Helvetica. Avoid using boldface, italics, underlining, or differences of color to emphasize individual words.

- **Center the text over or under the image.** If the label appears beside the image, align the text against the edge of the image:

WriteText

WriteText Program
Version 3.2

WriteText
Program
Version 3.2

- **Make the type at least 0.35 degrees visual angle.** The actual size of the type will vary with the viewing distance. At a distance of 60 cm (24 in.) the minimum type size would be 10 points. For screens read at a greater distance, you must increase the size proportionately.

- **Use no more than 40 characters of text per line.** Lines longer than this will be hard to fit onto a crowded screen and will severely overlap the labels of other icons.

- **Make the space between lines at least 1/30 the line length.** Doing so provides a distinct downward angle for the eye as it searches for the beginning of the following line. If lines are too close together, the eye may skip the next line or reread the current one.

- **Use uppercase and lowercase letters** Capitalize labels as if a sentence or a title. Do not use all capital or all lower-case letters:

✗	All caps	ALL LETTERS ARE CAPITALIZED
✗	No caps	only proper nouns capitalized
✔	Sentence	Capitalized as if a sentence
✔	Title	Capitalized as Though a Title

Writing style

Write all labels in a simple, consistent style. Be careful that differences in phrasing, spelling, abbreviation, and punctuation do not miscue the user:

✗ No	✔ Yes
Inconsistent labels	**Consistent labels**
Rename file	Rename file
Object delete	Delete object
Draw a map	Draw map
Item: duplication	Copy item
New directory	Create directory
Create file!	Create file

Phrase all the labels for a particular kind of icon the same. Here are some examples of standardized labels:

Kind of icon	Form of label	Example
Object	Noun phrase	Facsimile machine
Command	Action [Object]	Show animation
Program	Company, Product, Version	VividVision Vizionary 2.0
Auxiliary data file	Product, Type	Vizionary preferences

Among a related set of labels, use each word for only one meaning and use only one word for each meaning. Use each word for only one part of speech.

If space is tight, you may be tempted to omit small, secondary words. Don't do this unless you have no alternative. Omitting words can reduce the labels to a choppy telegraphic style that can be ambiguous and make them harder to interpret. If you must trim words, start by eliminating articles (a, an, the), conjunctions (and, or), and prepositions (on, at, of, in). Then consider abbreviating longer words. Test your reduced label to ensure it is still clear, even to users with less than perfect language skills.

Also standardize punctuation. A few suggestions are:

- **Omit ending periods**.
- **Include question marks** if the label is phrased as a question.
- **Avoid exclamation points**. The exclamation point adds little emphasis to a tiny icon label.
- **Avoid colons (:) and semicolons (;)**. Few people know the difference anymore. Even if they do, few users can see a difference at normal screen resolution.

Timing

Concise labels and clear images are a powerful combination. Each helps to explain the other. The label is especially helpful in first learning the meaning of a new icon. However, permanently displaying a complete label for every icon on the screen may create problems. The labels take up considerable space, especially for complex systems with dozens or hundreds of icons. Unless labels are short, they will tend to overlap one another.

For these reasons, we may choose to display labels only under certain circumstances. By not always displaying all labels we save space but can create some problems. Without all labels displayed, the user cannot scan for an icon by name. So, before you eliminate labels, make sure users seldom need to scan by name.

When the user decides

One simple technique is to let users decide whether to display the labels for icons. Typically this is done by a setting in a configuration file or by selecting an option in a preferences menu. Here's an example from Helix Express:[1]

Labels on **Labels off**

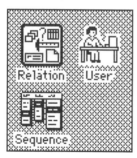 

Users typically will leave icon labels displayed while first learning the system. After they have learned the meanings of most icons, they tend to turn off the labels.

---

[1]Screen shots are reprinted with permission from Helix Technologies, Inc.

Only when the cursor points at the icon

Another approach is to display the label only when the user points to the icon. The label can appear next to the icon, in a pop-up window, or in a separate message area. These alternatives are discussed later.

When the user points to the icon, its label appears. This response confirms the identity of the icon, and it confirms the user's aim. However, the continual flickering of labels as the cursor moves about the screen can distract and annoy. This "flicker fest" is especially painful when labels are long or when they appear in a pop-up window.

To avoid the problem of flickering labels, you can have the system display the label only when the user holds down a special function key while pointing to the icon. This is less convenient than automatic display of labels, and it requires learning the technique.

If you cannot display a label

If you cannot display a label, make doubly sure that users can correctly interpret the icon:

- **Use icons redundantly.** Use icons as shortcuts for commands available through well-labeled pull-down and pop-up menus.

- **Use only a few icons**. Do not require users to memorize the meanings of hundreds of similar images. Generally users can learn a dozen images with no difficulty.

- **Teach and explain the meaning of icons**. Define icons in documentation and training materials, in training courses, and over customer-support hotlines.

- **Make the icons as obvious as possible**. Test and redesign until most users can guess the meanings of the icons.

- **Make icons fail-safe.** If the user mistakes the identity of an icon, it should not lead to disaster. Confirm all irreversible actions before carrying them out.

Location

For labels to identify, the user must notice the label and associate it with the icon. For users to make that association we must place the label near the icon.

Caption position

The most common position for icon labels is centered beneath the image. Macintosh, Windows, and OS/2 icons all display labels this way:

Zippy Draw

This position imitates the caption placed below many graphics. Most of us scan a scene from top to bottom, so we would notice the image before its label. This works well where the image is primary and the label provides reinforcement.

Title position

Some icons appear with the label above the image. This places the label in the position of a title. This is the position used in the icons for Computervision's CADD system:

Zippy Draw

Putting the label atop the image gives it more prominence. Use the title position when users know and search for concepts primarily by name and where the visual image is secondary in importance.

Annotation position

An icon has at least four sides, and left and right are two of them. Why not put the label beside the image, either to the right or to the left?

When you are stacking icons in a single vertical column, the only position for labels is beside the image. However, placing labels beside the image precludes arranging icons in a horizontal row.

You often see labels beside icons when small icons are included in a pop-up or pull-down menu. Here, though, the word labels are primary and the icons secondary:

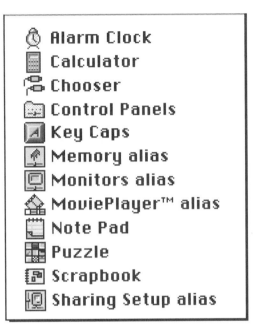

As image component

The label can also be incorporated into the area of the graphic, either fitting itself into the background area around the image or overlapping the image slightly:

Merging the label and graphic tightly couples the label. It ensures that the user can take in both image and label in a single glance. Putting labels into the image area can save space on an otherwise crowded screen. However, merging requires very concise labels. Because the text becomes part of the graphic, it is harder to change—the designer must redraw it rather than retype it. Such tightly fitting labels are difficult to translate, as the translated text may require more space. Incorporating the label into the graphic can obscure the graphic while making the text harder to read.

Elsewhere on the screen

If the labels appear only when the user points to the icon, we need to display only one label at a time. That label can appear in a separate area on the screen. Typically this area is a permanently displayed message field at the top or bottom of the screen:

This approach is useful because:

*   It avoids the clutter of permanently displayed labels.

*   It makes learning the identity of an icon simple.

*   It allows infrequent users to confirm the identity of an icon.

This approach can become tedious, however, when first confronting a screen of new icons. The user points at an icon, searches for the name, points at another icon, looks at the message field, points, looks, points, looks, points, and looks. Another problem is that the field continually changes as the cursor moves across a bank of icons. Even though the flickering is off in another corner of the screen, it still annoys and distracts. We are actually more sensitive to flickering when it occurs in peripheral vision.

SIZE AND SHAPE OF THE ICON

The size and shape of an icon determine how easy it is to notice, understand, and select. Size and shape may be determined by design standards, by restrictions inherent in the computer system, or by the designer's judgment. Let's look at some of the considerations we face as designers.

The size

An icon should be large enough to do the job but no larger. All icons of a related set should be the same size, but deciding that size may require considering several conflicting requirements.

Follow standards

In many cases, the required size of icons is spelled out either by standards or by the software that displays and activates icons. Before beginning any design project, determine what requirements are imposed by safety standards, user-interface style guides, and GUI software.

Safety standards

You may face governmental or corporate standards for the size of all critical signs and accompanying text. These standards are usually aimed at ensuring legibility for persons with limited visual acuity, and selectability for those with limited motor control.

User-interface style guides

Most graphical user-interface (GUI) systems offer precise guidelines to ensure that application developers deliver consistent applications. These guidelines are found in the official or unofficial style guide for that GUI. These are listed at the end of this chapter.

GUI software

Graphical user-interface systems typically include software to display icons representing files, directories, cursors, and other types of graphical images common to many applications. These routines accept only icons of a very specific format. This format limits the size and shape of the icon. It is typically spelled out in the software-development documentation for the GUI system.

Make icons legible

Make icons large enough that users can readily recognize them. How large is that? The size required to make an icon, or any visual image, legible depends on the user s eyesight, the viewing distance and conditions, and the resolution and contrast of the display.

User's eyesight

Visual acuity varies considerably from person to person. It also varies as we age. It is at its maximum when we are about 22 years old. From there it tends to decline.

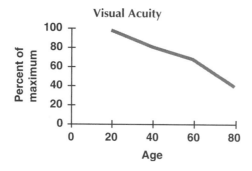

Keep in mind that corrective lenses do not fully compensate for a loss of visual acuity. Your glasses may give you 20-20 vision but leave your visual acuity substantially below what it was when you were in your 20s.

If a significant number of your users have less than perfect visual acuity, increase the size of your iconic images.

Viewing distance

The effective viewing size of an icon depends on the viewing distance. An icon that is twice as close will appear twice as large. An icon that works on a laptop computer used on the serving tray aboard an airplane may fail when displayed on a desktop computer read by a user who is leaning back with the keyboard in his lap and feet propped on the desk.

Typical viewing distances

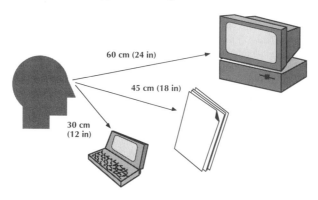

Consider how your users will view the icons and size them accordingly. Establish a legible size at one distance and then scale that size to different distances. If a 10 x 10-mm icon proves legible on a laptop viewed at 30 cm, then for the 60-cm reading distance of a desktop computer, you must make it twice as large, or 20 x 20 mm.

Display quality

Small icons test the quality of display monitors. Unless the image is clear on the screen, it will not be clear in the eye of the user. Consider carefully these characteristics of display monitors:

- **Resolution**. The density of pixels on the screen results in two opposing effects. A higher resolution tends to sharpen the image; but, it also makes it smaller.

- **Contrast**. Light-dark contrast is critical in reading text and in recognizing small visual images. A printed image is more legible than a displayed one because it has higher contrast. Monitors vary considerably in the maximum light-dark contrast they can display. The lower the contrast, the larger the image must be to be legible.

- **Focus**. Color monitors drift out of focus if their three electron guns stray from perfect alignment. The resulting fuzzy image is harder to recognize. Hence, you may have to enlarge images for display on older, poorly maintained monitors.

- **Glare**. Light reflecting off the screen increases eyestrain and severely reduces legibility. Unfortunately, most offices are designed to make reading from horizontal sheets of paper easy but reading from vertical screens hard.

You should match the size of your image to the actual quality of monitors in the field, not the ideal monitor.

Viewing conditions

Legibility depends on viewing conditions. These include environmental factors such as visual and audible noise, smoke, dust, and wind. They also include physiological and psychological factors such as fatigue, eye strain, workload, and anxiety.

Before designing icons, spend a day or two observing users at work. Do they work leisurely in comfortable offices with ergonomically designed workstations? Or, is the work hectic, the pace frantic, and the setting something out of Dante's *Inferno*? We take a risk when designing for ideal settings.

Size for easy selection

Icons that activate functions must be easy to point to and to select. Despite years of research we have no simple formula for calculating the ideal size of a selection target. The correct size depends on many factors, including the device steering the cursor, the manual dexterity of the user, and the required level of performance. Here, though, are some typical sizes:

Pointing device	Size		Pixels
Mouse, trackball	7 mm	(0.25 in.)	20 pixels
Finger	13 mm	(0.5 in.)	40 pixels
Stylus, pen	4 mm	(0.13 in.)	15 pixels

Use these values as a starting point. Increase or decrease them to fit your users and your system. Consider the following factors:

Gain

The ratio of the movement of the cursor on the screen to the movement of the hand is called gain. A mouse or trackball with high gain requires less movement to send the cursor scampering across the screen, but makes it harder to point the cursor precisely. High gain thus requires a larger target. Some GUI s allow the user to control gain, some don t. This adjustability will affect how you draw your icons.

Motor control

Some users lack the ability to point precisely. Precise pointing is affected by fatigue, stress, anxiety, old age, and certain medical conditions such as stroke and palsy. This means we must enlarge icons for use by those with limited motor control and icons used in emergencies and other trying circumstances.

Speed of selection

The smaller the target, the longer it takes to point to it. If users must select icons quickly, then increase the size by 50 to 100 percent. Likewise where high accuracy is important, increase the target size. If selecting the wrong icon has disastrous consequences, make icons *large*. Testing will tell you how large.

Fit available space

Sometimes you may have little choice for the size of icons. Often you have a certain number of functions you must represent and only a certain amount of space in which to do it. Simple division tells you how much space you have for each icon; but, it does not tell you how to make them clear. If you must fit multiple icons into a small space:

- Provide alternative ways of performing the same functions activated by the icons.

- Keep the images as simple and regular as possible.

- Teach the meaning of the icons. Define them in documentation, both printed and online. Explain them in tutorials and training courses.

What shape should an icon be?

Most icons have a square shape. This stable, stalwart shape accommodates a range of images and offers great flexibility in arrangement. But a square is not the only possibility. Just about any rectangular shape with a height:width ratio of 0.5 to 2 can be used. One popular shape is that of the golden rectangle, which has a width:height ratio of 1.618 or 0.618.

Type	Portrait		Square	Landscape	
Shape		(Golden rectangle)		(Golden rectangle)	
Height:width ratio	2	1.618	1	0.618	0.5

Of the nonsquare shapes, landscape (horizontal), rectangles are easier to work with than portrait (vertical), rectangles. Landscape rectangles are not only better because they more closely match the shape of the human field of vision, but also because labels fit better.

Typical sizes and shapes

These icons from Apple's System 7 illustrate some typical sizes for icons in a graphical user interface:[2]

Type icon	Example	Typical size (pixels)
File (large)		32 x 32
File (small)		16 x 16
Cursor		16 x 16
Window-bar control		11 x 11
Tool in drawing program		24 x 16

Test

Because the proper size and shape of an icon depend on so many factors, you must always test to ensure that your choices are correct. Make the test realistic and meaningful. Measure the speed and accuracy with which users can identify and select icons. Chapter 12 includes instructions on testing icons. We suggest two levels of testing: typical and worst-case scenarios.

Typical case

To test the typical situation, pick icons of moderate complexity and familiarity to the user. Test these under normal operating conditions with test subjects who resemble typical users. Test subjects should correctly identify and select icons without hesitation 85 to 95 percent of the time.

Worst case

For worst-case testing, increase the difficulty of the task. Test your most complex icons with your least capable users. Test with novices. Test with users who have poor eyesight and lack a steady hand. Simulate a noisy, hectic work envi-

---

[2]Screen shots are reprinted with permission from Apple Computer, Inc.

ronment. Acceptable levels of performance will depend on the importance of the task being performed and on the difficulty of correcting errors. In any case, performance should not fall below 50 percent success.

SIZES AND CLEARANCES

For a consistent, predictable display, we must control the exact location, alignment, and spacing of all elements of the icon:

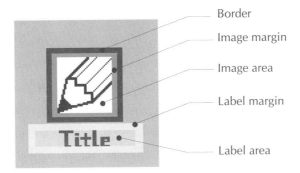

Typically these dimensions are set by the operating system software or by the graphical user-interface style guide. Here are the default settings (in pixels) for the versions of three popular operating systems in use in my office.

Part of the icon		Operating system		
		Macintosh System 7.1 Finder	**OS/2 2.0 Presentation Manager**	**Windows 3.1 Program Manager**
Image	Height	32	32	32
	Width	32	32	32
	Margin	1	3	1
Border	Width	none	1	none
Label	Height	9	11	13
	Width	248	?	438
	Margin	2	2	3

Keep in mind that these numbers are defaults and some of them depend on the display monitor (EGA vs. VGA and so forth).

FOR MORE INFORMATION

Apple Computer. *Macintosh Human Interface Guidelines.* Reading, MA: Addison-Wesley, 1992.

Human Factors Society. *American National Standard for Human Factors Engineering of Visual Display Terminal Workstations* (ANSI/HFS 100-1988). Santa Monica, CA: Human Factors Society, 1988.

IBM. *Common User Access Advanced Interface Design Reference.* Cary, NC: IBM Corporation, 1991.

IBM. *Common User Access Guide to User Interface Design.* Cary, NC: IBM Corporation, 1991.

Marcus, Aaron. *Graphic Design for Electronic Documents and User Interfaces.* New York: ACM Press, 1992.

Mayhew, Deborah. *Principles and Guidelines in Software User Interface Design.* Englewood Cliffs, NJ: Prentice Hall, 1992.

Microsoft. *The Windows Interface: An Application Design Guide.* Redmond, WA: Microsoft Press, 1992.

Open Software Foundation. *OSF/Motif Style Guide.* Englewood Cliffs, NJ: Prentice-Hall, 1990.

Rubenstein, Richard. *Digital Typography: An Introduction to Type and Composition for Computer System Design.* Reading, MA: Addison-Wesley, 1988.

Sun Microsystems, Inc. *OPEN LOOK Graphical User Interface Application Style Guidelines.* Reading, MA: Addison-Wesley, 1990.

ICONS FOR SPECIFIC PURPOSES

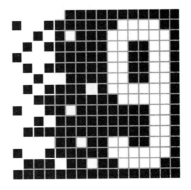

Icons can be used for many different purposes in computer systems. Each purpose imposes its own requirements and constraints on the design. This chapter provides guidelines and suggestions for designing icons used for identifying programs and data files, for activating commands, for controlling fields and windows, for switching between alternatives, as indicators of status or activity, for showing progress or numerical value, as cursors, for controlling movement of the display, and for representing mouse and keyboard actions.

PROGRAM IDENTIFIER

Most graphical user interfaces (GUI's) use icons to represent application programs. These icons let the user start the application, typically by selecting it and then an "Open" command from a pull-down menu or by double-tapping a mouse button while pointing to the icon. They also let the user change where the application program file is stored, usually by dragging the icon and dropping it into another file folder icon. They can also represent the program when it is *minimized*, that is, running but occupying no screen space other than the icon.

To fully identify the program, your icon needs to make clear the name and role of the program and its relationships with other components of the system. It may not be possible to include all the needed information within the icon, but at least consider how you will make clear these pieces of information:

Program, not data On many systems, the user must differentiate between programs and data used or created by the programs. Most GUI style guides provide conventions for making this distinction. You can reinforce these conventions by emphasizing action or activity in the icon for programs.

Name Users search for programs by name, so the name should be prominent. Usually the best place for the name is in the label for the image. If icons are displayed without labels, the name should be designed into the image.

Vendor Although less important than the name of the program, the name of the company producing the program may also appear in the icon. It commonly appears with the name in the label. It can also be indicated by including trademark objects, colors, or patterns. All the products by a vendor should have a noticeable consistency, especially when they are marketed as a suite or family for use together.

Function performed The image of the icon should communicate the general function performed. Icons for programs should show what operation is performed on what type of data. The function is general, not specific. General functions are actions like create, convert, modify, and distribute.

Version   If the version of the program is important to the user, the icon should include the number. This occurs if data created with a later version of the program cannot be read with an earlier version or if the user keeps multiple versions of the program on the same computer. The version number can appear in the image or as part of the label.

Related data files   The users should be able to recognize the icons for data created by or used by the program. This requires similarity between icons for programs and those for their data. Usually this is best achieved by repeating a prominent object, color, or pattern in all the icons related to a particular program.

Let's look at an example. Imagine that we work for a company called VividVision which produces a program called Vizionary. This program is used to create animations and other multimedia productions. We need an icon for Version 2.0 of the program running on the Macintosh. Our first draft might look something like this:

Vizionary

It combines several elements to fully identify the application program:

   The VividVision corporate logo identifies the vendor of this product.

   The segment of movie film indicates that this tool produces audio-visual works, rather than paper documents. The 45-degree cant is part of the Macintosh convention for distinguishing application programs from data files.

   The writing hand is also part of the Macintosh convention for application programs.

2.0   Because Version 2.0 differs significantly from earlier versions, the icon includes the version number.

Vizionary   The label contains the name of the program.

Program identifiers may also serve as a trademark for the product. If so, the image of the icon may appear on the box containing the product, in catalogs, or on trade-show banners. We must then design an image that is legible, prominent, and attractive in a wide range of sizes and styles.

CASE STUDY: PAGEMAKER PROGRAM AND DATA ICONS

The images in the icons for Version 4.0 of PageMaker for the Macintosh use visual elements to identify the function of the program and to link data and program files:[1]

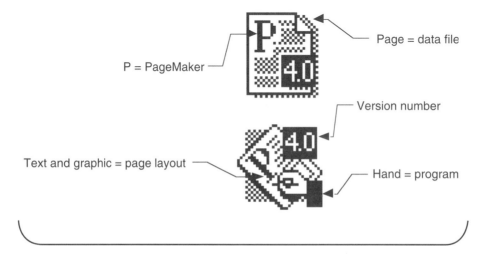

DATA FILE

Icons for data files identify the data created by users as well as reference data used by application programs. Users can select and then open their own data files. They can also move data icons about the screen to control where the corresponding files are stored, to make copies of them, and to print them.

The icon for a data file should clearly identify the file, tell what kind of data it contains, and distinguish it from related files. The icon should make clear:

---

[1] Screen shots are reprinted with permission from Aldus Corporation.

Data, not program
This is a data file, not an application file. The icon indicates this by following conventions of the particular GUI in which the icon appears. Avoid images that imply action. Instead show a picture or symbol of the kind of data contained in the file.

Name
The label of the icon typically displays the name of the data file. This is where users distinguish among their data files. For reference files provided by the vendor, the name can supply additional information, such as the title of the related application, and the type of data contained in the file title.

Vendor
Every icon is a miniature billboard. We can use it to remind users of the vendor of the product.

Program that created data
The user should readily recognize the icon for the program for the data file. The data file should share visual objects and properties with the icon for the primary program that creates or uses this data.

Access to data
The icon should make clear what the user can do with the file. Is the icon a template that the user can only copy? Is it a published version that the user can embed in another file but cannot modify? Can the user even open and examine the contents of the file? These restrictions can be communicated by giving the image an appropriate border or annotations.

General type of data
What kind of data does the file contain? Is it unformatted text, formatted text, a bitmap, vector art, sound, music, or a mixture of types? The image of the icon should communicate at least the general type of data contained in the file.

Specific file format
If the general type of data can be stored in different specific formats, the icon should indicate the exact format. Such formats are usually represented by including their name or initials in the image or the label.

Version
If the file requires a specific version of the associated program, the number of this version should appear in the image or label of the icon.

Let's look at an example of a typical data identifier. Here we want to identify animation files in the PICS format created by Version 2.0 of VividVision's Vizionary. Our first draft looks like this:

Maria's show

It combines these elements:

 The segment of movie film indicates that this is an audio-visual work, rather than a paper document.

Maria's show   The label names the file.

 The VividVision corporate logo identifies the vendor of this product.

PICS   The letters *PICS* identify the specific data format of the file.

2.0   Because Version 2.0 files cannot be opened with earlier versions, we include the version number.

COMMAND SELECTOR

In most systems, users control the program by issuing a series of commands. They issue these commands by typing them on a line or in a field on the screen, by selecting from a textual menu listing commands, or by selecting an icon. How do we design the icons to represent such commands?

Every command consists of an *action* upon an *object*. The action specifies what should be done, and the object specifies the receiver of the action. One of these two may be implied. Often the default for an object is the currently selected object. Sometimes the command has a third part, called a *qualifier*, that specifies how the action is carried out.

Let's see how some common commands can be divided into these three parts:

Command	Action	Object	Qualifier
Save	Save	(The currently active file)	
Save as	Save	(The currently active file)	As (a new file)
Copy	Copy	(The currently selected object)	
New folder	(Create)	New folder	
Open file	Open	File	
Open file in new window	Open	File	In new window

Our icons for commands must represent the action, the object, and sometimes the qualifier. What is the best way to do this? Show concrete actions on concrete objects directly. For commands with abstract actions or ones with no visible results, show a clear operation on a concrete object:

Save in file   Press mouse   Break link   Cut
                button

For commands that require manipulating controls, use abstract symbols to represent a typical action sequence.

WINDOW AND FIELD CONTROLS

On many systems, users control windows through small icons at the edge of the window. Look at this example of Canvas 3.0 window:[2]

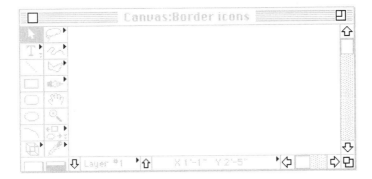

Such small icons are sometimes called *glyphs*. To fit in the border or title bar of a window, they must be small. Because they lack space for a label, each must communicate its function clearly. Each must provide a distinct target or handle for the user to interact with.

---

[2]Screen shot is reprinted with permission from Deneba Systems, Inc.

Where possible, use the standard icons defined for a particular style of GUI. If you invent new ones, make them consistent in style and operation with the standard ones.

CASE STUDY: CONTROLS IN COMMON GUIs

Function	Graphical user interface		
	Windows[3]	OS/2[4]	Macintosh[5]
Close window	(Done by command)		☐
Display menu of window-related commands	⊏⊐	⌄	
Expand or collapse window	▼ ▲	⸬ ☐	⊟
Stretch window	(Done by dragging edges)		⧉
Scroll up and down	⬆ ⬇	⌃ ⌄	⇧ ⇩
Pop up or drop down menu	⬇	⯆	▼
Show next level of pull-down menu	▶	➔	▶
Show mutually exclusive choice (radio button)	○ ◉	⬣ ⬤	○ ◉
Show one-of-many choice (ballot box)	☐ ⊠	☐ ☑	☐ ⊠

---

[3]Screen shots are reprinted with permission from Microsoft Corporation

[4]Screen shots are reprinted with permission from International Business Machines, Inc.

[5]Screen shots are reprinted with permission from Apple Computer, Inc.

MODE SIGNAL OR TOGGLE SWITCH

Mode output indicators show the current state of a system. Toggle switches let users alternate between two states. Both require an image for each alternative state:

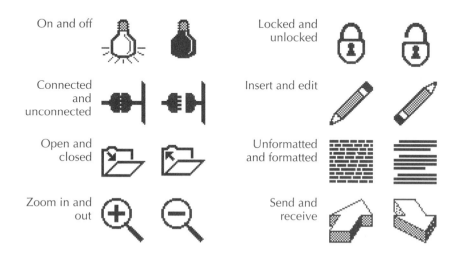

To design mode outputs and toggle switches, you must confront one really tough question: Do you show the image for the current state or for the target state? My rule of thumb is to show the current state if the icon is merely an indicator. If it is a switch, show the target state. If both, style it so it looks like a switch or button and show the target state.

If the product cannot change the image when the icon is selected, you can still indicate toggle switches by showing both states separated by a diagonal slash. This is analogous to the verbal construct "and/or," indicating that either alternative is possible:

On/Off   Edit/Insert   Unlock/Lock

STATUS INDICATOR

Users need clear feedback. One way we can provide it is to vary the icon to show the status or condition of the system. In this way, we provide feedback on the status of the concept represented by the icon.

Change display to show condition

One way to show the condition or status of the concept represented by an icon is to vary the way we display the icon:

To show that the icon is ...	Vary the design this way	Example
Normal	Plain display	
Active, primary	Thicken border, reverse video, fill background	
Being selected	Blink a few times	
In use	Fill with gray or stripes	
Unavailable	Gray or stipple the image and border	

Follow the conventions spelled out in the style guide for your particular GUI. For example, to show open programs OS/2 systems show striped icons and Macintosh systems gray the icon.

Vary details to show status

By varying objects within an icon or by switching to slightly different versions of the same icon, we can give the user specific feedback. For example, the icon for an electronic mail system can show whether there is mail waiting to be sent or to be read:

	No mail waiting to be sent	**Mail waiting to be sent**
Mail waiting to be read		
No mail waiting to be read		

The upraised flag indicates outgoing mail. The open door announces incoming mail.

Similarly, we can vary the basic icon for a printer to show whether the printer is busy or to alert the user to common problems:

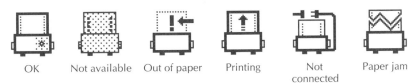

OK	Not available	Out of paper	Printing	Not connected	Paper jam

Vary visual properties to show display characteristics

In drawing programs, the icons for primitive shapes often do double duty. Users can select them in order to draw the shape. Users can also look at the icons to preview the properties of the shape to be drawn. For example, the icon for drawing rectangular shapes can, within limits, show the foreground and background color of the rectangle and its border, the fill pattern of the rectangle, and the line width and style of its border:

ACTIVITY INDICATOR

Activity indicators tell the user that the computer is busy doing something. They reassure the user that the system has not crashed or hung. Some systems indicate activity by changing the cursor to a small watch or hourglass. However, because these are static images, they do not demonstrate that the system is active.

A better approach may be to have an animated icon or cursor that continuously changes its display. To animate an icon, for example, an hourglass, have it cycle among a series of slightly different images. For the appearance of continuous movement, display each separate image between 1/4 and 1/30 of a second.

To indicate generic ongoing activity, many Macintosh applications turn the cursor into a spinning beach ball:[6]

The CompuServe Information Manager produces this spinning globe by cycling among images, each rotated 45 degrees more than the last:[7]

VALUE OR PROGRESS INDICATOR

Icons can represent numerical values. By changing the icon, we can show changes of value or progress toward a goal.

One way is to add objects to the icon to represent an increase in quantity. Notice how the increasing number of sound waves represents the volume in this icon for sound level:

---

[6]Screen shots are reprinted with permission from Apple Computer, Inc.

[7]Screen shots are reprinted with permission from CompuServe, Inc.

Off   1   2   3   4

Or an object can be moved along a scale or across an area. See how this icon for battery level moves a pointer along a scale like the fuel-level indicator in an automobile:

Empty   25%   50%   75%   Full

We can show quantity by progressively filling an area. This area can be a horizontal rectangle:

0%   25%   50%   75%   100%

Or a vertical rectangle:

0%   25%   50%   75%   100%

We can also show quantity by filling a circle like the hands of a clock sweeping over its face:

0%   25%   50%   75%   100%

To show continuous progress toward a goal, as represented by an icon, you can gradually fill in the background of the icon with a distinct color or tone:

0%   25%   50%   75%   100%

However, avoid changing the tone or color over the entire background because few people can accurately judge the relative positions of one of these icons along a scale without seeing all of them together:

| 0% | 25% | 50% | 75% | 100% |

Remember to post the number if precision is important.

CURSOR

The cursor is a small visual image that shows what the next tap of a mouse button will affect. It must make clear to the user what object will receive the mouse actions.

Because the cursor is at the user's center of attention, it is an excellent place to provide useful feedback on the status of the system and what actions the user can perform on the selected object.

Shape for the task

No sane carpenter would use a saw to drive in nails. The shape and design of a workman's tools reflect the task the tool best performs. A hammer does not look like a saw. In graphical user interfaces, most of the work is done by pointing and moving the cursor. The shape and design of the cursor must assist in the task being performed. Using a cursor of the wrong shape is like cutting wood with a hammer.

Let's look at some common shapes for cursors and what they do best:

  For selecting objects

  For selecting tiny objects or specifying points precisely. The cross-hairs help line up with horizontal and vertical edges.

  For selecting in text. The I-bar shape fits between characters. The user positions the horizontal strokes at the top and bottom of the line of text.

The text cursor can be fine tuned for more specific uses:

I̱   The extra horizontal line nestles against the baseline of a line of text.

I̱   The slanted cursor simplifies selecting italic, oblique, or slanted text.

⊢⊣   The horizontal cursor is useful for selecting between lines of text.

I   We can vary the height of the cursor to match the height of the text being pointed at.

Point precisely

If the user must select small objects or specify points precisely, the cursor must have a distinct, unambiguous *hot spot*. The user should know exactly which pixel is the hot spot. We ensure this by giving the cursor an obvious point or center:

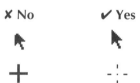

We must also avoid shapes that lack an obvious point or center:

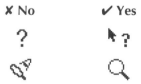

However, if targets are all large enough to fully contain the cursor, just about any shape will do.

Give feedback

In addition to letting the user select and activate objects on the screen, the cursor can provide valuable feedback. Because it is the focus of the user's attention, the user will notice subtle changes in the cursor's image. We can thus vary the image to show the condition of the system or to show what actions the user can take in a given situation.

System state

The image of the cursor can convey messages from the operating system about system-level activities or overall conditions of the system. Such messages are valuable in explaining delays that result when the operating system is performing common activities. Such messages can help the user understand the delay and why clicking the cursor over an object does not activate the object immediately.

Here are some examples of cursors that report system status:

   Processing a request

   Processing halted by system error

   Writing to disk

   Reading from disk

Mode or action to take place

The image of the cursor can reflect what happens if the user taps the primary mouse button or drags with the mouse button down. Some examples:

   Cut or break a line or other object

   Zoom out

   Zoom in

   Item pointed to cannot be selected

We can also annotate the basic selection pointer with small images of what is about to be created or activated:

Tapping makes basic selection.

Dragging diagonally will create a rectangle.

Dragging diagonally will create an oval.

Tapping or dragging will insert text.

Tapping pops up a menu.

Tapping reveals helpful information on the object pointed to.

Case Study: Photoshop tools and cursors

Adobe Photoshop uses a toolbox metaphor. To edit visual images, users select tools from boxes at the side of the drawing window. How does the user keep track of what tool is currently selected? For many of the tools, Photoshop makes this clear by changing the cursor to the tool image. Select a tool and the cursor becomes that tool.

Here we see the tools in the center and the cursors around the edge:[8]

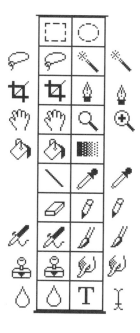

Permitted movement

In many systems objects on the screen can be moved by pointing to them with the cursor, holding down a mouse button, and moving the mouse. This process is called *dragging*. The cursor can change to show what movement is possible if the object pointed to is dragged. This change lets the user select the right object or handle on the object. It also confirms that the cursor is at the right spot.

---

[8]Screen shot is reprinted with permission from Adobe Systems, Inc.

Such feedback is especially helpful when low contrast or glare makes the point of the cursor hard to see.

The cursor can show the direction in which the grabbed object will move:

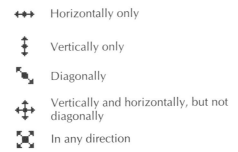

Horizontally only

Vertically only

Diagonally

Vertically and horizontally, but not diagonally

In any direction

The cursor can also hint at what object is being dragged by showing the general shape of the object:

    A small object or point, such as a corner of a rectangle

    A vertical object or line

    A horizontal object or line

    A rectangular object

Button assignments

The effect of tapping and double-tapping various mouse buttons can change as the user moves from program to program and as the cursor moves from object to object on the screen. The image of the cursor can change to show the results of various mouse actions at any moment. To communicate the effect of a mouse action, post small images near the cursor. For example:

The four small images below the pointer symbolize the general function that results from tapping a button:

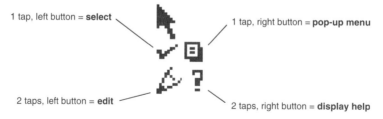

1 tap, left button = **select**

1 tap, right button = **pop-up menu**

2 taps, left button = **edit**

2 taps, right button = **display help**

For this scheme to work, you must develop and teach users a vocabulary of symbols for common actions. These must be small but recognizable, as in this sample starter:

✔	Select, activate, OK, approve
✘	Delete, halt, cancel, reject
🖉	Edit, modify, change
🗐	Pop up a menu of choices
?	Display helpful information
↰	Undo, reverse
🔓	Unlock
🔒	Lock
⇥	Move forward in sequence
⇤	Move backward in sequence
+	Increase, advance
–	Decrease, reduce

If you implement such a scheme, make it optional. Let users turn off display of the extra images. Experienced users who already know what mouse buttons do will resent the clutter.

Data being dragged

In *drag-and-drop* interfaces, the user requests action by dragging from one icon to another. To print a file, for example, the user may drag the icon of the file to the icon of the printer. While the icon is being dragged, the cursor can show the type of information being dragged by changing to resemble the icon. This correspondence between the file icon and cursor reminds the user of the association. Some examples:

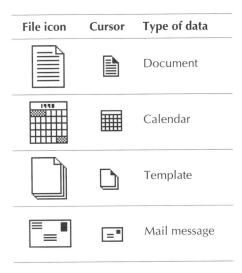

File icon	Cursor	Type of data
		Document
		Calendar
		Template
		Mail message

MOVEMENT CONTROL IN A DISPLAY

When the user's work involves inspecting and reviewing large amounts of data or many complex displays, we must give them control over how the data is displayed. When the data will not all fit in a window or on a screen, we must provide a way for them to bring unseen data into view. This is especially important when the data is complex and each display requires undivided attention.

Movement along a sequence

Often the data is organized in a sequence of items to be examined one at a time, for instance, pages in a document, records in a database, or frames in an animation or video. Fortunately we have a ready-made set of symbols for navigating linear sequences: the well-known controls for audio and video cassette recorders.

For moving through the series of items continuously, we can use the continuous-play controls:

| Fast backward | Backward continuously | Forward continuously | Fast forward |

For stepping through by whole units, we can use stepping controls:

| To start | Backward one unit | Forward one unit | To end |

To stop along the way, we can use the pause, stop, and quit controls:

| Pause | Stop | Stop | Quit |

For repeatedly viewing the sequence, we can use the common controls for looping and cycling:

| Loop once | Loop continuously |

Movement in two dimensions

Some data is naturally two dimensional, for instance, maps, plots, spreadsheets, and other flat displays. For these we must make it easy for the user to examine the whole surface. We could use scroll bars along vertical and horizontal edges, but coordinating movements, especially diagonal ones, requires much mouse movement. We could also just let the user drag the display in the window, but dragging does not lend itself to precise movements. An alternative is to provide a cluster of arrow buttons:

Each moves in the direction shown. The center intersection button centers the data in the window.

Movement in three dimensions

Three-dimensional data is common in mechanical engineering, industrial design, architecture, geology, medicine, and other fields dealing with solid objects. Movement in three dimensions is best indicated by three-dimensional arrows:

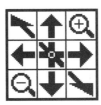

Here the arrows produce movement up, down, left, right, in, and out. The center intersection resets the display to its home position. The magnifying glasses enlarge or shrink the display without moving the viewpoint in or out.

Rotations of three-dimensional objects are especially difficult to visualize and to communicate. They usually require a frame of reference and three-dimensional arrows drawn in that frame of reference:

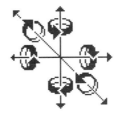

Movement coordination

When using icons to move and rotate data displays, you must consistently resolve several thorny design issues.

Does the data move or does the viewpoint move?

Should selecting the movement icon move the data in the direction shown, or should it move the user's viewpoint relative to the data? The answer is to do what users want and expect the control to do. The up arrow in a scroll bar, for example, moves the viewpoint relative to the data. The display behaves as if it is a TV picture of the data and the arrow controls movement of the camera over these data.

This convention of moving the viewpoint is common for one- and two-dimensional data. It makes a good default choice. For three-dimensional data, however, the case is less clear. I suggest testing with users on simulated systems (pen-and-ink tests are usually OK). Or let the user choose whether the icons move the data or the viewpoint.

How far does the display move?

How much does the display change for each mouse click over the movement icon? Each click of the icon should shift the display or the viewpoint by a predictable amount. The correct amount depends on the type of data displayed and on the expectations of users.

One possibility is to have two rates of movement. One is the default. It is the response to normal selection. The other is for accelerated movement. It is the response to an alternate method of selecting the icon, for example, by double-tapping it or holding down an accelerator key (Shift, Option, or Control) while the icon is selected.

Here are some typical movements:

Type of data and display	Example	Normal selection	Accelerated selection
Discrete units. Each unit completely fills the window.	Frames of animation or video	One complete unit of data	To beginning or end of sequence
Discrete units. The window displays a range of units.	Scrolling lines of text or cells in a spreadsheet	One unit of data	One complete window full of data
Continuous data	Partial view of map or picture	10% of width or height of window	One complete window full of data

Activate from the keyboard

Let users trigger the same movements from the keyboard as with the mouse. Assign keys as synonyms for selecting the icons. Obvious candidates include:

- Arrow keys, especially for horizontal and vertical movements.
- Numeric keypad keys for vertical, horizontal, and diagonal or depth movements.

MOUSE ACTION

Icons usually receive mouse actions. They are sometimes needed to provoke mouse actions. In manuals, computer-based training (CBT), and tutorials we often use small images to teach or suggest mouse actions:

| Press left mouse button | Tap left mouse button | Double-tap left mouse button |

Basic icons are often annotated with special marks showing to which mouse actions these icons respond:

Press   Tap   Tap twice

The following icons incorporate such annotations. Because tapping is the default and all the icons respond to tapping, the symbol for tapping is not shown. The first and third respond to pressing and holding down the mouse button (↳). The second one responds to a double tap (⇧). The fourth responds to both pressing and double-tapping:

BUTTON PRESS

We sometimes show icons on the screen to refer to buttons on the keyboard. These icons serve as reminders or alternatives to pressing the same button on the keyboard.

Keyboard shortcuts for menu actions

Many commands available from pull-down menus can also be triggered by pressing buttons on the keyboard. Often pull-down menus show the keyboard equivalents for menu entries:

```
 File
  New              ⌘N
  Open...          ⌘O

  Close            ⌘W
  Save             ⌘S
  Save As...       ⌘⌥S

  Page Setup...
  Print...         ⌘P

  Quit             ⌘Q
```

We often need icons for keys other than letters, numbers, and punctuation marks. Apple's Macintosh uses these icons to stand for special-function keys:[9]

⌘   The Command key. Labeled ⌘ on keyboards sold by Apple but labeled "Command" or "Cmd" on those sold by some other manufacturers.

⌥   The Option key. It is labeled "option" on Apple keyboards.

⌃   The Control key. It is labeled "ctrl" or "control" on Apple keyboards.

⇧   The Shift key. It is labeled "shift" on Apple keyboards.

---

[9]Screen shots are reprinted with permission from Apple Computer, Inc.

I find that many users have trouble remembering and recognizing the icons for the Option and Control keys.

On-screen synonyms for keyboard actions

In documentation, CBT, and tutorials, we often have to tell the user to press this or that button on the keyboard. Sometimes we want to provide an on-screen synonym for buttons or keys so the user does not have to shift from mouse to keyboard. For these purposes we can use icons to represent keyboard buttons.

A rounded or beveled border is usually all we need to suggest a key or button:

Here are some synonyms for keys. Notice that the border provides a clear target for the cursor:

| Enter | Tab | Shift | Function key 3 |

When icons are instructions to the user to press keys, we must identify the exact order of actions, especially when multiple keys are involved. A simple convention can help. When keys are pressed separately, leave space between them. If one is held down as the other is pressed, butt them together:

Press and release   Hold down Shift
Esc and then press   as you press F3
and release F3

FOR MORE INFORMATION

Galitz, Wilbert O. *Handbook of Screen Format Design.* Wellesley, MA: QED Information Sciences, 1989.

Helander, Martin, ed. *Handbook of Human-Computer Interaction.* Amsterdam: North-Holland, 1988.

Laurel, Brenda, ed. *The Art of Human-Computer Interface Design.* Reading, MA: Addison-Wesley, 1990.

Tognazzini, Bruce. *TOG on Interface.* Reading, MA: Addison-Wesley, 1992.

ICONS FOR INTERNATIONAL PRODUCTS

Icons might seem a panacea for the problems facing international products. After all, are not pictures a universal language? All we have to do is replace text with tiny pictures, right? No. Many pictures and symbols lack any universal meaning. And eliminating text entirely can rob many icons of any clear meaning. True, icons can help products surmount barriers of language and culture, but not without carefully accounting for these differences. This chapter suggests how.

Consider who uses your product. What symbols and objects will they recognize? Do they speak a different language? Are they familiar with the same symbols you are? Is your user an illiterate peasant farmer or an educated scientist or business executive? Has your user traveled extensively? Do they watch movies and television? Foreign users are no less intelligent and worldly than local ones. We must understand them well enough to select symbols they will recognize and understand.

EMPHASIZE ICONS

For more and more companies, the only market that matters is the international market where over 100 languages are used in business. Even products that do not cross borders must overcome barriers of language and culture. No country speaks just one language and possesses a unified culture. India, for example, has 15 official languages that require 11 different scripts. If current trends continue, in about 15 years, less than half of Americans will have English as their first language.

With careful design icons can help bridge these barriers of language and culture. Well-designed icons can:

- **Reduce translation**. The more you communicate visually, the less you must translate. Clearly designed icons reduce the amount of text that must be translated and reduces the odds of incorrect translation.

- **Simplify learning**. A good icon is easier to interpret and remember than a verbal label in an unfamiliar language.

- **Improve intelligibility of text**. The meaning imparted by the icon helps users translate and understand related text. Second-language readers rely on graphics to help them understand text.

- **Give products an international look**. Interfaces with icons greet the user, not with indecipherable text, but with simple, recognizable images like signs at international airports and the Olympic games.

REMOVE OR TRANSLATE TEXT

Icons that rely on text for their meanings must be redesigned or translated for users who speak another language.

Words and abbreviations

Avoid including words and especially abbreviations in the image of your icons. Either design an image free of text or plan to translate to all target languages. These icons would require translation.

Exit program   Halt process   Items to be   End a process   Remedy
                                processed

Translation may not be as simple as it seems. Because the text is incorporated into the image itself, the translator must edit the actual bitmap of the icon. The translated text may not fit.

Abbreviations are especially difficult. The translator may not recognize the abbreviation or the target language may not allow abbreviations.

If you do include text in the icon, style the text to make it familiar to international users. For example, shape the characters for the "Exit" and "Stop" sign exactly as they appear on the real sign. If you show individual letters, show capital letters (A, not a) as these are more familiar to those whose language does not include these letters.

Letters

There are other cases where individual letters appear in icons, not as abbreviations, but as an intrinsic part of the design. These letters, used to represent various text formatting options, would need to be replaced with the initial letter of the appropriate word in the language of the user:

Boldface   Italics   Underline   Outline

Notice how these icons assume the use of the roman ABCs:

DOS   Outline   Dictionary   Check spelling

Punctuation marks

Also take care with punctuation marks used as symbols. Many scripts do not have these marks:

			#	
Important	Help	And	Number	Duplicate

AVOID CULTURE-SPECIFIC SYMBOLS

The meaning of an icon depends on the associations it triggers in the mind of the user. The same image can have vastly different associations in different cultures. We must pick symbols that have the same meaning for all users. Not all symbols do.

The symbols we may use to encode meaning or to decorate a graphic can have vastly different associations in different cultures. We must ensure that the different associations do not contradict our intended meaning.

Puns and verbal analogies

Visual puns show objects whose name sounds like that of the concept you want to represent. Puns are whimsical and fun when used as a puzzle or game; however, avoid puns in icons for international products. Puns require such a subtle knowledge of language that they prove difficult for those who read in their second language. Puns are impossible to translate. Consider these examples:

Icon	Intended meaning	Problems
⚖	Scale of a map	The words for balance scale and the relationship between distances in the world and the map are not the same in all languages.
📦	Post entries in an accounting program	Posting a package means mailing it but posting data means writing it into a ledger. Such different concepts will not have the same name in all languages.

	The "mouse" that controls the pointer on the screen	In some languages the name for the box that controls the screen pointer is not the same as that of a small rodent
	Oncology department of a hospital	Oncology is made of the Greek words for "study of" and "cancer." Cancer is the Latin word for crab. Few know Latin and Greek. Anyway the image looks like a malignant growth.
	Microsoft Excel[1]	The image is made from the superimposed letters X and L. XL is pronounced the same as "Excel." The image loses its cleverness in languages that pronounce the names of letters differently or that lack these letters.

Gestures

There is almost no arrangement of the human hand that is not an obscene, rude, or impolite gesture somewhere in this world. Consider the various meanings of a few gestures common in the USA:

Icon	Intended meaning	Problems
	Yes, OK	In Sicily, this is an invitation to insert the thumb into a private part of the anatomy.
	Precisely, yes	In France, this means zero or worthless. In Japan it is a reference to money. In South America it means that the viewer is a part of the anatomy of this shape.
	Stop, halt	In Greece, this gesture, which goes back to Byzantine times, means, "Here's excrement in your face."

If you must show hands, show them holding, pressing, or moving something.

---

[1] Screen shot is reprinted with permission from Microsoft Corporation.

Mythological and religious symbols

We do not all share the same religious and mythological symbols. Avoid such symbols in international interfaces:

Icon	Intended meaning	Problems
	Fatal error	Would someone raised a Hindu, Buddhist, or Zoroastrian recognize the grim reaper?
	Minor glitch	Some may not recognize this as a gremlin, but see instead a bat with a long tail. A gremlin can be a symbol of a minor problem or a monstrous evil.
	First aid	Images incorporating crosses and six-pointed stars can offend in Arabic countries. In such countries, the local version of the Red Cross is known as the Red Crescent.
	Transform	The magician's wand has its roots in sorcery.

Animals

Tribal societies, sports teams, political parties, and nations commonly adopt animals as emblems. Such totems imply the group possesses the desirable characteristics of the animal: the courage of a tiger, the ferocity of a lion, the swiftness of a hawk, or the power of an elephant. Icon designers likewise use images of animals to represent characteristics traditionally associated with these animals. Unfortunately many such associations are local to a single culture:

Icon	Intended meaning	Problems
	Loyalty Search, retrieve	To Americans, dogs are pets or hunting companions; to many Asians, they are food.
	Wisdom Expert system Training	In southeastern Asia, the owl is considered a particularly brutal and stupid bird.
	Copy, reproduce rapidly	Rabbits are also symbols of sexual promiscuity. In Germany, rabbit is a dinner entrée. In Australia, rabbits are vermin.
	Savings account	To Muslims and many Jews, the pig is considered unclean and unholy.
	Deception	In the orient, the snake is a symbol of life and rebirth.

Remember that many animals have religious significance, for example, cows to Hindus, pigs to Muslims and Jews, lambs and fish to Christians. Animals are often used as negative stereotypes of certain nationalities and professions: kangaroos for Australians, frogs for Frenchmen, and vultures for lawyers. Because these cultural associations are strong, animals seldom work as icons in international products.

Colors

Conventional meanings of colors often vary. In the UK, first place is often awarded a red ribbon, in the US first place earns a blue ribbon. The use of green to symbolize money works in America only because American paper money is colored green. By using color codes for tribal candidates on ballots, the United States Indian Service inadvertently biased the voting among the Navajo for whom colors carry meanings of virtue and evil, blue being good and red bad.

The meanings for color come from a culture's religion, literature, and fine arts. Here are some common associations for colors in different cultures:

Color	Western European	Japanese	Chinese	Arabic
Red	Danger	Anger, danger	Joy, festive occasions	
Yellow	Caution, cowardice	Grace, nobility Childish, gaiety	Honor Royalty	Happiness Prosperity
Green	Safe Sour	Future Youth, energy		Fertility, strength
Blue	Masculinity Sweet Calm Authority	Villainy		Virtue, faith, truth
White	Purity Virtue	Death, mourning	Death, mourning	
Black	Death Evil			

If you use color, follow these guidelines:

- Make the icon work in black and white first. Then use color only to reinforce the primary message.

- Use color only for applications used in business and technical settings where the context does not suggest symbolic or religious interpretations.

- Clearly define your color codes and make the color scheme explicit.

- Test with typical users and revise colors that are misinterpreted.

Body parts

Using parts of the human body as symbols is doubly dangerous. We have no universal standard of modesty, and the symbolic meaning of body parts varies from culture to culture. Some cultures forbid images of the human face or form. Some take offense at certain parts of the body. Some examples make the point:

Icon	Intended meaning	Problems
	Move ahead	The underside of the foot can offend in the Orient. Showing bare feet can also seem crude and unprofessional.
	Inspect, examine	This looks like "the evil eye."
	Welcome	Take care with body language, especially conventional poses. This figure could be waiting to ask a question, hailing a taxi, delivering an insult, or giving a Nazi salute.

Provincialism

Universal concepts do not always lead to universal symbols. The same general idea may appear quite different in different countries. An activity may be performed in a different manner and the appearance of particular objects can vary too. We should avoid symbols that are too limited. Consider these universal concepts represented by provincial symbols:

Mail

Marriage

Family

Currency

Reminder

CONSIDER READING AND SCANNING DIRECTION

The accustomed reading direction of the user influences the interpretation of the sequence of events in a graphic, the relative importance and virtue of objects in a graphic, and the recognition of objects representing text. Western cultures, which write left to right, draw charts and graphs with time flowing from left to right. They write numbers with the most significant digits on the left. In an outline, they subordinate items by indenting them toward the right. The left knob of a faucet controls the hot water and the right controls the cold. In religious art and drama, good is most often on the right and evil to the left.

These conventions are just conventions and not shared by the whole world, especially countries whose languages are traditionally written right to left or in columns top to bottom. In the Middle East, an advertisement for laundry detergent presented dirty clothes on the left, clean clothes on the right, and the box of detergent in between. It confused Arabic readers who read text right to left. How do we avoid causing the same confusion in our icons?

Showing text

Take special care with symbols that show or refer to text in a way that implies a left-to-right reading direction. These symbols for buttons on the keyboard, for example, assume a left-to-right language:

Return   Tab

The assumption of a left-to-right reading direction shows up in icons for bodies of text:

Book   Memo   Body text   Table of   Bullet list
                                       contents

Implying order or sequence

The left-to-right arrangement of objects implies an order and sequence to the objects:

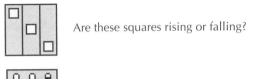

Are these squares rising or falling?

Is it getting hotter or colder in this icon?

The answer depends on whether time flows from left to right or right to left.

Consider how the meanings of these icons depend on the presumption that the user is moving left to right:

Continue   Go back   Undo

Implying value or virtue

In Christian cultures, good is on the right and evil on the left. In theater and painting, good things appear to the right and evil to the left. Language reinforces this distinction. The word *right* is both a direction and a synonym for proper and correct. The words *rectitude, adroit,* and *dexterous* are based on the word for *right* in other languages, just as *sinister* and *gauche* come from the words for *left.* In Arabic culture the left hand is used only for "unclean" tasks. In Chinese art, however, the right is violent and self-destructive while left is honorable.

Do not rely solely on horizontal position within the icon or on the screen to represent the virtue or correctness of an object or concept.

Solutions

To avoid falling into the trap of assuming a left-to-right reading direction for users who read in another direction, take precautions.

First, determine if you really have a problem. Although Arabic and Hebrew read left-to-right, they do reverse direction for proper nouns. Many publications in Arabic and Hebrew include charts and graphs with time moving left to right. Test with intended users.

For a quick test, mirror-image the icons and test them with left-to-right readers. If the reversal causes no serious problems, then the original icons will probably work with right-to-left readers. If you discover a problem, however, take steps to correct it.

Some steps you might take would be:

- **Show sequence with arrows**. If you must arrange the sequence of objects left to right, indicate the reading sequence by an arrow:

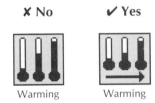

- **Use vertical sequence**. Make the icon read from top to bottom. All languages read from top to bottom of the page:

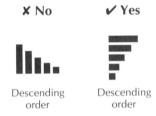

- **Mirror-image icons**. For the Arabic and Hebrew editions of your applications, flip left-to-right all icons that depend on horizontal arrangement for meaning.

- **Draw images symmetrically** or in other ways that do not depend on a left-to-right sequence:

GENERALIZE IMAGES

Go into any modern business office around the world and you will find more familiar sights than unfamiliar ones. Although a million variations are possible, you would not be shocked to see this scene: people sitting at desks as they write and read from paper. On the desk is a telephone and either a typewriter or a computer. Also on the desk you may find a calculator and a calendar. Periodically people attend meetings where they sit around tables and listen to one another talk. The men wear dark, single-breasted suits, white shirts, dark ties, and dark, leather, lace-up shoes. The image of business is similar around the world—provided you do not look too closely.

When you look at the details, you find many differences. Common office objects look and work differently. The shape and ring of the telephone is not exactly what you are familiar with. Clip boards, thumb tacks, and file folders have a different shape than the ones in your office. The rulers measure in different units than yours and power plugs have a different configuration of prongs than the ones back home. The business attire of women may be quite different—if women participate in business at all.

Highly realistic icons that draw attention to such details can confuse and mislead. Those that maintain the soft-focus can yield images understood by business users around the world.

Suppress unimportant details

Specific details help users recognize icons—provided the details are familiar ones. Detailed icons can fail when users are unfamiliar with the details or the details show objects that vary from country to country. For international icons, we must remove unnecessary details.

Pick graphics your international readers can identify. A strategy of including specific details to make objects more recognizable may backfire for international icons when readers are unfamiliar with the details shown. For such readers we may have to deliberately make images more general and abstract:

- Draw the image in a simplified style, not a photographic or realistic style.

- Reduce or hide national differences, such as the on-off position of power switches or the shape of power plugs.

- Show the object from a viewpoint that hides unnecessary details.

- Remove text. Omit or gray-out labels. Show keyboards with blank keys. Indicate to buttons and function keys by position instead of name.

Show generic people

In international icons, show people only where necessary and represent them by simple, generic figures, not realistic portraits. Realistic detailed images of people show a person of a particular race, gender, age, and social class. Unless such particulars are relevant, they make the true meaning of the icon harder to recognize.

Consider Hewlett-Packard's icon for a software agent, a program that auto-mates separate activities in your computer. From a viewpoint above and to the right, it shows a man with slicked-down, shiny black hair wearing sunglasses, a shirt, and a tie.

It is supposed to look like a secret agent. Many users did not recognize it as such. One woman from Japan called it the "hoodlum" icon. A New Yorker referred to it as the "California Joe Cool" icon. Another person said it showed a "white male yuppie with a bad attitude."

How then can we avoid similar problems with our icons?

- Use inanimate objects instead of people as symbols. Unless the subject is a person, do not show a person. For an emblem of data security, you could for example, use a padlock instead of a policeman which might have associations of political repression in some societies.

- Draw the human form as a simple line drawing, cartoon, or stick figure. Forego realistic details.

- For actions, show just the hands of the person performing the action.

See "Faces" in Chapter 13 for more suggestions on how to show human faces.

Take care with hands

If you must show hands, avoid hand gestures and instead show generic hands manipulating familiar objects. Make sure the hands are ones the user can recognize and identify with. Some guidelines:

- Consider alternatives. Can you represent the concept without showing a hand? Try arrows to show motion. Or present the tool used to perform the action:

✗ No   **✔ Yes**

- Show hands only when they are performing procedures. Show the hand touching, holding, pushing, grasping, or twisting something:

- Make clear what object the hand is touching or manipulating. If you omit the object the hand becomes a gesture, and most gestures are offensive somewhere. These are gestures:

Smear   Move

These are hands or fingers doing recognizable work:

Repair   Press button

- If you use a pointing finger, make clear what it is pointing toward:

✗ No   ✔ Yes

- Draw the hands so they are not clearly male or female. Do not show long, painted nails, hairy knuckles, or any jewelry:

✗ No   ✔ Yes

- If a procedure can be performed easily with either right or left hand, show it being performed with the right hand. In Arabic culture the left hand is for unclean tasks only:

- Do not indicate skin color. Pure white and pure black better represent generic skin than gray, tan, or brown:

Show the best-known version

Many objects come in several versions. When using such an object in as icon, we should pick the version most widely recognized.

If one version of an object is more common throughout the world, show that version. For an automobile, select a small boxy model like the Honda Accord or Ford Escort, which are sold in many different countries. For a truck, show a typical delivery truck rather than a pickup truck which is not as common in Europe as in America. Show 10 or 5 divisions per unit in a measuring ruler rather than 12 or 4. The divisions can thus represent millimeters or tenths of an inch:

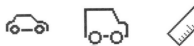

If there is no international version, then pick the most common version familiar to the largest number of users. Although these versions are not universal, they are quite common:

Also consider the oldest of several contending versions. Older versions are more likely to have appeared in movies seen abroad. Older versions may be more common in some countries. The enterprising citizens of less affluent societies often repair rather than replace mechanical devices. Such devices remain in service longer than in many "state-of-the-art" societies. Here are some old, but recognizable objects:

One rule of thumb I have is that objects commonly seen in Hollywood movies of the 1930s, 1940s, and 1950s are safe to use in international icons.

Mix several versions

If there is no universal symbol for a concept, you may have to create several different versions of the icon and use a different one for each market. Another approach is to combine the several versions into one. The plurality of images produces a symbol more general than either alone. Even if the user does not find his own version represented, he may still recognize the concept in what the separate images have in common:

Currency   Users   Religion

Use abstract symbols

Most simple geometric shapes are mercifully free of cultural connotations. Icons using abstract shapes and lines often work well in international interfaces:

Consolidate   Mix   Network   Unformat   Rotate   Row

If you use abstract symbols, forego shapes that resemble political and religious emblems:

- Five- or six-pointed stars
- Crescent shapes, which resemble the symbol for Islam
- Pentagrams

- Shapes that resemble flags:

CREATE INTERNATIONAL SYMBOLS

Despite the clear differences of language and culture, human beings have much in common. We are all born and we all die. In between we eat, sleep, educate ourselves, work for a living, travel, shop, get sick, get well, see movies, watch TV, and participate directly or vicariously in sports. As designers we can rely on these common activities to suggest images familiar to all.

Natural features

We all live in the same world. We all see the sky and the sun and moon and clouds that travel through it. We have all seen mountains, lakes, islands, trees, and deserts—at least in pictures:

Nature   Day   Night   Zoom
                                            out and in

Modes of transportation

We all travel. We travel to work and back home again. We visit our relatives and our friends. If we are lucky we go on vacation. Throughout our lives we learn about automobiles, airplanes, buses, boats, trains, and bicycles:

Fly   Drive   Cruise   Truck

Sports and games

Athletic competition is a global activity. Many forms of competition are familiar around the world. Popular Olympic sports include soccer, track, swimming. The checkered flag of automobile racing is as familiar as are the pieces of the chess board:

| Exercise | Games | Goal | Run |

Avoid symbols based on less common sports, especially those with implications of wealth and class distinction, such as yachting, horseback riding, and golf.

Consumer goods

Some products are marketed throughout the world. Many are electronic entertainment devices: televisions, video cassette recorders, audio cassette recorders, satellite dishes, and camcorders. Another familiar set are those used by tourists. These include cameras, binoculars, and film:

| Record | Snapshot | Film | Video |

Still others are found in households almost everywhere:

| Light | Portable | Battery | Inspect |

Office implements

Many of the tools of business are similar around the world. Consider the objects you would find on desks, on shelves, and on the walls of offices everywhere:

    Calculator   FAX   Package   Time

World news

Watching the evening news on TV is a common activity throughout the world. Images that appear on televisions around the world are good candidates for use in icons. Happenings of international importance supply just such images. Watch your evening news and notice the coverage of overseas events. This coverage probably includes wars, natural disasters, other disasters, negotiations, scientific breakthroughs, and space travel. If we have international images they are those of tanks advancing, rifles firing, ambulances and police cars speeding through narrow streets, rockets rising on columns of flame, and people shaking hands across a conference table. Such images, though not always pleasant, provide a vocabulary of shared images we can use in icons:

    Launch   Danger   Death   Industry

Communication media

Another universal need is to communicate and to be entertained. The means and media we use are often similar:

    Newspaper   Reading   Movie   Music

Science and technology

Scientists around the world must share their findings and discoveries. The languages of science are often based on mathematical symbology that transcends human language. The formulas, charts, graphs, and equations speak a universal, neutral language:

| Flowchart | Formulas | Circuit | Graph |

Scientists and others in high-technology pursuits often use the same tools and devices. Telescopes, microscopes, micrometers, beakers, flasks, stethoscopes, and other tools of the trade are the same from Bombay to Birmingham:

| Measure | Diagnose | Design | Inoculate |

Other professions

Many professions are practiced worldwide: soldier, sailor, tinker, tailor, beggar man, and thief—not to mention policeman, physician, house painter, carpenter, automobile mechanic, writer, and graphic designer. Each profession has practices, tools, and conventions that are shaped by the need to work quickly and efficiently. These aspects of the profession are similar in many lands. Consider these professional tools used as icons:

| Write | Paint | Anchor | Repair |

Body language

Contrived poses and gestures are as provincial as a particular dialect or accent. The spontaneous facial expressions and body postures, however, are more general:

Study	Walk	Teach	Happy	Asleep

Use international signs

Some traffic and safety signs are widely used throughout the world. We can borrow them for use as icons:

OK	No	Stop	Caution	Radiation

Several organizations have begun to develop a standard set of icons for actions and concepts of using computers:

Off	On	Contrast	Brightness

Not all of these international-standard symbols are recognized without prior study.

TRANSLATE LABELS

In an interface for international products it is tempting to omit labels for icons. Labels are difficult and expensive to translate. Still, translating labels may prove less expensive than having an unusable product. Labels in a familiar language clarify unfamiliar images based on different culture's visual symbology.

Leave room for translation

Leave extra space for labels that must be translated. Notice how these English labels expand as they are translated to other European languages:

English	File	Edit	View	Print	Help
German	Datei	Editieren	Anzeige	Drucken	Hilfe
French	Fichier	Édition	Visualisation	Impression	Aide
Italian	File	Editare	Visualizzare	Stampare	Aiuto
Spanish	Archivo	Editar	Ver	Imprimir	Ayuda

For international icons, size the label area to fit the largest label in English and multiply this size by the amount text expands as it goes to other languages. Here is a table I use to estimate the space required when translating from English to other European languages:

Characters in English	Characters in other European languages	Characters in English	Characters in other European languages
5	10 – 13	40	55 – 61
10	18 – 24	45	61 – 66
15	26 – 32	50	66 – 71
20	33 – 39	55	72 – 77
25	39 – 45	60	77 – 83
30	44 – 50	65	82 – 88
35	49 – 55	70	88 – 95

You must consider other factors as well. English tends to use shorter words than some other European languages. It is easier, for example, to fit English into a narrow column than to fit German which employs more long compound words, especially for business and technical concepts. Oriental scripts use more detailed characters than Western alphabets. Chinese and Japanese characters tend to be about 30 percent taller than roman characters of the same legibility.

Write labels for reliable translation

The way you phrase labels can make them easier to translate. Whether you rely on human or machine-assisted translation, a simple, consistent style of labeling icons will make translation smoother and more reliable.

Set up and enforce standards for consistency of labels. Use each word as only one part of speech and let is have only one meaning. For each type of icon phrase all labels the same. See Chapter 8 for more suggestions on standardizing labels.

Use simple, common words that are easy to translate. Avoid abbreviations, acronyms, and mnemonics. Some terms may not have abbreviations in the target language. Some languages do not allow abbreviation at all. Avoid slang, jargon, and colloquialisms. Overly informal language seldom translates well.

Select qualified translators

The translation is no better than the translator. For translators, insist on people who know:

- **The languages**. The translator must be a native speaker of the target language, familiar with idiom and other subtleties, and thoroughly up to date in technical terminology. The translator must be fluent in the source language too.

- **The product**. The translator must understand who uses the product and why they use it.

- **The technology**. The concepts represented by icons are often highly technical. They are rarely ones found in a standard dictionary.

Remember, though, that translators cannot read minds. Give them complete information about the interface. Show them icons in context and let them learn to use the product.

Consider how you display labels

The most difficult text in the interface to read or to translate is usually the captions of icons. We can take precautions to prevent many difficulties:

- **Never put labels in the bitmap of the icon**. Store them separately and display them above or below the image.

- **Do not fit labels tightly into enclosed areas**. If the translated label requires more space, it may overflow the enclosed area or part of it may get chopped off.

- **Use simple, plain character shapes**. Stylized characters are harder to recognize, especially for those users reading in other than their native language.

- **Make provisions to right-align the lines of labels** when they are translated into Arabic or Hebrew (which read right-to-left) if you are currently left-aligning them.

REVIEW AND TEST

If you market your product internationally, you should test your icons with users from each country, not just local people who have vacationed in the country. Thorough testing in the target countries is often impractical given the rapid pace of product development. What can you do then to ensure that your icons are understood and do not offend?

The first step is to learn about your markets. Your international marketing department can help. They know a lot about potential buyers in each market. However, remember that the person who buys the product is often not the one who uses it. The buyer may speak perfect English and be thoroughly familiar with Western culture. Is the same true of the end user?

Study the culture and values of potential users. Learn what visual symbologies are familiar to them. Subscribe to technical and business magazines read by prospective users. Look at the symbols used in illustrations and advertisements. Examine icons in products that are popular in the target country.

Solicit as much feedback as you can on your icons. Here are some suggestions:

- Test icons with foreign customers visiting your site for training or sales demonstrations.
- Test at international conferences and users-group meetings.
- Fax copies of the icons to foreign sales offices or distributors.
- Post copies of icons on bulletin boards in the international marketing department and invite comments.

Testing is never easy, especially when users are thousands of miles, kilometers, or leagues away. However, the more problems you identify and fix, the better your product will sell around the world.

WHAT IF ICONS ARE NOT 100% UNIVERSAL?

For a complex product, designing icons that are totally language independent and culturally neutral may prove impossible.

Fortunately users do not require perfect icons, only recognizable ones. You can use images not common in the target culture provided your users can still recognize them. Most users would recognize the words *STOP* and *OK* on icons. Some objects, though not common, may be well known, especially among those in business:

 An Arab businessman will recognize this image of a book, even though books in Arabic, which reads right to left, would have the spine on the right.

 Likewise, his Japanese counterpart will recognize this image as a symbol of greeting among business associates, even though in the orient a bow is more common as a greeting than a handshake.

 A Chinese user will recognize this as an emblem for food even though chopsticks and a bowl may be more common in China.

Trying to be 100 percent international may make you 100 percent unclear. The solution is simple and relatively inexpensive: redraw a few of your icons. Changing 5 percent of your icons is a bother, but it is often a better solution than the alternative of refusing to change the icons and thereby confusing or offending users. It is certainly less expensive than avoiding icons altogether and having to translate 100 percent of the equivalent text into multiple languages.

Make your icons as universal as you can. Test and revise them. Then test again. And if a few have to be changed for certain countries, change them.

FOR MORE INFORMATION

Axtel, Roger E. *Do's and Taboos Around the World.* New York: John Wiley, 1990.

Axtel, Roger E. *Gestures: The Do's and Taboos of Body Language Around the World.* New York: John Wiley, 1991.

Jones, Scott, Cynthia Kennelly, Claudia Mueller, et al. *Developing International User Information.* Bedford, MA: Digital Press, 1992.

Morris, Desmond. *Manwatching: A Field Guide to Human Behavior.* New York: Harry N. Abrams, 1977.

MANAGING DEVELOPMENT

PROCESS OF DESIGNING ICONS

This chapter is for anyone who has to manage complex icon design projects —
even if you are the only person on the project. Designing more than a handful
of icons requires a methodical process. Doing it on time and within budget requires careful management and supervision.

The process of designing icons is more cyclical than straightforward. It consists
of several activities in sequence, but at any point you may have to drop back to
redo an earlier activity.

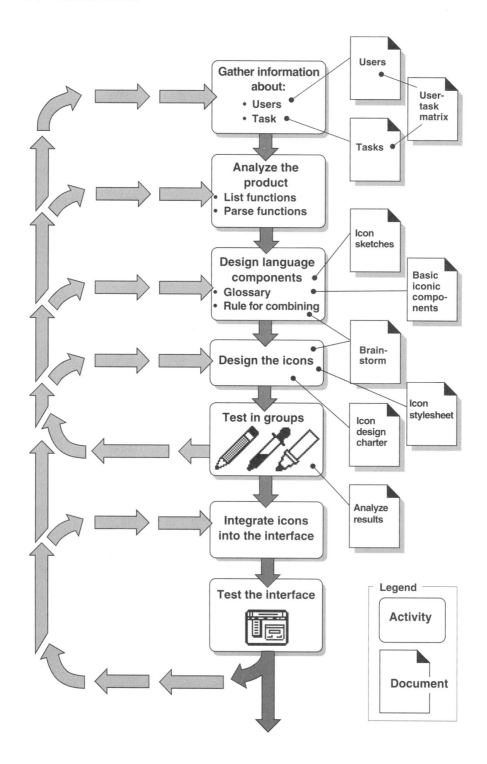

Gather information about users and tasks

Inexperienced designers jump right in and start sketching icons. Good designers realize the first step is to understand who uses the product and why they use it.

Learn who uses the product

You are designing icons for people, and unless you are the only user of the product, you must design for other people. The only thing you know with certainty about the user is that the user is different from you. How different? That's what you have to find out. Invest the time and effort to understand users. Anything you learn about them may prove helpful. The form "Users" in Chapter 14 lists what software designers need to know about users. Because you design icons, you should continually ask, "What visual symbols will this person recognize? What symbols have they already learned?" There are several ways to study users or potential users:

- **Questionnaires**. Have users describe themselves by answering a series of written questions. Keep the questions simple and unambiguous. Make filling in the form easy. Let users check off alternatives and fill in numbers and short words or phrases. Unless you have the authority to demand a response, send out lots of questionnaires because response rates are usually low, typically 1 to 5 percent.

- **Phone survey**. Asking users questions over the phone lets you ask more open-ended questions and lets you follow up on vague or unexpected responses. Many users will talk about subjects they avoid in writing. Phone surveys take more time than questionnaires buy yield deeper information.

- **Site visits**. Visit users where they work. Get to know them and understand their work. Share coffee and lunch with them. Observe them on the job. Better still, work alongside them on the job yourself. Pay attention to how users work together in teams, what pressures they feel, and what sustains them through a hard day. Site visits are time-consuming and costly but yield the most realistic impression of users.

You can mix these methods. Start mailing out questionnaires to a broad sample of users. Select a smaller number of users and phone them for more detailed questions. Visit a handful of typical users.

Tasks they perform

What will users do with the system? What tasks must your icons enable? Here you can call on three sources of information:

- **Users**. Users can tell you what they think they will do with the product. If users have experience with comparable or competitive products, they can tell you exactly how they will use the product. However, if your product is unlike anything users have experienced, you must build and test prototypes to know for sure what users will do and how your icons will be used.

- **Marketing analysts**. Marketing can tell you why people buy the product and what problem they expect it to solve for them. However, the person who buys the product is not always the one who uses it. You may need to dig deeper.

- **Software developers**. What people *do* with a product depends on what they *can do* with it. Learn what capabilities are being included in the product. What assumptions have guided the design of the product?

Keep in mind that using a product is more than pressing keys and buttons. It involves an intricate series of decisions and actions, some quite concrete and specific, and others quite abstract and general. Users with a goal must translate that goal into a specific plan of action and carry out that plan successfully. They must make clear decisions and recover from likely missteps. The better we can anticipate these activities, the better we can design icons to support them.

The form "Tasks" in Chapter 14 shows the kind of information user-interface designers typically gather about tasks performed by users.

User-task combinations

As you analyze users and the tasks they perform with the product, you soon realize that not all users perform all tasks. Some tasks are performed only when the system is first installed, while others are performed every day. Some users repeatedly perform basic tasks, and others apply more advanced features. Some activities are rarely performed at all. For good design you must sort out which groups of users perform which tasks. The form "User-task matrix" in Chapter 14 lets you summarize the correspondences between users and tasks.

Analyze the product

With a good understanding of who uses the product and why, you can turn to a detailed study of the product. Learn what components of the product will need icons. Make a list of the concepts that need icons. Here is a checklist:

Component of the product	Icon needed
Program	Each program requires an emblem for display on the Desktop or Program Manager level of the graphical user interface. It may also need a trademark or advertising emblem.
Data files	Each type of data file created by or used by the program may need a separate image for display at the Desktop or Program Manager level of the graphical user interface.
Commands	Each command the user can give to the system may require an icon. These icons would appear on palettes, toolbars, and other menus.
Data objects	If the user performs work by manipulating data objects, you may need icons so the user can point to, select, move, and combine these objects. For example, icons for files can be dropped onto icons for printers to print the files or onto an icon of a trash can to delete the files.
Prompts for action	Some icons can be used to remind users of the kind of input the system is waiting for. If you use icons to prompt the user, you will need a separate icon for each kind of action the user can take and each kind of data the user can enter.
Error and status messages	Icons can provide immediate feedback. They are certainly clearer than numeric codes and can supplement verbal messages. You may need an icon for each category of status or error message.
Cursors	The shape of the cursor can provide valuable feedback and can simplify various tasks. You may need a series of cursors of different shapes and sizes.

Design the iconic language

If you are designing more than a dozen icons, resist the temptation to jump in and start designing icons right away. Take a little time and set up a scheme for creating icons as discussed in Chapter 5. Such a scheme establishes a language for your icons, and greatly simplifies the task of designing large number of icons. A language also makes learning your icons easier for users.

Designing an iconic language requires defining a vocabulary of basic symbols and specifying a grammar of rules for combining the parts. Both of these tasks are explained in detail in Chapter 5. The forms "Basic iconic components," "Brainstorming," and "Icon sketches" in Chapter 14 aid in this task.

Design icons

The next step is to design the individual icons. If you have set up a language, many icons can be designed by simply combining elements from your vocabulary of basic symbols according to the rules of your grammar. Otherwise, you must design each icon from scratch. The bulk of this book is devoted to guiding you through the process of designing icons. Several chapters of this book may prove useful:

Activity		Read
Design	Simple images	Chapter 3
	Complex images	Chapter 4
	Specific kinds of icons	Chapter 9
	For international users	Chapter 10
	Color icons	Chapter 7
Draw	Images	Chapter 6
	Borders, backgrounds, labels	Chapter 8
Edit	Icons and images	Chapter 13

Several of the forms in Chapter 14 are designed to aid in designing the icons:

Brainstorming	For gathering ideas on how to represent a concept
Icon style sheet	For specifying the appearance of a series of related icons
Icon design charter	For planning the design of an individual icon

Test groups of icons

As soon as you have designed a few icons, start testing them. Do not wait until all the icons are designed, or until the product is up and running. You can begin testing related groups of icons almost immediately. You can test them on paper or on simulated screens. Chapter 12 details how to test icons.

Integrate icons into the interface and test again

As soon as your individual icons appear to work, design them into a prototype of the actual product and test them in action. Don't wait until the product is nearly finished. You can simulate interactivity by using a skeleton user-interface that simply jumps from window to window in response to inputs from the user. Or you can simulate the product using nothing fancier than index cards and rough sketches of screens. For best results:

Test early and often.

Chapter 12, especially the sections on usability testing, will guide you through this testing process.

Revise, revise, revise

Invite comments and even criticism. Test and test again. Then test some more. The more you test, the more you find to fix. The more you fix, the easier the product is to learn and to use. Either you find and fix problems, or the user finds them … and you still have to fix them.

Designing visual symbols is hard work. Even if you are an artist, do not expect to get it right the first time. The quality of a visual symbol often depends on the number of times you have revised it. Do not be satisfied with your first idea. Sketch several ideas before you draw the symbol. Test the symbol, and do not be too proud to replace it if someone else has a better idea. The recipe is simple:

1. Think of five good ideas for the icon.
2. Pick the best one and draw it.
3. Test and redraw it five times.

WHO SHOULD DESIGN ICONS?

Who should have the task of designing icons? Let's consider the various candidates for the job.

Group	Advantages	Disadvantages
Software developers	Familiar with the internals of the system and the command or data object set.	Seldom see whole picture. Icons designed by individual developers will be inconsistent.
User-interface designers	Concerned with the user's view of the system. Have a big-picture view of the entire product.	Lack graphic design skills.
Graphic artists	Strong visual design skills.	Often lack detailed knowledge of the product's functions. Often prefer making pretty pictures to representing concepts simply.
End users	Understand what other users will recognize. Know what is important to end users.	May lack understanding of new concepts or potential uses of obscure features.

The best solution may be a team. The user-interface designer consults with the software developer to learn the functions of the software and then specifies the icons. The graphic artist draws the icons which are then tested by end users. The user-interface designer suggests revisions to the graphic artist who redesigns for further testing.

GETTING IDEAS

Designing icons demands creativity. The best designers seem to be those who have many ideas and just throw away the bad ones. How do you get lots of visual ideas? The creative process may be somewhat mysterious, but we can all make the most of the creativity we have.

To augment our native creativity we can actively seek out new ideas. Here are some techniques to try:

- **Brainstorming**. Put creative people together and they become more creative. One way to generate ideas is to hold a brainstorming session. In such a session the only rule is that no one can speak ill of another person's idea. The purpose of brainstorming is to elicit as many ideas as possible, not to critique them. Participants can offer new ideas or they can add to an earlier idea. All ideas are welcome, even crazy, wild, impractical ones. Often such ideas spark further ideas that are practical. Even obviously wrong ideas can provide a path to better ideas.

- **Checklists**. Another approach is to use a checklist of possibilities. You could use the encoding techniques mentioned in Chapters 3 and 4. Simply start at the beginning and for each technique ask, "How can I use this technique to symbolize the concept?"

- **Standards and conventions**. Many professions, such as medicine and engineering, already have rich vocabularies of visual symbols that you can adapt as icons. Look for these symbols in industrial standards and technical handbooks.

- **Magazines and trade journals**. Look at the use of symbols in the communications media your users read. Pay attention to symbols in titles, headings, illustrations, and, especially, advertisements.

- **GUI style guides**. The handbooks for designing various graphical user interfaces often contain guidelines on using icons. Some even provide samples of icons you can use.

- **Software-development toolkits**. The tools and resources used to prepare applications with graphical user interfaces often contain libraries of icons ready for you to plug into your application. Even if you find no icon for your particular function, you may find one for an analogous function. You can then modify or add to the design to achieve the icon you need.

DEVELOPING AND MAINTAINING SKILLS

Designing dozens or even hundreds of icons requires visual creativity. So, how can icon designers systematically improve their visual skills?

Get training

No universities offer degrees in icon design. Few even offer courses on designing icons for computer screens. Even though specific education and training is largely unavailable, we can still take advantage of books and courses in allied fields. A curriculum for icon designers should include courses in these fields:

- Ergonomics and human factors

- Graphic design, especially of corporate logos and visual symbols

- Drawing techniques
- Color theory

Play games

Games are a great way to improve your skills and exercise your creativity while having fun at the same time. The best are games that test your ability to represent concepts simply and quickly.

Pictionary

In the game of Pictionary, you must communicate a name or a phrase to your partner without using words but by drawing pictures. You have to do this faster than other participants can communicate the concept to their partners. Here are two sketches done to prompt the response "Electric chair:"

Pictionary is ideal for icon designers because it emphasizes the need to communicate clearly and quickly. The pressure of competition does not allow intricate drawings. The person who can make a recognizable image in a few strokes wins.

Children are very good at Pictionary. Though they lack precise drawing skills they have a knack for identifying the essence of an idea and expressing it in simple shapes. It is that childlike ability to cut through extraneous details that makes for superb icon design.

Tangrams

The game of Tangrams, which is based on the ancient Chinese puzzle Chih-hui-pan (wisdom board), requires participants to arrange small tiles to form an image of a familiar object. Participants can use only the shapes provided and must use all of them:

For example, using just these tiles ...   **How would you form this image?**
(answer on next page)

Pixel-Less

Pixel-Less is a contest I invented to test the ability of icon designers to design simply. By filling in squares on a sheet of graph paper, the designer tries to make a recognizable image of an object. The winner is the one whose image requires the smallest number of squares. Here are some winners. Can you do better?

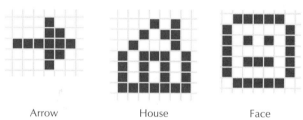

Arrow   House   Face

TOOLS OF THE TRADE°

Whether you are chopping wood or making icons, you need tools to do the work. What are the tools that an icon designer needs and how do we tell good tools from bad ones?

Sketching supplies

For quickly recording an idea or sharing it with a colleague, nothing beats pen and paper. No computer drawing program is as responsive or as convenient as a sketchpad and pen.

Any smooth surfaced paper will work well, but pens are not all equal. I recommend an inexpensive pen with a broad, soft nylon or felt point and opaque black ink. You can buy them for less than a dollar at most drug stores.

One reason I recommend this pen is that it leads to good habits. Fine-point pens encourage finely detailed drawings that cannot be translated into small images on a grainy computer screen. A broad line encourages quick, crude sketches. And if your design works as a crude sketch, it will probably work as a refined icon.

Color pens and pencils lead to bright, multi-hued designs that rely so heavily on color that they fail when the icon must be displayed on a monochrome monitor or when viewed by a color-blind user.

This is the solution to the puzzle on the previous page.

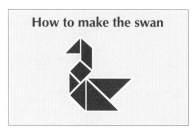

How to make the swan

Scanners

Scanners convert sketches on paper to electronic images that you can edit on the computer. Although I know of no case of images going directly from sketches on paper to icons on a computer screen, the scanned images provide a starting point for refining designs. Once you have the design in the computer you can edit and refine it.

For icon design, a simple scanner is usually adequate. A scanning resolution of 300 dots per inch is three or four times the resolution of finished icons on the computer screen. If you are scanning only sketches, you do not need color.

Drawing programs

If you are designing more than a few icons, invest in a general-purpose drawing program. On large projects, you will do most of your work in this program. You will refine your sketches, draw the icons, edit and revise them, draw alternatives, and add color and other refinements. When the icons are nearly perfect, you transfer them to an icon editor program for fine tuning and saving in the prescribed format.

Canvas 3.0 was the program I used to design most of the icons in this book. A sample screen is shown below:

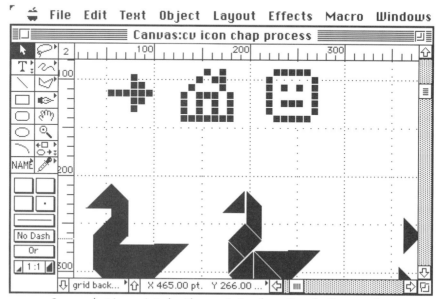

Screen shot is reprinted with permission from Deneba Systems, Inc.

Why use a drawing program instead of doing all the work in an icon editor? One advantage of a drawing program is that it makes it easier for you to design and view groups of related icons together. You can save an entire set of icons in a single file. Drawing programs typically have advanced drawing capabilities lacking from icon editors.

What should you look for when picking a program for drawing icons?

- Can it edit both raster (paint) and vector (draw) graphics? Can it mix the types? Can it convert vector graphics into raster graphics?

- Can you define independent layers? Can you draw the icon over a template without affecting the template?

- Does the program have a full complement of commands for editing graphics?

- Does the program let you revise raster graphics? Can you rotate, stretch, and skew raster graphics? How many steps can you undo?

- What file formats can the program import? What ones can it export? Can the program input directly from the scanner?

Icon editors

Icon editors are computer programs designed especially for creating icons. They provide tools for drawing and editing the image of the icons. Here is the icon editor from OS/2 2.0:

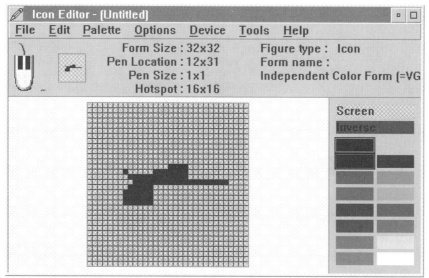

Screen shot is reprinted with permission from International Business Machines, Inc.

Most current icon editors are simple, relatively limited, and are more than adequate for designing a few dozen icons. If you are designing more icons than that, you will probably want to do most of the design in a drawing program and then transfer your results to an icon editor for touch up.

A good icon editor provides these features:

- **Tools and commands**. The program provides a rich set of tools and commands for drawing and revising images.

- **Import**. You can use the icon editor to revise images created elsewhere. A good editor can accept input from scanners, drawing programs, and even font files.

- **Preview**. The editor should show the image in realistic color and actual size

- **Enlarged view**. The editor should let the user zoomin on the image or should magnify it so that the user can easily select individual pixels.

- **Multiple versions**. Often you will need several versions of an icon. The editor should make it easy to produce the same image in several numbers of colors and at different sizes. It should also help you define related images such as the masks that specify what parts of the icon are transparent when it overlaps other objects on the screen.

Database

On large projects, one of the hardest tasks is keeping track of all the required icons. This is especially true if several programs have icons in common and if icons must exist in different versions. Cataloging and tracking hundreds or thousands of icons requires a database.

Most flat-file or relational databases are adequate for this task. Setting up the database does not require any special technical skills, but does require understanding what you need to keep track of and how you need information presented. For managing the development of an extensive set of icons, your database should track:

- **The icon**. Some databases let you store the icon directly in the database. Others let you store the name of the file containing the icon.

- **Name**. What is the label for the icon? You may want to store the name in multiple languages.

- **Related icons**. Are there other versions of this icon? Is it similar to other icons? When this icon is revised, should other icons be revised at the same time?

- **Where used**. What programs use this icon?

- **Designer**. Who designed this icon? Who should revise it?

- **Status**. Is this icon a sketch, a prototype, or a finished design? Is it approved for release? When was it last revised?

- **Description**. Include key words or phrases you can use to retrieve this icon later.

Once you have established your database, print a concise summary. Put these reports in notebooks or thumbtack them to a wall. When you need to locate a particular icon you may find it easier to scan a printout than to retrieve it from the database by textual descriptors.

STAYING ON SCHEDULE AND WITHIN BUDGET

How long will it take and how much will it cost? As with any creative activity, it is impossible to answer precisely. The budget and schedule of an icon design project depend on the number of icons, the number of versions of each, the quality required, the number of colors used, the experience of the team, and a hundred other factors.

One way to estimate the costs is to set up a spreadsheet that lists the various activities and tallies the time and cost of each. An example of such a spreadsheet is included in Chapter 14.

Here are some tips for controlling costs and improving productivity that I have learned from the projects I have managed or participated in:

- **Start early**. Pace the work so that you do not need costly overtime or outside contractors.

- **Set up an iconic language**. The synergy effects of having a language can reduce the amount of effort by a factor of 10.

- **Test early and often**. Discover problems before they become too expensive to fix. Redrawing 10 icons is easy. Redrawing 1000 is not.

- **Get good tools**. Invest in a good general-purpose drawing program.

- **Stay organized**. Keep good records and learn from your mistakes.

- **Automate repetitive procedures**. Write macros and scripts for the simple tasks that are performed repeatedly for every icon.

- **Assign tasks appropriately**. Drawing icons requires drawing skills. Thinking up icons requires creativity, but not necessarily drawing skills. A junior designer could assemble icons from a library of components designed by the senior designer.

STANDARDIZING ICONS

Wise standards intelligently implemented increase consistency among icons and make them more predictable and easier to learn and use.

What to standardize

Users expect computers to be consistent. Tiny differences can provoke major distractions. We should ensure that every difference the user notices among a set of icons has meaning, and should standardize features repeated within an application or between related applications, in particular:

- Size and shape of icons
- Number of colors
- Where and how color is used
- Where to use icons
- Design of border, background, and margins
- Labeling

Format for standards

Give designers tools, not rules. The worst way to promote standards is to hand out fat rule books. Instead of a rule book, consider these:

- **Glossary of approved icons**. Give designers examples of icons that demonstrate good design. Let designers copy and reuse these icons. Supply the icons as paper printouts and computer files.
- **Standard icons**. Define icons for the most common functions and provide them for designers to include in their designs.

- **Design grid and templates**. Give designers properly sized templates to use in creating their own designs. Such templates ensure that icons all have the same size, shape, and margins.

- **Rule booklet**. Keep the rules few, short, simple, and clear. Publish them in a convenient, attractive format. Make them look more like a pamphlet than a tome.

Enforcing standards

The secret to enforcing standards is not to become "standards police" or "icon Gestapo." The secret is to make standards easier and less costly to follow than to ignore.

The most important thing you can do as a standards setter is to make your standards wise. Avoid arbitrary or pedantic rules, and base your standards on common sense and proven experience.

Build a consensus for your standards. This requires actively publicizing and promoting them. Explain the reason for your standards while trying not to over-explain or become defensive. Keep your standards open-ended and yourself open-minded, allowing exceptions and amendments where appropriate. Encourage suggestions and promote healthy discussion of standards. Remember that no standards can resolve more than about 85 percent of the issues faced by designers.

COPYRIGHT ISSUES

Many icon designers live in dread that they will spend the rest of their lives in a dungeon because they inadvertently designed an icon that looked like one in another product. Concern about violating someone else's copyright is healthy, but fear and panic are not.

The best way to avoid copyright problems is simply to design your own icons in your own style. Make them as clear and effective as you can regardless of what others may have done. Document your work. Date your sketches and keep the sketches.

Then, after designing your icons, compare them to those of others, especially competitors with hair-trigger lawyers.

If you have designed your own icons in your own style, chances are you will notice few duplications. If some of the icons are similar, you can always ask permission of the other company. Unless the company is a direct competitor, they will probably grant permission. After all it is in their interest to have as many users as possible recognize their symbols.

If permission is not forthcoming, you should consult your corporate attorney before you use the icon. Be prepared to answer these questions:

- **How similar are the two icons?** Merely changing a pixel or two does not sufficiently distinguish one icon from another.

- **How many icons are similar?** If only a small percentage is similar, you cannot be accused of wholesale copying. Are the similarities clearly incidental, not intentional?

- **Is your design the only logical way to express an idea?** How many different ways are there to represent a concept like "telephone"?

- **How many others use this same design?** Have ten other companies all used the same basic symbol for several years without anyone suing anyone else?

I cannot emphasize how important it is to have this conversation with your attorney **before** you use any questionable icon.

TESTING ICONS

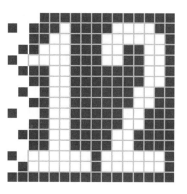

How do you know if an icon is good or bad? Designers and users often express opinions, but how do you know whether an icon will work? The guidelines for good design presented in this book will help you design icons, but no guidelines can absolutely ensure good design. The only way to do that is to test your icons. And then revise them. Then test again and revise again. Only by several cycles of testing and redesign will you make icons reliable and efficient.

TEST EARLY AND OFTEN

The most common problem I've seen with testing icons is that in most organizations it is done too late to be any help whatsoever. The purpose of testing is to uncover problems in time for you to correct them. Yet when do most organizations do testing? Only at the very end of the project. As the deadline approaches, the cost of fixing problems or revising icons rises exponentially—so too does the resistance to change. By the end of a project, egos are fully vested in the current design and any change is a direct criticism of the designer.

> The two most important tools the architect has are the eraser in the drawing room and the hammer on the construction site.
> —Frank Lloyd Wright

The result of late testing is a tendency to look for only small, easily fixed problems. I have heard product designers tell testing coordinators, "Don't bother testing for anything major because we don't have time to fix it." Late tests tend to be superficial and cosmetic. We redesign a few icons, change a pixel here or there, and fine-tune the colors—when we should completely revamp the scheme of our entire iconic language.

Testing is as much a part of research and design as it is a method of evaluating the design. We should begin testing on the first day of the project and continue through the last version of the product. Of course, the kind of testing we do during the first week of a project differs considerably from that done the week before releasing a major version. In general, three phases or types of testing are required. These overlap in time and method, but each answers a specific type of question:

- **Formative**. What works? What can we try?
- **Comparative**. Which alternative is better?
- **Evaluative**. Is the design good enough?

The three types of testing occur at different times during the development process:

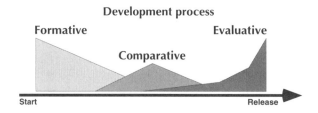

Formative testing

Formative testing asks the question, "What will work?" It strives to stimulate ideas rather than to refine or verify them. Formative testing is at the core of any rapid-prototyping effort. The idea behind formative testing is that development is cumulative, empirical, and iterative—we learn what to do by repeatedly testing a series of prototypes, ever refining them. The basic cycle of formative testing involves four activities:

- **Build**. Create a prototype, no matter how crude.
- **Test**. See how well the prototype works.
- **Analyze**. Understand how the prototype failed or how it can be improved.
- **Redesign**. Incorporate the lessons learned into the new design.

This technique is sometimes called the "two steps forward, one step back" approach:

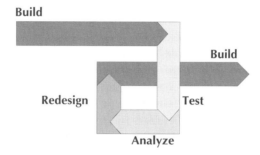

The cumulative effect of the repeated testing and improvement is continual progress toward perfection:

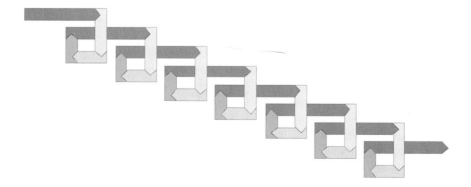

Formative testing works best when we keep it simple, informal, and quick. The more times we go around the build-test-analyze-redesign loop, the better our design gets. In formative testing, we are not trying to prove that the icon or the product works. To the contrary, we want our design to fail so we can learn how to improve it. In formative testing, eschew polished designs and decimal points. Five quick-and-easy tests are better than one scientifically valid one. Remember that in formative testing, we are not perfecting the design, we are trying to come up with a design to perfect later.

Comparative testing

Comparative testing measures the performance of two or more alternative designs. The best summary of and argument for comparative testing was given by a participant in one of my design seminars:

> Don't argue, argue, argue.
> Test, test, test.

Comparative testing requires clear, objective criteria for evaluating the results. Agree on these criteria before the test, and plan how you will measure them. Or else, expect to argue, argue, argue about the results.

Comparative testing is most valuable in the middle phase of development, after you have a simple prototype that is worthy of refinement but before you must verify the complete success of the product. Comparative testing helps you refine a product and make it more efficient.

Evaluative testing

Evaluative testing ensures the quality of your icons. It tells you whether the icons are good enough to release. Evaluative testing compares the performance of the icons with your initial usability objectives for them. (You do have usability objectives, don't you?) As with comparative testing, you must have well-defined criteria. How good is good enough?

Evaluative testing requires precise and unambiguous test objectives:

- **Test subjects**. How will you simulate actual users?
- **Scenario**. What will the test subjects be asked to do?
- **Measurement**. How will you measure success?
- **Criteria**. What degree of success is your goal and what level must be achieved before you will release the product?

MAKE TESTING REALISTIC

To be of any use, tests must reliably simulate actual use of the product. Test subjects must act like actual users, and the prototype must evoke the same responses as the actual product. Simulating an uncompleted product requires careful recruiting of test subjects and simulating the actual work environment.

Recruit reliable test subjects

No testing is effective without adequate test subjects. The ideal test subjects accurately reflect the preferences and behavior of future users of the product. Where can you find such people?

- Users attending training classes for current products

- Potential customers at a trade show

- Users of earlier versions of the product or of competitors products

If you are developing an entirely new product, however, no users may yet be available. In any case, you must have some test subjects who simulate novices. When you cannot test with actual users, you must recruit test subjects who resemble the future users. Look for people with:

- **Similar physiology**. The performance of icons depends on the eyesight and reflexes of the users. If 60 percent of your users wear bifocals, so should 60 percent of your test subjects.

- **Same psychology**. Test subjects should have the same motivation, intelligence, and problem-solving strategies as actual users. The results you achieve with a temporary office worker will not match those of a tenured university professor.

- **Similar education and job background**. Test subjects need the same depth and breadth of knowledge as actual users.

- **No inappropriate knowledge of the product**. Test subjects should know as much about the product as actual users are likely to—but no more.

- **No stake in success of the product**. The purpose of testing is to uncover weak links. You want test subjects who will break the product. People with a stake in its success, however, try hard to make the test a success. They may overcome difficulties and overlook flaws that will stump or annoy actual users.

Educate test subjects

Test subjects never match users perfectly. One way to overcome the mismatch is to carefully brief test subjects so that they can better simulate actual users.

Whom they are to simulate

If the test subject is not exactly like the future user, ask the test subject to pretend to be the user. Have the test subject play the role of the actual user. Tell the test subject as much as possible about the actual user.

I remember watching one test in which a 55-year-old woman pretended to be a 15-year-old male sales clerk. She smacked imaginary gum. She listened to music through invisible headphones, swaying rhythmically. She flirted with every female customer. This test showed us that the user interface had to work for a distracted user. When I asked her how she was able to simulate a teenager of the opposite gender, she told me, "It was easy—I've shepherded my two daughters and one son through adolescence."

Background knowledge

Users bring certain background knowledge to the task at hand. We must ensure that test subjects have the same knowledge. Ask yourself, what will the actual user already know at this point? Make sure the test subject has the same knowledge. This knowledge comes from three sources:

- Education and training
- Experience in a profession or on a job
- Prior experience with the product or others like it

Spend the time necessary to bring the test subject up to this level of knowledge. Although preparing the test subject takes time away from testing, it improves the value of the test and is usually less time consuming than recruiting and testing with actual users.

Task they are performing

For usability testing of working prototypes, give users clear, realistic tasks to perform. Unless you explain to users what they are to accomplish, the results will depend more on their misunderstanding of the task than on the quality of the user interface. Define:

- **The goal**. Tell the users exactly what action they are to accomplish. You need not prescribe the exact steps for them to reach the goal.

- **The available resources**. Spell out what resources the users can employ to accomplish the goal. Can they rely on paper and online documentation, tutorials, and other job aids? Can they ask for help from a (simulated) knowledgeable coworker? Can they call a customer-support hotline?

- **The time available**. How much time do the users have to accomplish the goal? Is there a deadline?

- **The performance objective**. What are the criteria for success? How will the users know when the result is achieved?

- **The data**. Give the users realistic data to use in the task. Don't say, "Type a memo." Give them a handwritten memo and have them type it.

Help test subjects to act naturally

Imagine that you have been selected as a usability test subject. You are directed to an unfamiliar building, whisked to the fifth floor, taken to an interior room with no outside window but with a mirror the length of one entire wall, seated in front of a computer, and glared at by three video cameras. Then a disembodied voice out of the wall says, "Act natural." Yeah!

In conventional usability testing, test subjects follow instructions to an unrealistic degree. They follow only approved procedures. They obey instructions literally. They conceal their doubts and objections. Many say they fear looking foolish or ignorant.

How, then, do we ever get realistic test results? There are several things we can do:

- **Test pairs of test subjects**, rather than individuals. The two users learn the product together. Their discussions show what they are thinking and reveal their growing knowledge, as well as their misunderstanding. Having a buddy lessens self-consciousness:

- **Test users on their territory**. We are all more confident, more spontaneous, more secure on our own turf. Where possible, test users in their own offices, on their regular computers. If you need to record the test, use a small camcorder, unobtrusively positioned.

- **Test icons, not users**. Make test subjects understand that you are not testing them but the icons. Do not tell users that the purpose of the test is "to see how well you recognize icons," but to spot ways to improve icons. Never refer to the icons as "my icons" or "our icons." Just call them "the icons." When test subjects ask how well they did, reply like this: "Huh? [mock surprise] Oh, you were perfect. You really helped us spot the icons that need improvement." Continually remind test subjects that you are evaluating the icons, not them.

TEST PERFORMANCE

Opinions are plentiful and easy to gather. Everyone has some and is willing to share them. Opinions are not so helpful in refining icon designs, though. More helpful are concrete measurements of performance.

Measure performance objectively

Avoid beauty pageants, which ask users which icon is more striking or cute or which they prefer. Although the aesthetic judgments of users should not be ignored, first impressions seldom mirror final judgments, and preferences do not accurately predict performance.

Look at what users do, not just what they say. In testing icons, record such objective measurements as:

- Percentage of users who complete tasks successfully
- Amount of work done
- Time required to do the task
- Number, rate, or time of errors
- Number of pages or screens of documentation consulted
- Amount of assistance required

Look for subjective cues too

Whereas objective measures tell us how well icons work, subjective cues hint at why one succeeded and another failed. When watching users, pay attention to subtle indicators of their emotional responses:

- Sighs, grunts, groans, mumbles
- Expressions of frustration, boredom, or delight
- Facial expressions
- Rate and smoothness of eye and hand movements
- Body language
- Any sudden change of behavior

Compare subjective and objective observations. Unless the two agree in every point, probe deeper. If the user says, "Everything is fine," but body language tells another story, find out why. A fear of looking foolish may mask deeper concern or confusion.

TEST IMAGE-MEANING ASSOCIATION

Image-meaning associations measure how closely the user associates a visual image with a verbal concept. Such tests help us pick images that will reliably trigger the right associations in the mind of the viewer.

Image-meaning tests are quick and easy. They can be done from paper or even automated. However, they are seldom the only kind of testing you need. In my experience, they work best in eliminating poor designs and in rapidly narrowing down the candidates for an image to represent a concept.

Open-ended meaning-for-image tests

Meaning-for-image tests show the user an image and ask, "What does this image mean?" They test the associations a user already has for a visual image.

These tests can be open ended or multiple choice. In open-ended tests, users tell what the image means to them. Do not require users to type or write by hand their responses. This makes the test too burdensome for users and blocks their spontaneous responses.

Here is an example of an open-ended question:

Imagine that you are looking at the navigation palette, which lets you move forward and backward in a series of records. Record 63 (of 183) is displayed. What happens if you select this icon?

As you observe the user's response, try to answer these questions:

- Is the user's association the one you intended? If not, is the association too broad, too narrow, too abstract, or just totally wrong?

- How quickly did the user make the association?

- How confident did the user seem?

I like to videotape users so I can watch facial expressions and gestures as they describe the meaning. If you cannot videotape or if the videotaping inhibits the users' responses, try audiotaping or just observe closely.

Multiple-choice meaning-for-image tests

Multiple-choice tests present an image and a list of possible meanings for the user to pick from. Multiple-choice tests are easier to administer and evaluate, but they may reveal less then open-ended tests. The hardest part of multiple-choice tests is coming up with realistic choices. You need four or five plausible choices for the testing to be valid.

Here is an example of a multiple-choice question:

Imagine that you are looking at the navigation palette, which lets you move forward and backward in a series of records. Record 63 (of 183) is displayed. If you select this icon …

… what happens?

a.   Record 62 is displayed.

b.   Record 64 is displayed.

c.   Record 1 is displayed.

d.   Record 183 is displayed.

e.   Records are displayed one at a time in reverse order.

Image-for-meaning tests

Image-for-meaning tests ask the user to identify which of several images best represents a concept. You can use it to test completely different symbols or to select among different ways of drawing a single symbol.

Here is an example:

The navigation palette provides icons to enable you to move back and forth among a series of items. Which of these icons would take you to the item immediately before the currently displayed item?

a   b   c   d   e   f

Image-meaning matching

Another way to test the association between an image and a concept is to give users images and verbal labels for the same concepts but in different orders and observe how quickly and accurately they match the image with the appropriate label. Here is an example:

The navigation palette provides icons to enable you to move back and forth among a series of items. It contains these icons.

a   b   c   d   e   f

Which icon would you select to make each of these movements?

1.   Move to next item in sequence   _____
2.   Move to previous item in sequence   _____
3.   Move to first item in sequence   _____
4.   Move to last item in sequence   _____
5.   Move continuously toward last item   _____
6.   Move continuously toward first item   _____

You may let users match icons and labels in several ways. You can number the labels and letter the icons, as is done in the example. If you have only a few icons to test, you can arrange the icons and labels in facing columns and let users draw lines connecting each icon to its label. My favorite way is to put each label and each icon on separate slips of paper, shuffle them, and hand the pile to a user. I like this approach because it requires users to look for patterns and similarities among the icons and labels. Users like it because it is more like a game than an aptitude test.

In such tests, observe which items are matched first and which later. Notice which are matched quickly and which are matched only by a process of elimination. (You may want to give the users a different number of icons than meanings to prevent them from working by process of elimination.) Pay special attention to cases where users change their mind.

CATEGORIZATION TESTS

Categorization tests ask users to arrange icons into meaningful groups. These tests measure users' recognition of the images and also their understanding of the concepts represented by the images. The tests help determine how to group icons into menus and palettes.

For categorization tests, give users copies of the icons as they will appear on the screen and ask the users to arrange the icons into groups—by whatever criteria they think important.

Analyze the resulting groupings carefully. How large are the groups? Are they all at the same level, or are there subcategories? Did users group merely by visual similarity or by deeper meaning? Are items grouped by logical category or by the task that would employ them? Do groupings tend to cluster around a common action or object?

If users have arranged the icons spatially, observe where they put each group. Most people tend to put abstract and general categories higher than more concrete and specific ones. If a time sequence is involved, earlier items come to the left of later ones, at least in a left-to-right reading culture.

USABILITY TESTS

In usability testing, we install the icons in a prototype of the user interface and test whether users can do meaningful work with the system. Usability testing emphasizes the smooth integration of icons with other aspects of user-interface design.

Usability testing is the best indicator of the overall performance of the user interface. Usability testing evaluates icons the way they will actually be used. It integrates them with other aspects of the user interface and lets us observe their interaction with other components.

Usability testing requires: a user, a task, and a prototype of the product. Earlier in this section we saw how to simulate the user and the task. How do we simulate the product when the product is not finished?

You can simulate the product at any stage of its development. If you cannot concoct a working prototype on the computer, you can still simulate the product manually. Sketch displays on a deck of index cards. Have the user-interface designer simulate the role of the computer. The designer can describe displays and controls, simulate sound effects, and mimic the computer's responses to various inputs from the user. Even this type of low-fidelity simulation can yield useful results—while there is still time to take advantage of them:

In usability testing, measure performance of tasks and activities influenced by the quality of the icons:

- Speed with which selections are made
- Accuracy of selection
- Time required to reach proficiency
- Complexity of tasks performed

ANALYZING RESULTS

We test to inspire better design. Test results should suggest ways of making icons work better. We must pay special attention to how users react to our designs. It is more important to observe what users do than to ask what they like. For each icon that fails to communicate clearly, we must analyze the failure and prescribe a remedy. The form "Analyzing results" in Chapter 14 provides a format for analyzing results of testing and suggesting improvements to the icon.

EDITING ICONS

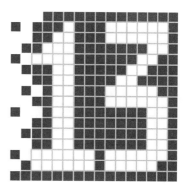

A good icon is a useful icon, enhancing the usability of the interface for which it is designed. As explained in Chapter 2, people do four things with icons:

- Decode them during the first time they encounter them
- Recognize ones they have seen and learned before
- Find them in a visual display
- Activate them

Designing an icon that performs all these tasks well requires great creativity. In refining icons, though, we must temper creativity with judgment.

This chapter will help you to take a second look at your designs, to identify potential problems, and to find alternatives.

CHECKLIST FOR GOOD ICONS

A checklist is just that: a list of characteristics to verify. It will guard against obvious goofs and blind spots, ensuring you have not forgotten any conventional design guidelines. However, it cannot ensure quality and success. Only a clear focus, persistent testing, and skillful refinement can do that.

So what are the characteristics of a good icon?

Understandable

If the user must look up the meaning of an icon in a manual, the icon offers little advantage over a clearly worded label. To ensure users readily associate the correct meaning with each icon, we must ask ourselves:

- Does the image spontaneously suggest the intended concept to the viewer?

- Will it appear with an understandable label?

- Is the association between the image and the concept it represents consistently strong for different users?

- Is the meaning based on a direct association such as physical similarity? On a strong analogy? On a universally learned association?

Unambiguous

A good icon suggests the same concept to all viewers under all circumstances; therefore, an image should implicate only one idea in the minds of users. To that end, ask:

- Is the image associated with just one concept?

- Is that concept associated with only one image?

- Are additional cues (label, other icons, documentation) available to resolve any ambiguity?

Informative

A good icon can convey more than the identity of the thing it represents. It can answer other important questions, such as:

- Why is the concept important?

- How does this icon fit with related icons? What category does it belong to?

- How important is this icon relative to others?

- How does the user interact with the icon?

- What will selecting the icon accomplish for the user?

- After selecting the icon, what procedure does the user follow?

Remember, though, to balance the need for additional information against potential complexity.

CASE STUDY: ILLUSTRATION SOFTWARE

Icons for a technical drawing program can do more than identify commands. They can also show how to use the command:

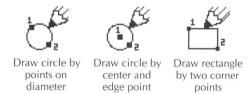

Draw circle by points on diameter

Draw circle by center and edge point

Draw rectangle by two corner points

Such icons show:

- Shape created by the command

- Type of inputs (position, text, numbers) required

- Number of the inputs

- Order of the inputs

Distinct

Often we use icons to represent several similar concepts or to let users select among alternatives. We must make such icons distinct from one another.

Doing so clearly distinguishes one choice from others and keeps them from getting jumbled or blurred in memory.

To ensure that icons are appropriately distinct, ask:

- Is every icon distinct from all others?

- Does the icon make clear how it differs from all others it might be confused with?

- Among sets of alternatives, are the distinguishing characteristics clear?

Notice how these alternatives for justifying lines of text exaggerate the raggedness of line endings to clearly distinguish the different alternatives:

Left   Right   Center   Full

Memorable

We remember some icons better than others. If users must learn the meaning of an icon and recall it later, you must design a memorable image for the icon. Characteristics that make and icon more memorable include:

- Concreteness, rather than abstraction

- Emphasis or exaggeration

- Unusualness or even bizarreness

- Vividness

- Activity or interactivity

- Repetition, especially if the repeated image is in a different form

- Organization, grouping and labeling by the characteristic to be recalled

This leads us to ask of each icon:

- Where possible, does it feature concrete objects in action? Are actions shown as operations on concrete objects?

- Is the image striking and vivid?

- Have you used it consistently throughout the interface, documentation, and training?

- Is the icon clearly identified by a label?

- Is its place in the scheme of the interface clear?

Coherent

All elements in a coherent icon work together to clearly communicate a single concept. A coherent icon is more than the sum of its visual components. For coherent icons, ask:

- Is it clear where one icon ends and another begins?

- Is the icon a unified visual image, rather than a collage of points, lines, and other visual objects?

- Does the design focus and hold attention on the subject matter of the icon?

- Are secondary design elements clearly subdued relative to primary subject matter?

- Do borders serve to unify objects contained within?

Familiar

To reduce the effort of learning an icon, pick images the user has already learned. Such images are recognized more quickly and let users apply their knowledge about the objects shown in the icon. For example, in a program for petroleum geologists, the concept of storage was shown by oil drums rather than disk drive cylinders, and data transfer was indicated by a pump.

In checking the familiarity of images, ask these questions:

- Are the objects in the icon ones familiar to the user?

- Are the objects common in the user's work or home environment?

- Can users apply what they know about the real-world object to its use in the icon?

Legible

In text, legibility refers to our ability to correctly identify the letters and punctuation marks on the page. In icons legibility refers to our ability to recognize the objects depicted in the icon. If we cannot recognize the objects drawn in an icon or we misidentify them, we are unlikely to guess the intended meaning of the icon. To ensure legibility ask:

- Is the icon always displayed with sufficient foreground-background contrast?

- Does it use sufficiently thick lines and shapes?

- Is the icon legible under actual viewing conditions of less than perfect monitors, poorly adjusted monitors, screen glare, and so forth?

- Are icons legible at real viewing distances? Can a user prop his feet up on his desk, plop the keyboard in his lap, lean back and still make out icons on the screen?

- Can users with common visual defects, such as myopia, astigmatism, presbyopia, and color blindness still recognize the icon?

- Have you tested all combinations of color and sizes in which the icon will be displayed?

CASE STUDY: TISSUE BOX

On many systems the icon for a printer has been misinterpreted as a box of facial tissue. It is too similar in appearance to a more familiar object. When this occurs, we must emphasize distinctive characteristics:

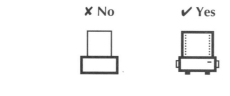

Few

With ample study and sustained practice, a user can learn an almost unlimited number of icons. However, when an icon must be learned quickly or when the system is used infrequently, we should reduce the number of icons. To do this ask:

- Is the number of arbitrary symbols less than 20?

- If large numbers of icons are used, are they built from a small number of familiar images?

- Are all icons explained in readily available online or paper documentation?

- Are all these icons necessary? Are they really the best way to meet the need?

Compact

Good icons do not waste space. They do not cover up other valuable information. Ask:

- Is every object, every line, every pixel in the icon necessary?

- Is the border necessary? Or could its space be put to better use?

- Are icons really more compact than equally effective word labels?

Attractive

We cannot prescribe beauty. Nor do we want to make aesthetics the sole or primary concern in designing icons. We can, however, suggest some common-sense guidelines for avoiding unattractive images:

- Does the image use smooth edges and lines?

- Are the parts visually balanced and stable?

- Is the image proportioned to fit available space?

- Does the image use harmonious colors, patterns, and values?

Extensible

Good designs can serve multiple purposes. They are extensible. That is, the basic design of the icon can be extended for use in different forms and for different purposes. To determine whether your icons are extensible, ask these questions about your basic design:

- Can I draw the image smaller? Will users still recognize it?

- Does the image work in black and white as well as in color?

- Can the image serve as an element in an iconic language?

- Can I redesign the image as a border to surround other objects?

- Can the image serve as an emblem, trademark, or decorative element on boxes, in manuals, and in brochures?

PROBLEM OBJECTS

There are objects that are more difficult to use in icons than others. Some of these objects we should forego, and others we should use only in limited and restricted ways. For each of these problem objects, we must consider whether we can substitute some other object. In any case we must take care how we draw them.

Letters and arbitrary shapes

When we encounter an icon, we try to recognize its image in our visual memories. If the icon resembles a familiar image in memory, we recognize the icon as that image. This process can lead to problems when objects in an icon inadvertently resemble very familiar symbols like letters and numbers:

Such shapes are especially difficult because we have so many associations for each of them. For instance, a crescent shape could be the letter C, a third-rate grade in school, a musical note, the Roman numeral for one hundred, the moon, a symbol for monthly activity, an object in astronomy, or an emblem for Islam.

Animals

Unless the icon actually refers to an animal, as it might in an online catalog for a zoo, you should avoid animals as symbols. Animals make poor symbols for two reasons: The symbolic associations of an animal vary from culture to culture and the emotional associations of animals vary from person to person.

The symbolic meaning of an animal depends on the culture, social class, and religion of the viewer. Chapter 10 details some of the problems of using animals in icons for international products.

Animals arouse differing emotional associations in viewers. A cat fancier is likely to feel affection toward the image of a kitten, whereas an asthma sufferer may just see it as a noxious allergen. A fish will have different associations for a fisherman, fishmonger, cook, and dietitian.

Hand gestures

Do not use hand gestures at all. Just about every configuration of the human hand has a rude or obscene meaning somewhere in this world. For example, the thumbs-up gesture, which means OK in America, has an obscene meaning in Mediterranean countries.

Although you want to avoid hand gestures, you need not totally avoid showing hands. If you are showing hands, follow the simple guidelines found in Chapter 10.

Humorous icons

One of the most controversial and emotional issues among icon designers is the use of humor. Everyone claims to like a good joke, but few agree on what makes a good joke and fewer still can craft that good joke. A light, somewhat whimsical touch in designing icons can help users overcome the tendency to interpret icons literally rather than symbolically. It can also make decoding icons enjoyable—more like playing a game than deciphering an alien script.

However, in my experience, nine out of ten attempts at humorous icons fail, sometimes causing considerable embarrassment to the vendor of the product. Before you use humor in your icons, ask yourself:

- **Is a humorous tone appropriate for your product?** A game for children demands a tone different from one for helping aging adults prepare their last will and testament.

- **Will *all* users get the joke?** Just because your buddy in the next office laughed, do not assume everyone will.

- **Have you tested the humor?** Test with a spectrum of users of different cultures, nationalities, religions, and political philosophies Did they all get the joke? Was no one offended or confused?

- **Have you used humor consistently?** If one icon is funny, all should be.

- **Are you sure the joke will not grow tiresome?** Ideas that seem fresh and clever the first time may grow stale the 27th time and become positively obnoxious the 356th time we experience them.

- **Does the humor improve the product?** Or are you just indulging your need for self-expression?

Emotional associations

Except when emotion is the subject of the icon, avoid symbols with strong emotional associations. If users react emotionally to an icon, they will probably misinterpret its meaning. Avoid:

- Religious figures or symbols

- Political emblems or signs

- Objects of strong emotional attachment like infants or pets

- Symbols of social status or political power

Faces

Human faces are the most recognizable, most expressive, and most powerful images we experience. Our visual cortex even gives special priority to images of human faces. For these reasons, faces might seem ideal for use in small icons. In fact, for these very reasons, they are quite difficult to use in icons:

- Faces convey emotion and attitude. The viewer may react emotionally and miss the intended meaning entirely.

- Realistic images of faces depict a person of a particular age, race, and gender. The type of person shown in the icon may not fit the intended role in the viewer's culture. The viewer may fail to identify with the person shown.

- Faces may draw too much attention to themselves. If an icon contains a face, we look at the face first and assume it is the subject of the icon.

Just as some UNIX programmers have immortalized themselves by using their initials for the names of commands, some graphical user interface designers have had their faces enshrined as icons. I recommend you avoid this practice for several reasons:

- Your users probably don't know you or care what you look like.

- You may not look as good as you think, especially in just a few pixels.

- Your icons would violate cultural taboos in certain Islamic countries.

- This practice labels you as insecure, egotistical, and arrogant.

For some concepts, however, there is no substitute for showing a human face, typically when we need to represent the user or some other human being or to show an emotion:

| User | Find biography | Happy | Sad |

When you do use faces in icons, take care to prevent problems common with realistic images of faces:

- **Show multiple faces**. If using color, you can vary the skin color to represent multiple races:

- **Simplify the face** to downplay individual characteristics and to generalize the reference. Avoid showing a distinctive hair style, facial hair, eye shape or color, skin color, lip size or shape:

- **Subordinate the face** by moving it off center and showing it doing something:

Seeing   Speaking   Searching

REFINING ICONS

When I ask experienced, successful icon designers what three pieces of advice they have for those just getting started in icon design, I always seem to get the same three answers. The order may vary. The phrasing may be different. But the advice is always the same:

- Make your icons consistent.
- Simplify your designs.
- Make icons that work in black and white.

The first two of these pieces of advice are elaborated in this chapter. The last one is covered in Chapter 7 on color.

Consistency

Everyone seems to agree that consistency is better than inconsistency. Not many would prefer a set of icons that look like this ...

...to ones that look like this:

But what is it that we make consistent? Consistency is of no value in itself, especially if we make irrelevant or distracting items consistent at the expense of crucial or meaningful details. The purpose of consistency is to make icons predictable. In this purpose, some kinds of consistency are more important than others.

Notice how consistency aids in uniting these icons for various types of data:

ALPH AN UMERICD ATALET TERS AN D123 45	A3 1FB2 49 EC8 D 00F1AD 45D70 A 0F0BCFF	1011001000I 01011001010 II0I0III0II0I 0II000II0I0 00III0II00II	▲●I◆■ ▶◆▼◢◆ ◆■●Г▲ ◢▶◆■◆ ●▼◢◆◢
Alphanumeric data	Hexadecimal data	Binary data	Graphical data

The symmetry and similarity among these icons lets the user concentrate on what is different among them:

Combine   Merge   Ungroup

Here the subtle differences among various types of lists stand out clearly because of the consistent way the lists are depicted:

Bullet list   Checklist   Glossary   Numbered list   Outline

Consistency becomes even more important with large numbers of symbols. Notice how the consistent drawing style and size helps us decode these icons for drawing tools:

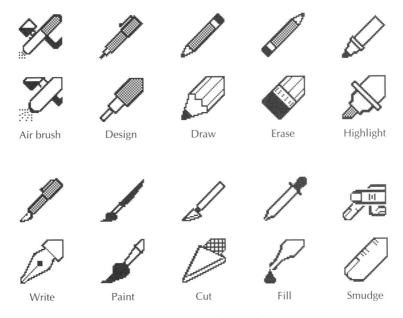

Air brush   Design   Draw   Erase   Highlight

Write   Paint   Cut   Fill   Smudge

We should design the icons of a series by combining similar elements in the same way, and we should draw these icons in the same style. Consistent use of the same symbols in a series of icons reduces the time required for users to learn the icons. It also reduces the effort required to design and perfect the icons. Consistency is reinforced by repeated design elements such as color, patterns, textures, and line styles and widths.

Simplicity

When asked for her advice on designing icons, one experienced designer said, "Practice the KISS principle with a vengeance. You know, Keep It Simple, Stupid." Another said she had three pieces of advice for all designers: "Simplify, simplify, simplify." The arguments for simplicity are strong:

- **Simpler icons are recognized more reliably**. They provide fewer distractions and potentially misleading details.

- **Complex icons can look formidable**, making the system seem difficult to learn and inefficient to use.

- **Simpler images are read quicker**. Complex icons waste the user's time.

- **Simpler icons can be made smaller** and require fewer colors.

- **Complex icons may require so much study** that users give up before decoding their meaning or may attend to the wrong details.

- **Complex icons may provide too specific a reference**. The user may interpret the icon as a particular, concrete object rather than the intended general, abstract category.

So how do we make icons simpler? Let's consider some techniques.

Filter

We can simplify an icon by reducing the number of objects and graphical elements used to represent each concept. Filtering is the process by which we decide what to put in and what to leave out. For example:

Include or emphasize	Exclude or downplay
Essential concepts, facts, and objects	Anomalies and exceptions
	Irrelevant objects and concepts
Details necessary to make objects recognizable	Distracting details, backgrounds, and reference marks
	Nice-to-know information
	Purely decorative or merely clever details

Include only those objects necessary to make your point. Do not show five objects if three are sufficient. Question every shape, every line, every dot. If in doubt, leave it out:

Intended meaning	Unnecessary detail	Adequate detail
Home		
Bar chart		
Printout		
Hot		

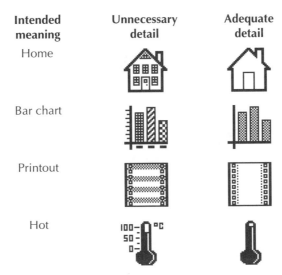

One way to enforce simplicity is to ration "ink." Imagine that every pixel costs $500. How many can you justify?

Generalize

Icons are not pictures. They need not be pictorially accurate. Icons usually fail when they include too much detail. Unnecessary details distract viewers and suggest that the icon refers to a particular object rather than to a class of objects.

For example, if your computer program runs on several different models of computer, you might show enough detail to suggest a computer but not enough to designate a particular model or brand:

✘ No   **✔ Yes**

To generalize, omit unnecessary details. Include only features needed to distinguish the icon from related ones. Omit details found in just one model, one version, or one variation. Omit distinctions unimportant to the user:

Safe   Report   Newspaper   Printer   Computer

Abstract

The best icons abstract the essence of an idea and express it in simple visual forms. One way to keep visual forms simple is to compose the image entirely from simple geometric elements. Limit yourself to just vertical and horizontal lines, 45-degree diagonals, and circular arcs:

| Attach | File server | Fax | Sound | Manual |

Or use only rectangles, right triangles, and circles:

| Exercise | Hot | Diskette | Erase | Library |

Categorize

Representing too many types, kinds, or categories of objects leads to complexity. Show symbols of abstract categories instead of specific instances. Rather than show many separate objects, group the objects into categories and represent all members of a category with an abstract shape, line, or pattern:

| Layers | Checklist | Group | Filter | Combine |

Stereotype

Draw things the way people think they look. When we try to recognize an image, we search our visual memories for a match. The closer the image matches the memory, the quicker and surer the match. Images that match our memories require fewer details to be recognized.

People's memories, however, may not reflect how an object actually looks. Thus we must learn how users remember an object (their visual stereotype of it) and then make our images match that memory:

| House | Marriage | Projector | Family | Alarm clock |

Some cautions are in order. First, beware of negative stereotypes when showing people. Catering to bias and prejudice seldom results in a more recognizable icon anyway. Second, remember that stereotypes vary from culture to culture. The way an object is traditionally shown in one culture may baffle or offend someone from another culture.

Abbreviate

Eliminate needless duplication and repetition. When representing a series of similar or related items, you seldom need to show all of them. Employ the *etc. principle,* showing just a few typical members, and users will complete the series. Three or four typical members are usually enough to represent a coherent group:

| Users | Library | Currency | Keyboard | Tools |

FOR MORE INFORMATION

Bailey, Robert W. *Human Performance Engineering: Using Human Factors/Ergonomics to Achieve Computer System Usability.* Englewood Cliffs, NJ: Prentice Hall, 1989.

Mayhew, Deborah. *Principles and Guidelines in Software User Interface Design.* Englewood Cliffs, NJ: Prentice Hall, 1992.

Harrison, M. D. and A. F. Monk, ed. *People and Computers: Designing for Usability.* Cambridge, England: Cambridge University Press, 1986.

Dumas, Joseph S. *Designing User Interfaces for Software.* Englewood Cliffs, NJ: Prentice-Hall, 1988.

Heckel, Paul. *The Elements of Friendly Software Design.* New York: Warner Books, 1984.

FORMS, FORMULAS, AND CHECKLISTS

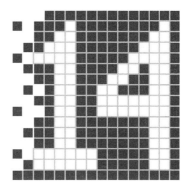

This chapter provides tools to guide the development of icons. Here you will find checklists and forms for gathering information and evaluating designs. You will also find aids for some common calculations you may need to make.

FORMS

Filling in forms is seldom fun, but on a large, complex project, it may be necessary. A form ensures that pertinent questions are asked and answered. It serves as a checklist to make sure designers consider alternatives. A form records information explicitly so that everyone on the design team makes the same assumptions. The following forms are ones I have found helpful on large projects. Chapter 11 shows where each of them fits in the development process.

Users

Date:	Page _____ of _____		William Horton Consulting
Client:			
Project:			PO Box 4585 Boulder, CO 80306-4585 1-800/398-2963

USERS

Name		ID	**Size** (number of users or % of total user base)
Job role	**Experience**	**Training**	
Physical characteristics (age, eyesight, limitations)	**Language skills**	**Cultural values**	
Work conditions Space Lighting Noise and interruptions	**Work environment** Hardware Software Documentation and other tools	**Work style** Individual vs collaborative Batch vs interactive tasks Frequency of use	
Value of time (Cost of 1 second of this user's time, including overhead, vacation, and so forth)	**Notes**		

Tasks

Date: _____

Page _____ of _____

Client: _____

Project: _____

William
Horton
Consulting

PO Box 4585
Boulder, CO
80306-4585
1-800/398-2963

TASKS

Task	ID #
Users who perform this task	**Is this part of a larger procedure? If so, its ID #**
Why do this task?	**When to do it?**
Steps in the procedure (actions and decisions)	**Resources required** Hardware Software Data
Results	**Related procedures**

Common problems

Problem	Likelihood	Cost to identify and correct

User-task matrix

Date:	Page _____ of _____
Client:	
Project:	

William
Horton
Consulting

PO Box 4585
Boulder, CO
80306-4585
1-800/398-2963

USER-TASK MATRIX

Tasks

Users

Basic iconic components

Date:	Page _____ of _____	William Horton Consulting
Client:		
Project:		

PO Box 4585
Boulder, CO
80306-4585
1-800/398-2963

BASIC ICONIC COMPONENTS

Actions	Objects	Qualifiers

Limiters	States of being	Relationships	Others

Brainstorming

Date:	Page _____ of _____
Client:	
Project:	

William
Horton
Consulting

PO Box 4585
Boulder, CO
80306-4585
1-800/398-2963

BRAINSTORMING

Component category	Description	
Component	**Description**	**Sketches**

Icon sketches

Date:

Page _____ of _____

Client:

Project:

William
Horton
Consulting

PO Box 4585
Boulder, CO
80306-4585
1-800/398-2963

Icon sketches

Name	Description	Icon

Stylesheet for icons

Date:	Page 1 of 5	William Horton Consulting
Client:		
Project:		

PO Box 4585
Boulder, CO
80306-4585
1-800/398-2963

STYLESHEET FOR ICONS

IDENTIFICATION

Name of this class of icons

Where they appear	How the user interacts	What they represent
☐ On desktop	☐ Clicks on	☐ Data
☐ On tool palette	☐ Points to and holds mouse button down	☐ Program
☐ In menu bar		☐ Status or value
☐ In pull-down menu	☐ Double clicks on	☐ Cursor
☐ _____	☐ Drags	☐ _____
	☐ _____	

OVERALL DESIGN

Size

Image width (pixels)	Image height (pixels)
Border width (pixels)	Border height (pixels)

Shape

☐ Rectangle
☐ Rounded rectangle
☐ Diamond
☐ Circle
☐ _____

Sketch

Colors

Maximum number of colors	☐ Use this color palette or lookup table

Versions needed
Specify a style sheet for each alternative version

Name	Width	Height	Number of colors

STANDARD PARTS

Border ☐ Yes   ☐ No   If answer is "no," go to next section, "Background"

Date:	Page 2 of 5

How used	☐ Uniform for consistency	Shape		
	☐ Varies to represent concept	How?		
	☐ Varies to represent status	Normal	Active	Unavailable

How drawn	☐ Solid	☐ Incised	☐ Embossed	☐ Raised area	☐ Sunken area

Line	Weight (pixels)	Style

Margin	Top	Bottom	Left	Right

Background	☐ Yes ☐ No If answer is "no," go to next section, "Labels"

Contrast	Foreground	Background

How used	☐ Uniform for consistency	Pattern	Color	Other
	☐ Varies to represent concept	How		
	☐ Uniform for consistency	Pattern	Color	Other

Labels	☐ Yes ☐ No If answer is "no," go to next part, "Drawing the image"

When displayed	☐ Never
	☐ Always
	☐ Only if the user has turned on the display of labels
	☐ Only when the cursor points at the icon

Where displayed	☐ Above the image or border
	☐ Below the image or border
	☐ Within the image area
	☐ In a separate message area

Date:	Page 3 of 5

How stored	☐ Automatically by the system ☐ Designed into the icon itself		
Size of label area	Width (characters or pixels)	Height (lines or pixels)	Clearance from image or border (pixels)

	Font	Size	Style ☐ Regular ☐ Bold ☐ Italic ☐ Outline ☐ _____
	Vertical alignment ☐ Top ☐ Center ☐ Bottom	Horizontal alignment ☐ Left ☐ Center ☐ Right	Hyphenation rules

Capitalization
☐ All caps (ALL LETTERS ARE CAPITALIZED)
☐ No caps (no letters are capitalized except proper names)
☐ Sentence (First letter and proper nouns are capitalized as if a sentence)
☐ Title (First, Last, and All Important Words Are Capitalized Like a Title)

Style of writing	Omit ☐ Articles ☐ Prepositions ☐ Conjunctions ☐ _____	Rules for punctuation	Rules for phrasing labels

DRAWING

Level of detail
☐ Photographic realism
☐ Simplified drawing
☐ Caricature
☐ Profile or outline
☐ Silhouette

Image area
If image does not fill image area, put image:

☐ Left	☐ Bottom	☐ Lower right
☐ Center	☐ Upper left	☐ Top center
☐ Right	☐ Upper right	☐ Bottom center
☐ Top	☐ Lower left	☐ _____

Date:	Page **4** of **5**

Image area, continued
If image overflows image area border, show border by:

- ☐ Feathering out image
- ☐ Stopping image at image border
- ☐ Regular line width to show image border
- ☐ One pixel line to show image border
- ☐ Jagged edge
- ☐ _____

Shadows

☐ Yes   ☐ No

Type

- ☐ Drop
- ☐ Attached
- ☐ Cast

Direction of light

In the plane of the screen	Into or out of the screen
___ degrees . . . ☐ clockwise ☐ counterclockwise . . . of vertically downward	___ degrees . . . ☐ toward ☐ away from . . . the screen

Distance of drop shadows

Horizontal	Horizontal
___ pixels to the . . . ☐ left ☐ right	___ pixels . . . ☐ downward ☐ upward

Three-dimensionality

Style	Direction of front face
☐ Flat, two-dimensional ☐ Isometric ☐ True perspective	___ degrees . . . ☐ left ☐ right

Layering

Number of layers	Vertical spacing	Horizontal spacing
	Offset deeper layer ___ pixels . . . ☐ upward ☐ downward	Offset deeper layer ___ pixels to the . . . ☐ left ☐ right

Viewpoint preferred

- ☐ Front
- ☐ Top
- ☐ Side
- ☐ Solid
- ☐ Abstract

Mechanics
Line weight

Primary lines		Secondary lines		Invisible or hidden lines	
Width	Style	Width	Style	Width	Style

Date:	Page **5** of **5**

Restrictions	Angles	Shapes	Separation
	Where possible draw lines only at these angles:	Where possible compose objects of only these shapes:	Minimum separation between objects:
	☐ Horizontal ☐ Vertical ☐ 45-degree diagonal ☐ 30-degree diagonal ☐ _____	☐ Straight line ☐ Square ☐ Rectangle ☐ Circle ☐ _____	

COLOR

	☐ Color	☐ Gray scale	☐ Black and white only

Purpose	☐ To add visual interest and beauty ☐ To make object easier to recognize ☐ To represent categories

Number	Maximum number of colors or levels of gray	Use only this color palette or look up table:
	☐ 8 ☐ 256 ☐ _____ ☐ 16 ☐ Thousands ☐ 32 ☐ Millions	☐

Style	☐ Flat	☐ Shaded

Color codes	Color	Represents

ICONIC LANGUAGE

Parts of speech (and preferred method for representing them)	☐ Action	☐ Object	☐ Qualifier (adverb)	☐ Limiter (adjective)
	☐ Relationship	☐ State of being	☐	☐

How to represent common concepts	Movement	Change	Toggles	Grouping of items
	Selection of one item			

Analyze test results

Date:	Page _____ of _____
Client:	
Project:	

William
Horton
Consulting

PO Box 4585
Boulder, CO
80306-4585
1-800/398-2963

ANALYZE TEST RESULTS

Icon	Intended meaning	How the user interpreted it	Changes needed	New icon

Icon design charter

Date	Page _____ of _____
Client:	
Project:	

William Horton Consulting

PO Box 4585
Boulder, CO
80306-4585
1-800/398-2963

ICON DESIGN CHARTER

REQUEST

	Person	Organization	Date requested
By			
For	Product	Version	Date needed
What	Concept to represent	User	Related icons

Style

☐ Command button
☐ Desktop file
☐ Desktop program
☐ Tool palette
☐ Custom
☐ _____

Hardware

Size: _____ x _____ pixels

☐ Border: _____ pixels

☐ Background _____

DESIGN

Sketch

Notes

Label [_____]

APPROVE

Design completed	Designer	Date created	Date last revised
Sign-offs	Person	Department	Date requested

CALCULATING TRANSLUCENCY

To calculate the color where a translucent object overlaps another object, apply this simple formula:

Overlap = Background x Translucency + Foreground x (1 - Translucency)
color color color

For an example, let's take a square of 60 percent gray that is 40 percent translucent and see what it would look like superimposed over a black (0 percent) and white (100 percent) background.

Over black, the gray level in the overlap is:

Gray = 0.0 x 0.4 + 0.6 x (1.0 - 0.4)
= 0.6 x 0.6
= 0.36

Over white, the gray level in the overlap is:

Gray = 1.0 x 0.4 + 0.6 x (1.0 - 0.4)
= 0.40 + 0.36
= 0.76

Applying the results to the sample yields this image:

The procedure for color is the same in principle: We scale each object's contribution by the degree of translucency of the top object. However, we have to calculate the contribution for each of the components of color. Unfortunately there is no universal way of representing color. The way you specify color affects the results you calculate for the area of overlap. In the RGB system, if you scale the separate red, green, and blue primary colors, you get one result. With the CMYK system you get a somewhat different result by scaling cyan, magenta, yellow, and black. Applying the technique to hue, lightness, and saturation values (HSV) yields yet another result.

Estimating costs

This spreadsheet shows one way to tally the costs of an icon design project. The only thing I guarantee about it is that it is wrong. The variables that affect cost are ... well, variable. The actual values for your particular project are bound to be different. Use this example only as a framework for organizing your own calculation.

Number of icons: 100

Activity	Times performed	Per ...	Time required (hours)	Total time (hours)	Done by	Hourly rate	Cost
Research & plan	1	project	40.0	40	Designer	$40.00	$1,600
Generate ideas	1	icon	0.5	50	Designer	$40.00	$2,000
Sketch ideas	5	icon	0.2	100	Designer	$40.00	$4,000
	5	icon	0.1	50	Designer	$40.00	$2,000
Draw icons	4	icon	0.5	200	Artist	$30.00	$6,000
Test icons	3	icon	0.5	150	Designer	$40.00	$6,000
	3	icon	0.5	150	User	$35.00	$5,250

Total	$26,850
per icon	$268

CHECKLIST FOR EDITING ICONS

This checklist summarizes the points discussed in Chapter 13 on editing icons.

Understandable

- ☐ Does the image spontaneously suggest the intended concept to the viewer?
- ☐ Will it appear with an understandable label?
- ☐ Is the association between the image and the concept it represents consistently strong for different users?
- ☐ Is the meaning based on a direct association such as physical similarity? On a strong analogy? On a universally learned association?

Unambiguous

- ☐ Is the image associated with just one concept?
- ☐ Is that concept associated with only one image?
- ☐ Are additional cues (label, other icons, documentation) available to resolve any ambiguity?

Informative

- ☐ Why is the concept is important?
- ☐ How does this icon fit with related icons? What category does it belong to?
- ☐ How important is this icon relative to others?
- ☐ How does the user interact with the icon?
- ☐ What will selecting the icon accomplish for the user?
- ☐ After selecting the icon, what procedure does the user follow?

Distinct

- ☐ Is every icon distinct from all others?

☐ Does it make clear how it differs from all others it might be confused with?

☐ Among sets of alternatives, are the distinguishing characteristics clear?

Memorable

☐ Where possible, does it feature concrete objects in action? Are actions shown as operations on concrete objects?

☐ Is the image striking and vivid?

☐ Have you used it consistently throughout the interface, documentation, and training?

☐ Is the icon clearly identified by a label?

☐ Is its place in the scheme of the interface clear?

Coherent

☐ Is it clear where one icon ends and another begins?

☐ Is the icon a unified visual image, rather than a collage of points, lines, and other visual objects?

☐ Does the design focus and hold attention on the subject matter of the icon?

☐ Are secondary design elements clearly subdued relative to primary subject matter?

☐ Do borders serve to unify objects contained within?

Familiar

☐ Are the objects in the icon ones familiar to the user?

☐ Are objects common in the user's work or home environment?

☐ Can users apply what they know about the real-world object to its use in the icon?

Legible

☐ Is the icon always displayed with sufficient foreground-background contrast?

□ Does it use sufficiently thick lines and shapes?

□ Is the icon legible under actual viewing conditions of less than perfect monitors, poorly adjusted monitors, screen glare, and so forth?

□ Are icons legible at real reading distances. Can a user prop his feet up on his desk, plop the keyboard in his lap, lean back and still make out icons on the screen?

□ Can users with common visual defects, such as myopia, astigmatism, presbyopia, and color blindness still recognize the icon?

□ Have you tested all combinations of color and sizes in which the icon will be displayed?

Few

□ Is the number of arbitrary symbols less than 20?

□ If large numbers of icons are used, are they built from a small number of familiar images?

□ Are all icons explained in readily available online or paper documentation?

□ Are all these icons necessary? Are they really the best way to meet the need?

Compact

□ Is every object, every line, every pixel in the icon necessary?

□ Is the border necessary? Or could its space be put to better use?

□ Are icons really more compact than equally effective word labels?

Attractive

□ Does the image use smooth edges and line?

□ Are the parts visually balanced and stable?

□ Is the image proportioned to fit available space?

□ Does the image use harmonious colors, patterns, and values?

Extensible

☐ Can I draw the image smaller? Will users still recognize it?

☐ Does the image work in black and white as well as in color?

☐ Can the image serve as an element in an iconic language?

☐ Can I redesign the image as a border to surround other objects?

☐ Can the image serve as an emblem, trademark, or decorative element on boxes, in manuals, and in brochures?

CASE STUDY IN ICON DESIGN

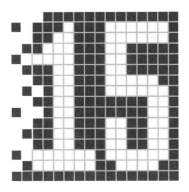

This is a journal chronicling the issues, ideas, and decisions on one project—*The Writer's Pocket Almanack Version 2.0.* Use it as an example to illustrate the icon design process. It employs much of what we've discussed in this book and applies it to a real-world project. Except for reformatting and cleaning up typos, it is pretty much as originally recorded.

ABOUT THE WRITER'S POCKET ALMANACK

The Writer's Pocket Almanack started as a paperback book by John Brockmann and me. It contained quotations, witticisms, good and bad advice, and illustrations on the business of writing and on writing in business. With help from Kevin Brock, we produced an online version using Apple's HyperCard. In addition to the "Quotations" stack, or database, this online version contained other stacks:

Broken Quill	Examples of bad business writing
Calendar	An on-screen calendar that displays a different quotation each day
Great Moments	Historical events in the development of communication
Mal Mots	Bad advice on writing, offered facetiously
Veni Vidi Scripsi	Latin sayings on the art and craft of writing
Pocket Stack Home	The home base for navigating through these stacks, to be renamed Almanack Home
Game	A question-answer game.

The original interface for the "Quotations" stack looked like this:

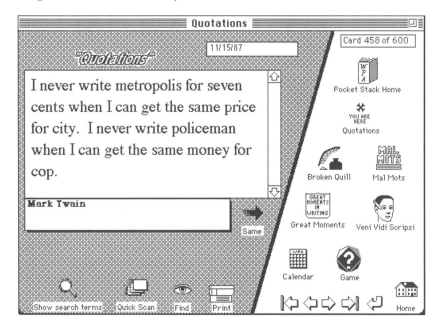

Although users said it was fun, experience showed that it needed an overhaul. This is the overhaul:

The new interface has a clean, uncluttered look. In addition to the original set of features, we added several new functions—in a way that does not overpower the user. We especially wanted to provide ways to accommodate users with varying levels of experience and motivation.

To accomplish our aims we placed commands on the menu bar, on pop-up menus throughout the main window, and on a floating pallet (the "remote control").

Pull-down menus

Most commands for navigating from quotation to quotation and performing other functions are available from pull-down menus:

Here's how they appear:

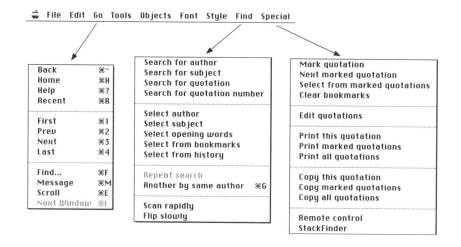

Pop-up menus

Many of these same commands are available from pop-up menus within the quotation window itself. To select one of these commands, the user points to the appropriate object in the display and holds down the mouse button. A list of applicable commands appears. The user then moves the pointer over the desired command and lets up on the mouse button:

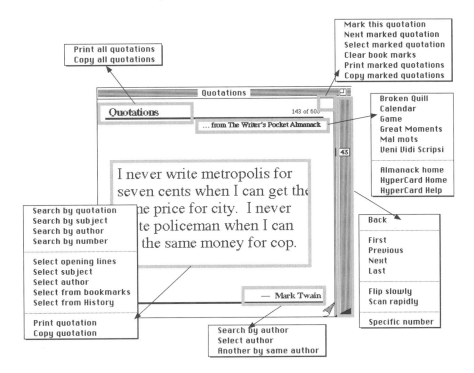

Buttons

In addition to the pop-up menus, the user can activate other functions by pointing to an area in the display and tapping the mouse button or by dragging a floating button:

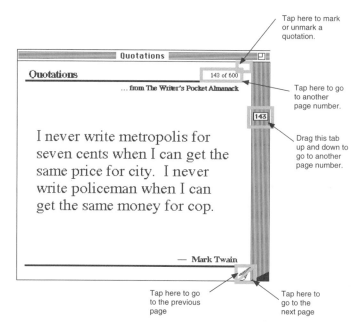

Tap here to mark or unmark a quotation.

Tap here to go to another page number.

Drag this tab up and down to go to another page number.

Tap here to go to the previous page

Tap here to go to the next page

Remote control

For frequent users, we plan to add a floating palette of buttons for immediate access to the most frequently used commands. Because the palette will probably be no larger than one of the pop-up menus, the button labels must be small. Icons should be effective for this purpose.

ANALYZE AND PLAN

We must design icons as needed by the revision of *The Writer's Pocket Almanack* (WPA) HyperCard stack. This stack is has been revised to improve the user interface and to serve as a prototype for similar interfaces for large online catalogs. In particular, we must design icons for the "remote control" palette.

Constraints

Before diving into the project, we must understand the constraints and limitations we face. Following are some of the constraints on this project:

- HyperCard does not provide color displays. This means that all icons must be black and white only.

- This is a prototype, so there is relatively little time to perfect a solution.

- The icons for commands must fit on small buttons on a floating palette.

- To keep the files small, we want to restrict the design to only those capabilities provided by HyperCard. We have added one external command to display pop-up menus, but that is all.

- We have limited staff and time to work on this project.

- We do not have the budget to hire a professional graphic designer.

Users and context

Because the meaning of an icon depends on both the user who views it and the context in which it appears, we must consider both these factors before proceeding.

We have key assumptions about our users:

- They are avid readers. Many are writers by profession.

- They are familiar with the Macintosh graphical user interface and possibly with HyperCard itself.

- Some are casual, infrequent users. Others are fervent browsers. The navigation palette meets the needs of the fervent browsers.

We realize these are some of the contextual issues:

- All commands will be available from pull-down menus and pop-up menus. This means that we can take more risks in the design of the icons.

- HyperCard applications have a typical style that may shape people's expectations.

- Casual use may demand an interesting visual design.

We used several forms to gather and analyze this information. Samples of these forms can be found in Chapter 14.

Functions

First, I list all the functions for which we may need icons. We don't worry too much whether our terms match the current command names. The current command names will evolve.

Writing the commands in a consistent grammatical form (action-object) and arranging the list alphabetically makes some common actions and objects stand out:

Bookmark this quotation

Copy all quotations

Copy bookmarked quotations

Copy this quotation

Edit this quotation

Flip through the quotations rapidly

Flip through the quotations slowly

Go back one step

Go to another quotation by the current
   author

Go to the first quotation

Go to the Help stack

Go to the HyperCard Home stack

Go to the last quotation

Go to the next bookmarked quotation

Go to the next quotation

Go to the previous quotation

Go to the stack Broken Quill

Go to the stack Calendar

Go to the stack Great Moments

Go to the stack Mal Mots

Go to the stack Veni Vidi Scripsi

Print all quotations

Print bookmarked quotations

Print this quotation

Remove all bookmarks

Repeat the previous search

Search for a quotation

Search for a quotation by number

Search for a subject

Search for an author

Select from a list of authors

Select from a list of bookmarked
   quotations

Select from a list of opening words

Select from a list of recently viewed
   quotations

Select from a list of subjects

Select from pictures of recent quotations

Difference between "search for" and "select from"

One distinction may not be clear: the difference between *searching for* an item and *selecting from* a list. To *search* for an item, the user names it in a dialog box. To *select* an item, the user picks it from a list of available items.

The user can employ either technique to locate quotations by words, subject, and author.

DESIGN THE ICONIC LANGUAGE

Rather than design icons for individual commands, I will analyze the commands and establish a consistent iconic language.

Analyzing the commands

All of the functions are combinations of five different kinds of information:

Action	Describes what the system does.
Object	Specifies what receives the action.
Qualifier	Tells how the action is performed.
Limiter	Specifies which objects are involved? This either broadens or narrows the recipients of the action.
Identifier	Identifies a specific, named object.

From our list of functions we identify these basic components and list them on a form similar to this one:

Actions	Objects	Qualifiers	Limiters	Identifier
bookmark	quotation	rapidly	this one	Help
copy	step	slowly	all	Home
display	author	from list	bookmarked	Broken Quill
edit	stack	from pictures	first	Calendar
flip through	bookmark		last	Great Moments
go back	search		next	Mal Mots
go to	number		previous	Veni Vidi Scripsi
print	subject		recently	
remove	opening words		viewed	
repeat				
search for				
select				

This form is similar to the one named "Basic iconic components" in Chapter 14.

Brainstorming

Having listed by category all the actions, objects, qualifiers, limiters, and identifiers—including their meaning—now we are ready to brainstorm.

Sketching with wide lines to better simulate the coarse pixels of the computer screen, we try to come up with at least five rough ideas for each concept. The goal is to generate lots of ideas so we can throw away the bad ones. These sketches are consolidated on a form similar to "Brainstorming" in Chapter 14.

Actions

Actions are the operations the commands perform. Grammatically they are the active verbs of the system:

Label (tentative)	Description	Sketches (at least 5 different ideas)
Bookmark	Flags an item the reader may want to find later	
Copy	Copies an item onto the clipboard or into a file	
Edit	Displays the quotation in a way that lets the user modify it	

Display	Displays the quotation formatted for easy reading	
Flip through	Shows one quotation, then another, and another	
Go back	Returns to the previous quotation or other card.	
Go to	Moves to a specific quotation	
Print	Prints out a quotation	
Remove	Clears or eliminates something (a bookmark in this case)	

Repeat	Performs the preceding operation (a search) again	
Search for	Lets the user enter text for which to search	
Select	Lets the user select from a list of available items	

Objects

Objects are the things acted upon. They are nouns and serve as the direct object of the sentence:

Label (tentative)	**Description**	**Sketches** (at least 5 different ideas)
Quotation	A saying	

Step	One jump or go-to operation	
Author	The person who spoke or wrote the words of the quotation	
Stack	An entire collection of quotations or other data	
Bookmark (noun)	A flag marking a quotation as one of special interest to the user	
Search	Operation of locating a quotation that contains certain text	
Number	A unique number assigned to a quotation, like a page number	
Subject	What the quotation is about, like indexed terms in a book	

Opening words	The first words of a quotation	

Qualifiers

Qualifiers focus or constrain the action. They say where, when, how, or to what degree the action is performed. They are adverbs:

Label (tentative)	**Description**	**Sketches** (at least 5 different ideas)
Rapidly	At a pace too fast for comfortable reading	
Slowly	At a pace that gives the user time to read the entire quotation	
From list	By pointing to one item in a scrolling list	
From pictures	By pointing to one item in an array of small visual images	

Limiters

Limiters constrain the scope of objects. They tell us exactly which objects are acted upon. They sharpen the destination of the action. Grammatically, they are adjectives.

Label (tentative)	Description	Sketches (at least 5 different ideas)
This one	The currently displayed item	
All	Every quotation in the stack	
Book-marked	Those that have been flagged by the user as of special interest	
First	The beginning item in a sequence	
Last	The final item in a sequence	

Next	The item after the current one in a sequence	
Previous	The item before the current one in a sequence	
Recently viewed	Those the user has looked at during the current session	

Identifiers

Icons are needed to show other stacks of information and destinations outside the Quotations stack:

Label (tentative)	Description	Sketches (at least 5 different ideas)
Home	The HyperCard Home stack	
Almanack home	The home base for navigating through these stacks	

Help	The HyperCard Help stack	
Broken quill	Examples of bad business writing	
Calendar	A calendar that shows a different quotation each day	
Great moments	Historic events in com– munication	
Mal mots	Bad advice on writing, offered facetiously	
Veni vidi scripsi	Latin sayings on the art and craft of writing	

I find a form like this helpful because it puts all the information into one document. It prompts for all the icons at once, and it makes me aware of conflicts in style and symbology early in the project.

Developing the grammar

From our brainstorming we have decided on the icon to represent each component, determining both its size and style. We now must decide the rules for combining these iconic components—the grammar. Here are the rules we have developed:

- Movement in sequence is shown by the standard VCR controls:

  These controls are also incorporated into other icons to represent movement in sequence:

- Searching for matching text is shown by a magnifying glass:

- Picking from a list of available item is shown by a checkmark beside a line of the available items:

- Simple symbols are used to represent common concepts:

Concept	Symbol	Examples
Quotation	Speech balloon	
Subject	Thought balloon	

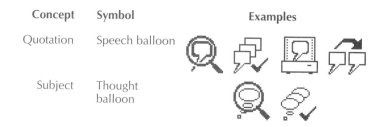

Concept	**Symbol**	**Examples**
Author	Profile of a face	
Bookmark	Dog-eared page	

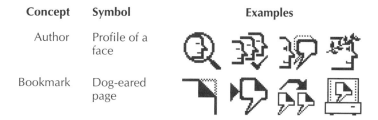

- Contained symbols tend to limit the scope of the outer symbol:

- Printing is indicated by a page coming out of the printer. The page contains a small image indicating what is printed:

- Copying is shown by an arched arrow connecting images of what is duplicated:

- Sequence is indicated by shading earlier items and by drawing current or future items solid:

- Commands that change the state or characteristics of an item are indicated by an icon showing the future state:

Some such commands include both a before and after image. The before image is shaded and the after is drawn solid:

- The emblem for *The Writer's Pocket Almanack* itself is the pen nib:

- Where a well-established symbol existed for a concept, it was used. These are traffic signs and established Macintosh icons:

Once users learn or infer the principle of this language, they will understand new icons with little effort.

DRAFT THE ICONS

Our goal at this point is not to design the final version but to produce a testable prototype. We enter these in a form like "Icon sketches" in Chapter 14:

Command	What it does	Icon	Command	What it does	Icon
Bookmark this quotation	Marks a quotation so you can find, copy, or print it later		Copy book-marked quotations	Puts the text of marked quotations onto the clipboard	
Copy all quotations	Creates a file containing the text of all quotations		Copy this quotation	Puts the text of the current quotation onto the clipboard	
Display this quotation	Arranges the display for viewing quotations.		Edit this quotation	Rearranges the display so you can edit quotations	
Flip through the quotations rapidly	Displays quotations in sequence, about 1 second each		Flip through the quotations slowly	Displays quotations timed to allow comfortable reading	
Go back one step	Returns to the previously viewed quotation		Go to another quotation by the current author	Displays the next quotation by the author of the currently displayed topic	
Go to another stack	Displays the icons for other stacks of *The Writer's Pocket Almanack*		Go to the first quotation	Displays the first quotation in sequence	

Command	What it does	Icon	Command	What it does	Icon
Go to the Help stack	Displays the Help stack for HyperCard		Go to the HyperCard Home stack	Displays the Home stack for HyperCard	
Go to the last quotation	Displays the last quotation in sequence		Go to the next book-marked quotation	Displays the next topic in sequence that has been bookmarked	
Go to the next quotation	Displays the next quotation in sequence		Go to the previous quotation	Displays the previous quotation in sequence	
Go to the stack Almanack Home	Displays the home stack for *The Writer's Pocket Almanack*		Go to the stack Broken Quill	Displays outstanding examples of poor business and technical writing	
Go to the stack Calendar	Displays a quotation for each day of the year		Go to the stack Game	Plays a "guess the author" game	
Go to the stack Great Moments	Shows great accomplish-ments in the art and science of communication		Go to the stack Mal Mots	Shows facetious advice on how to write	
Go to the stack Veni Vidi Scripsi	Displays Latin quotations on the subject of writing		Pause flipping	Stops automatically flipping through quotations	
Print book-marked quotations	Prints out only the quotations you have bookmarked		Print all quotations	Prints out all quotations	

Command	What it does	Icon	Command	What it does	Icon
Print this quotation	Prints the currently displayed quotation		Remove all bookmarks	Clears bookmarks from all quotations	
Repeat the previous search	Finds another quotation like the last one searched for		Search for a quotation	Enables entry of words contained in the quotation sought	
Search for a quotation by number	Enables entry of the number of the quotation sought		Search for a subject	Enables entry of words describing the idea of the quotation	
Search for an author	Enables entry of the name of the author of the quotation		Select from a list of book-marked quotations	Permits selection from a list of the topics you have marked	
Select from a list of authors	Permits selection from a list of available authors		Select from a list of opening words	Permits selection from a list of the opening words of all quotations	
Select from a list of recently viewed quotations	Permits selection from a list of quotations you have looked at recently		Permits selection from a list of subjects	Pick from a list of available ideas	
Select from pictures of recent quotations	Permits selection from postage-stamp sized images of quotations		Stop	Quits HyperCard	
Unmark this quotation	Removes the bookmark from the current quotation				

You may notice that some new commands have appeared. Such is the nature of an evolving product. We have made these additions

- **Mirror-image commands for actions that alternate between two states**. Such commands are often called toggle switches. On menus we can reflect the current state by changing the label on the menu. Unfortunately, HyperCard does not let us change the individual icon on the palette. Hence, we have added commands for "Display this quotation" and for "Unmark this quotation."

- **Synonyms for standard HyperCard navigational commands**. Several of the standard navigational commands in HyperCard are quite handy for zipping through the stack. Icons have been added for such commands as Quit HyperCard, Recent, Next, Previous, First, Last, and Back.

Fortunately our modular approach handles this in stride.

DISPLAY THE ICONS

Now we can arrange the icons in two palettes, the Remote Control and the StackFinder.

The Remote Control

The Remote Control provides instant access to all the commands of *The Writer's Pocket Almanack* stack:

How the commands are arranged

The arrangement of commands in the palette establishes a context for each icon. The positioning is an important part of the language of icons. It also has an effect on how efficiently the user can find and select commands. The following principles are used in this preliminary arrangement:

- **Put the most used commands where they are easily found and selected**. Here we put the high-use commands at the top, bottom, and left edge.

- **Arrange items by spatial analogy.** The navigation-control buttons are arranged the way they would appear on a VCR or tape recorder:

- **Group related functions**. Four bookmarking functions are clustered together:

  Searching functions are together in a row:

Commands for finding authors are stacked in a column:

- **Put parallel or mirror-image functions next to one another**. The commands for marking and unmarking a quotation are side by side, and the command for unmarking all quotations is above the one for unmarking a single quotation:

- **Repeat meaningful patterns**. The printing commands are in the same order as the analogous copying commands:

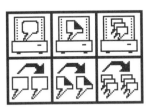

Problems with the arrangement

This arrangement has several potential problems (only testing will show whether they are really problems):

- **Not all commands are where they logically belong**. Because there are six selection commands, they could not be arranged in a neat row like the search commands.

- **The Edit and Display commands are one atop the other**, but the Mark and Unmark commands are side by side.

- **The number of buttons does not equal the number of commands**. Hence there is one blank button.

- **The palette is complex**. The sheer number of icons may overwhelm even experienced users.

Improvements to consider

Already we have ideas about how to improve the palette:

- **Pare it down to the essential commands**. Omit rarely used commands (Unmark all quotations) and potentially dangerous ones (Edit quotation, Quit HyperCard).

- **Divide the palette** into separate navigation, search, and utility palettes.

- **Consolidate mirror-image commands** into a single toggle command.

We will defer these potential improvements until after testing. Without the experience of observing actual users, we cannot be sure that these ideas would actually improve the product.

The StackFinder

The StackFinder makes it easy to hop to another stack of *The Writer's Pocket Almanack*:

The StackFinder palette is not really useful because selecting one of its icons closes the current stack (including this palette) and opens the one selected. One solution would be to redesign the palette with icons for all stacks, including Quotations, and make it available from all stacks of *The Writer's Pocket Almanack*.

The StackFinder palette also has the problem that the icons shown here do not match the ones shown for the individual stacks when viewed on the Macintosh

Desktop. We can fix this by installing these icons into the stacks with a utility such as ResEdit.

Observations

Ideas for enhancing the stack outstrip our ability to make changes. These are some of the changes we have recorded for later consideration:

- **Add a Quotation icon** (speech balloon) to the quotation stack.

- **Let users make notes about their favorite quotations**. This annotation field could pop up and might look like a note posted on a bulletin board.

- **Remove the "Edit quotation" command**. Let users read quotations, but not change them. Users could easily delete keywords or make the stack inconsistent with its index. We could leave the Edit command as a type-in command but strike it from all menus.

- **Automatically regenerate the indexes if users make changes**.

- **Add a command to speak the quotations aloud** using synthesized speech (or digitized speech on a CD-ROM version).

TEST THE DESIGN

The next step is to test the interface with actual users. No matter how good or how bad you think the icons are, your users will surprise you.

One way to test the relative clarity of the icons is to give test subjects a list of commands and pictures of the icons and ask them to match each command with its icon. Although not as useful as a realistic test with a live prototype, this test is easy to administer to a large number of potential users.

It will quickly point out which name/icon combinations are clear and which need improvement. If an icon is not matched with the correct command, the cause may be that the icon does not clearly suggest the right concept. The problem may also be that the command's name is unclear. Before you redesign the icon, you may want to try changing the command names. I like to ask test subjects, "What would you call this?"

Match the icons on the left with the commands on the right. Write the number of the command in the box of the icon that represents it:

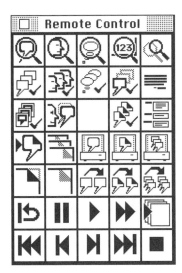

1. Bookmark this quotation
2. Copy all quotations
3. Copy bookmarked quotations
4. Copy this quotation
5. Display this quotation
6. Edit this quotation
7. Flip through the quotations rapidly
8. Flip through the quotations slowly
9. Go back one step
10. Go to another quotation by the current author
11. Go to another stack
12. Go to the first quotation
13. Go to the Help stack
14. Go to the HyperCard Home stack
15. Go to the last quotation
16. Go to the next bookmarked quotation
17. Go to the next quotation
18. Go to the previous quotation
19. Go to the stack Almanack Home
20. Go to the stack Broken Quill
21. Go to the stack Calendar
22. Go to the stack Game
23. Go to the stack Great Moments
24. Go to the stack Mal Mots
25. Go to the stack Veni Vidi Scripsi
26. Pause flipping
27. Print all quotations
28. Print bookmarked quotations
29. Print this quotation
30. Remove all bookmarks
31. Repeat the previous search
32. Search for a quotation
33. Search for a quotation by number
34. Search for a subject
35. Search for an author
36. Select from a list of authors
37. Select from a list of bookmarked quotations
38. Select from a list of opening words
39. Select from a list of recently viewed quotations
40. Select from a list of subjects
41. Select from pictures of recent quotations
42. Quit HyperCard
43. Unmark this quotation

REVISE AND REDESIGN

Testing reveals that the interface is too complex and the enormous palette of icons is about as intimidating as the instrument panel of a 747.

Changes

Before proceeding with further testing and development, we will make a few slight changes:

- Replace the single Remote Control palette with three specialized palettes:

Navigate—for stepping through the quotations

Find—for seeking out specific quotations

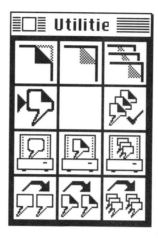

Utilities—for copying, printing, and bookmarking quotations.

- Add a pull-down menu just for palettes:

> **Naʋigate**
> **Find**
> **Utilities**
> **Other stacks**

- Change the user's privileges to "browsing." This removes from the pull-down menus commands for altering the stack:

 File   Edit   Go   Find   Special   Palette

- Redesign the icons for jumping to the next and previous quotation so they now look like the more common buttons on VCRs:

Old   New

More changes

More testing leads to more changes. These changes affect only a few icons (some affect only a few pixels), but they yield better performance:

Icon	Intended meaning	How the user interpreted it	Changes made	New icon
	Find a quotation by selecting from a list of authors (or other cues).	Approve authors. Check first author. Huh?	Replace the checkmark with an arrow. Draw the selected item with a thicker border. Point to rhe middle item, not the first.	
	The pen nib represents writing and writers.	Users recognized the pen nib but only with difficulty. The unsightly bulge at the point was the culprit.	Eliminate the bulge.	
	"Great Moments in Publishing"	Nothing.	Replace it with an exclamation point on a watch face, as suggested by a test subject.	
	Go to another WPA stack.	Go to another quotation in this stack.	Include the pen nib in the icon to associate it with the WPA product as a whole.	

This form is like "Analyze test results" in Chapter 14.

Besides the icons, a few other items needed changing:

- **Rename palettes**. The StackFinder and Utilities palettes were renamed to make their functions clearer and to make their names fit in the title area:

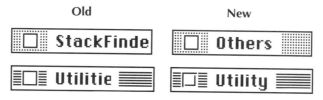

- **Fill the hole**. The hole in the Utility palette upset a lot of users who insisted that something was broken. It will eventually need an icon, but for the time being a neutral gray pattern seems to lessen the distraction:

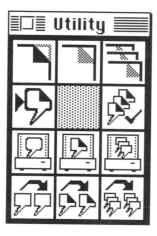

RECAP

The basic interface now works as expected. New and occasional users use the pull-down and pop-up menus, seldom venturing onto the icon palettes. The more determined and experienced users, performing repeated searches, bring forth the palettes and use them reliably. Most users familiar with the basic commands find their icon equivalents with little apparent effort. Because all commands are available on pull-down menus, pop-up menus, and icon palettes, users seem to start with word menus and pick up icon meanings as their experience grows:

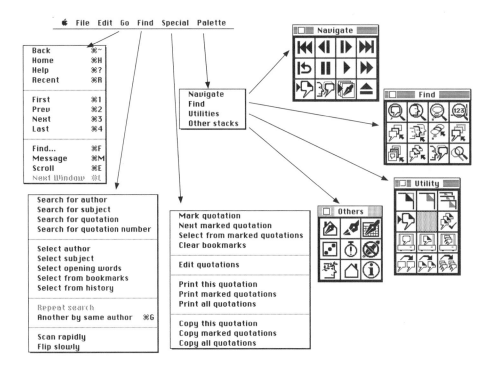

ICON
STARTER SET

The icon starter set includes iconic elements you can use to brainstorm, prototype, and inspire your own designs. Use these simple, black-and-white images as a starting point for your own creativity. Mix them. Match them. Combine them. Color them. Make them your own. They are arranged as a glossary of concepts. These same icons are included on the Starter Set disk included with this book. Instructions for using this disk appear at the end of this chapter.

access
(ACCESS)

Anger, angry
(ANGER1,
ANGER2)

activate
(ACTIVATE)

animation,
video
(ANIMATIO)

add to
(ADD_TO)

Apple
Macintosh
GUI
(APPLE)

air brush
(AIR_BR1,
AIR_BR2)

Apple
Macintosh
(APPL_COM)

airplane
(AIRPLAN1,
AIRPLAN2)

application
(APPLICAT)

alarm,
reminder
(ALARM)

atomic energy
(ATOMIC)

align objects
(ALIGN)

attach
(ATTACH1,
ATTACH2)

alignment of
lines of text
(ALIGN_LT,
ALIGN_RT,
ALIGN_CR,
ALIGN_JY)

audio
recording,
audio cassette
(AUDIO)

automobile
(AUTO1,
AUTO2)

anchor
(ANCHOR)

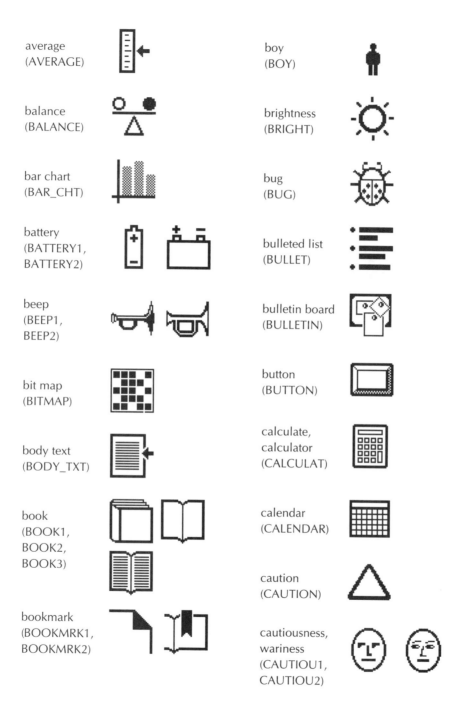

average
(AVERAGE)

boy
(BOY)

balance
(BALANCE)

brightness
(BRIGHT)

bar chart
(BAR_CHT)

bug
(BUG)

battery
(BATTERY1,
BATTERY2)

bulleted list
(BULLET)

beep
(BEEP1,
BEEP2)

bulletin board
(BULLETIN)

bit map
(BITMAP)

button
(BUTTON)

body text
(BODY_TXT)

calculate,
calculator
(CALCULAT)

book
(BOOK1,
BOOK2,
BOOK3)

calendar
(CALENDAR)

caution
(CAUTION)

bookmark
(BOOKMRK1,
BOOKMRK2)

cautiousness,
wariness
(CAUTIOU1,
CAUTIOU2)

CD-ROM
(CD_ROM)

color
(COLOR)

chart
(CHART)

column
(COLUMN)

check,
approve
(CHECK1,
CHECK2)

combat
(COMBAT)

checklist
(CHECKLIS)

combine
(COMBINE)

chemical,
molecule
(CHEMICAL)

command
(COMMAND)

chemistry
(CHEMISTR)

communicate
electronically
(COMMUN)

clipboard
(CLIPBOAR)

compress
(COMPRESS)

clock, time
(CLOCK1,
CLOCK2)

computer
(COMPUTE1,
COMPUTE2)

close a file
(CLOSE_FL)

conflict
(CONFLICT)

cold
(COLD)

connected
(CONNECT)

connector, port (CON_PRT1, CON_PRT2)		cut to clipboard (CUT_CLIP)	
continue (CONTINU1, CONTINU2)		damage (DAMAGE)	
contrast (CONTRAST)		danger (DANGER1, DANGER2)	
control panel (CONT_PNL)		dark (DARK)	
cooperation (COOPERAT)		data, alphanumeric (DAT_ALPH)	
copy (COPY)		data, binary (DAT_NUM)	
copy to clipboard (COPY_CLP)		data, graphical (DAT_GRAP)	
count (COUNT)		data, hexadecimal (DAT_HEX)	
crop (CROP)		day (DAY)	
cut (CUT)		death DEATH)	

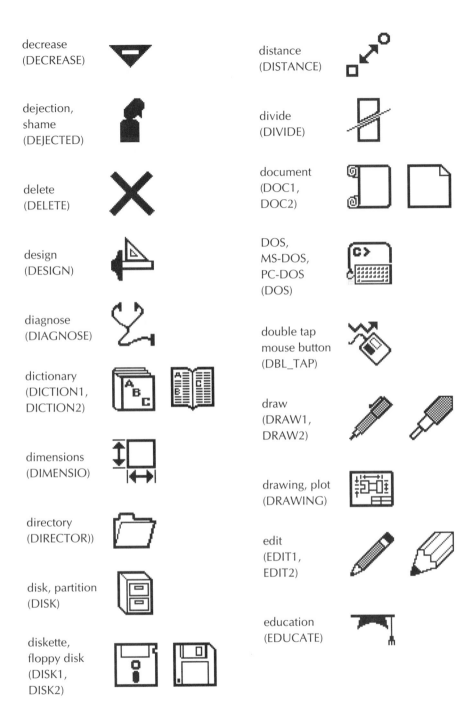

decrease
(DECREASE)

dejection,
shame
(DEJECTED)

delete
(DELETE)

design
(DESIGN)

diagnose
(DIAGNOSE)

dictionary
(DICTION1,
DICTION2)

dimensions
(DIMENSIO)

directory
(DIRECTOR))

disk, partition
(DISK)

diskette,
floppy disk
(DISK1,
DISK2)

distance
(DISTANCE)

divide
(DIVIDE)

document
(DOC1,
DOC2)

DOS,
MS-DOS,
PC-DOS
(DOS)

double tap
mouse button
(DBL_TAP)

draw
(DRAW1,
DRAW2)

drawing, plot
(DRAWING)

edit
(EDIT1,
EDIT2)

education
(EDUCATE)

electrical
hazard
(ELEC_HAZ)

error, system
crash
(ERROR)

electrical
outlet
(ELEC_OUT)

exercise
(EXERCISE)

electronic
(ELECTRON)

exit
(EXIT1, EXIT2)

electronic
circuit
(ELEC_CIR)

family
(FAMILY)

empty
(EMPTY)

fast forward
(FAST_FOR)

engineering,
drafting
(ENGINEER)

fast reverse,
rewind
(FAST_REW)

enlarge, scale
(ENLARGE)

fast, speed
(FAST1,
FAST2)

enter
(ENTER1,
ENTER2)

fax, facsimile
machine
(FAX)

erase
(ERASE1,
ERASE2)

fear
(FEAR1,
FEAR2)

fill an area
with a pattern
or color
(FILL1, FILL2))

film camera
(FILM)

filter
(FILTER)

fire
(FIRE1, FIRE2)

first aid
(FIRSTAID)

flip
horizontally
(FLIP_HOR)

flip vertically
(FLIP_VER)

food
(FOOD)

format,
organize
(FORMAT)

formula
(FORMULA)
$$a = \pi r^2$$
$$y = \sin x$$
$$e = mc^2$$

fragile
(FRAGILE)

full
(FULL)

game
(GAME)

gauge, dial
(GAUGE1,
GAUGE2)

get data from
(GET_DATA)

girl
(GIRL)

glossary
(GLOSSARY)

go back one
unit
(GO_BAK_1)

go back
where you
came from
(GO_BACK)

go backward
(GO_BAKWA)

go forward
(GO_FORW)

go forward
one unit
(GO_FOR_1)

go rapidly
(GO_RAPID)

go slowly
(GO_SLOW)

go to
(GO_TO)

go to end
(GO_END)

go to start
(GO_START)

goal
(GOAL1
GOAL2)

grid
(GRID)

group, bind
together
(GROUP)

handbook,
manual (HANDBK1,
HANDBK2)

handle with
care
(HAND_CAR)

happiness,
happy
(HAPPY1,
HAPPY2)

hard disk
(HARD_DK1,
HARD_DK2)

height
(HEIGHT1,
HEIGHT2)

help facility
(HELP1,
HELP2)

here, at this
point
(HERE1,
HERE2)

hide, render
invisible
(HIDE1,
HIDE2)

hierarchy
(HIERARCH)

infant
(INFANT)

highlight
(HILITE1,
HILITE2)

inoculate
(INOCUL1,
INOCUL2,
INOCUL3,
INOCUL4)

home
(HOME1,
HOME2)

hot
(HOT)

insert
(INSERT)

IBM PC
(IBM_PC)

is, equals
(IS)

idea
(IDEA)

joy
(JOY)

incomplete
(INCOMPLE)

keyboard
(KEYBRD1,
KEYBRD2)

increase
(INCREASE)

label
(LABEL)

index
(INDEX)

laptop
computer
(LAPTOP)

industry,
industrial
(INDUSTRY)

laughter,
laugh
(LAUGH1,
LAUGH2)

launch
(LAUNCH)

local, near
(LOCAL)

layers
(LAYERS1,
LAYERS2)

locate
(LOCATE1,
LOCATE2)

letter
(LETTER)

lock
(LOCK)

library
(LIBRARY1,
LIBRARY2)

look at,
inspect
(LOOK1,
LOOK2)

light
(LIGHT)

magnet
(MAGNET)

light source
(LITESOUC)

mail
(MAIL1,
MAIL2)

line chart
(LINE_CHT)

man
(MAN)

line, freehand
(LINE)

manual page
(MANUAL)

link
(LINK1,
LINK2)

manufac-
turing
(MFG1,
MFG2)

listen
(LISTEN1,
LISTEN2)

map
(MAP)

marriage
(MARRIAGE)

maximum
(MAXIMUM)

measure
(MEASURE1,
MEASURE2)

memo
(MEMO)

menus
(MENUS)

merge
(MERGE)

message
(MESSAGE)

Microsoft
Windows
(MS_WINDO)

minimum
(MINIMUM)

mix
(MIX1, MIX2)

modularity
(MODULARI)

module
(MODULE)

money
(MONEY)

month
(MONTH)

mouse
(MOUSE1,
MOUSE2,
MOUSE3)

move
(MOVE1,
MOVE2)

move on the
screen
(MOVE3,
MOVE4)

multimedia
production
(MULTIMED)

music
(MUSIC1,
MUSIC2)

noise
(NOISE)

names and
addresses
(NAMES)

notes
(NOTES)

nature
(NATURE1,
NATURE2)

notice,
annotation
(NOTICE)

network
(NETWORK)

number,
apply
numbers to
(NUMBER1,
NUMBER2)

neutral
emotion,
calm
(NEUTRAL1,
NEUTRAL2)

numbered list
(NUM_LIST)

new
(NEW)

object
(OBJECT1,
OBJECT2)

newspaper,
news
(NEWSPAPE)

old
(OLD)

night
(NIGHT)

open a file
(OPEN_FIL)

no, not
(NO1, NO2)

organization
(ORGANIZE)

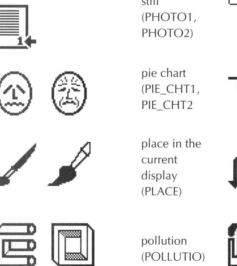

outline list
(OUTLINE)

ownership,
possession
(OWNER1,
OWNER2)

package,
bundle, group
(PACKAGE1,
PACKAGE2)

page footer
(PG_FOOT)

page header
(PG_HEAD)

page number
(PG_NUM)

pain, painful
(PAIN1,
PAIN2)

paint
(PAINT1,
PAINT2)

paradox
(PARADOX1,
PARADOX2)

paragraph
(PARA1,
PARA2)

paste from
clipboard
(PST_CLIP)

pause
(PAUSE)

people
(PEOPLE)

person
(PERSON)

photography
still
(PHOTO1,
PHOTO2)

pie chart
(PIE_CHT1,
PIE_CHT2

place in the
current
display
(PLACE)

pollution
(POLLUTIO)

portable item
or resource
(PORTABLE)

puzzlement,
puzzle
(PUZZLE)

preferences
(PREFS)

quit
(QUIT)

press mouse
button and
hold it down
(PRESS)

radioactive
hazard
(RAD_HAZ)

print, printer
(PRINT)

read
(READ1,
READ2)

printout,
report
(PRNTOUT1,
PRNTOUT2)

read data
from a disk
(READ_DSK)

process
(PROCESS)

read data
from a file
(READ_FLE)

program,
macro, script
(PROGRAM)

receive
(RECEIVE1,
RECEIVE2)

publication,
newsletter
(PUBLICAT)

record sound
(RECORD)

put data in
(PUT_DATA)

remembering,
remember
(REMEM1,
REMEM2)

remote, far
(REMOTE)

repair,
maintain
(REPAIR)

repeat, loop,
cycle
(REPEAT1,
REPEAT2)

replace
(REPLACE)

report,
specification
(REPORT1,
REPORT2)

reproduce
(REPRODUC)

rotate
(ROTATE)

row
(ROW)

ruler
(RULER)

sadness, sad
(SADNESS1,
SADNESS2)

safe, secure
(SAFE)

save data in a
file
(SAVE_FLE)

save data to
disk
(SAVE_DSK)

scatter chart
(SCTR_CHT)

screen
(SCREEN)

SCSI
(SCSI)

search for
(SEARCH)

select
(SELECT1,
SELECT2,
SELECT3)

select characteristics of an object, for instance the color of a pixel (SLCT_CH1 SLCT_CH2, SLCT_CH3, SLCT_CH4)

send and receive (SEND1, SEND2)

ship (SHIP)

shock, shaken (SHOCK1, SHOCK2)

show, project (SHOW1, SHOW2)

skepticism, skeptical (SKEPT1, SKEPT2)

sleep (SLEEP1, SLEEP2)

slide, photographic (SLIDE)

small (SMALL1)

smudge or smear (SMUDGE1, SMUDGE2)

snap to grid (SNAP_TO)

snapshot, capture a screen (SNAPSHOT)

sort in ascending order (SORT_ASC)

sort in descending order (SORT_DSC)

sound (SOUND)

speech
(SPEECH1,
SPEECH2)

surprise
(SURPRIS1,
SURPRIS2)

spelling
check
(SPELL_CK)

surrender
(SURREND1,
SURREND2)

spreadsheet
(SPREADSH)

swap
(SWAP)

start,
beginning
(START)

tab
(TAB)

stop
(STOP1,
STOP2)

tab stops in a
ruler
(TAB_STOP)

strong,
strength
(STRONG)

table
(TABLE)

study
(STUDY)

table of
contents
(TOC)

subtotal
(SUBTOTAL)

tap mouse
button, click
(TAP)

success,
victory
(SUCCESS)

tasks
completed
(TASK_OUT)

summary
(SUMMARY)

tasks waiting
(TASK_IN)

teach
(TEACH)

telephone
(TELE1,
TELE2)

telephone
directory
(TELE_DIR)

television
(TV)

template
(TEMP_1,
TEMP_2,
TEMP_3)

text font
(TEXT_FON)

text size
(TEXT_SIZ)

text style
(TEXT_STY)

text,
formatted
(TXT_FMT1,
TXT_FMT2)

text,
unformatted
(TXT_UFT1,
TXT_UFT2)

think
(THINK1,
THINK2)

thought
(THOUGHT)

time, elapsed
(TIME)

toddler
(TODDLER)

tool, tools
(TOOL1,
TOOL2)

total
(TOTAL)

transform
(TRANSFOR)

trim
(TRIM1,
TRIM2)

truck
(TRUCK1,
TRUCK2)

user interface
(USER_INT)

unconscious,
asleep
(UNCONSC1,
UNCONSC2,
UNCONSC3)

users
(USERS)

vertex, point
in a
geometrical
element
(VERTEX)

unconnected
to a network
(UNCONNCT)

vibrate, shake
(VIBRATE)

undo
(UNDO)

video
(VIDEO)

unformat
(UNFORMAT)

video tape
(VID_TAPE)

ungroup
(UNGROUP)

visible, make
visible
(VISIBLE1,
VISIBLE2)

Unix GUI
(UNIX_GUI)

unlink
(UNLINK1,
UNLINK2)

wait
(WAIT)

unlock
(UNLOCK)

water
(WATER1,
WATER2)

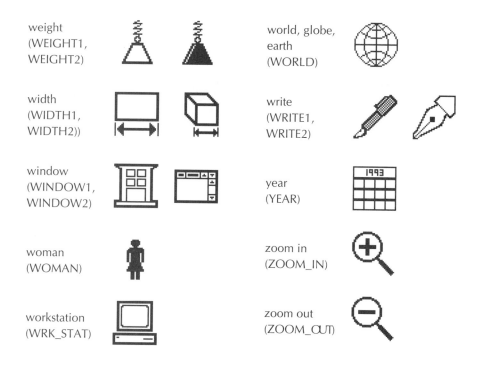

weight
(WEIGHT1,
WEIGHT2)

world, globe,
earth
(WORLD)

width
(WIDTH1,
WIDTH2))

write
(WRITE1,
WRITE2)

window
(WINDOW1,
WINDOW2)

year
(YEAR)

woman
(WOMAN)

zoom in
(ZOOM_IN)

workstation
(WRK_STAT)

zoom out
(ZOOM_OUT)

INSTRUCTIONS FOR THE STARTER SET DISK

To use the Starter Set icons, you must first install them onto your hard disk.

Installing the Starter Set

To install the files on this disk, you will need at least 1megabyte of free space on your hard disk.

1. Start your computer and Windows.

2. Insert the Starter Set disk into your disk drive.

3. From File Manager or Program Manager, choose **Run** from the **File** menu.

4. Type **A:\INSTALL** if the disk is in the A: drive or **B:\INSTALL** if it is in the B: drive. Click the **Install** button.

5. Follow the prompts to name the directory for the Starter Set and to create a Windows program group for The Icon Book.

Viewing the Starter Set

To see what icons are included in the Starter Set, open The Icon Book program group and double-click on the Icon Starter Set icon.

The Viewer program will open. To learn how to use the Viewer, click on its Help button.

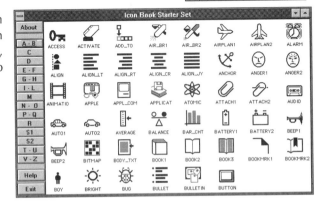

Editing the icons

The actual icons are stored in two subdirectories within the **ICONBOOK** directory.

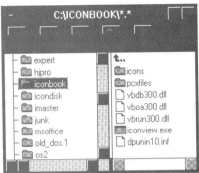

The **ICONS** subdirectory contains the individual icons in **.ICO** format.

The **PCXFILES** subdirectory contains pictures of groups of icons. Each file contains the icons shown on the corresponding viewer screen. These pictures are in **.PCX** (PC Paintbrush) format. You can edit them with Windows Paintbrush.

INDEX